I'M CHEVY CHASE . . .
AND YOU'RE NOT

Also by Rena Fruchter

Dudley Moore: An Intimate Portrait

I'M CHEVY CHASE ...
AND YOU'RE NOT

Rena Fruchter

First published in Great Britain in 2008 by
Virgin Books Ltd
Thames Wharf Studios
Rainville Road
London
W6 9HA

A catalogue record for this book is available from the
British Library.

ISBN 978 0 7535 1323 1

The paper used in this book is a natural, recyclable product
made from wood grown in sustainable forests. The
manufacturing process conforms to the regulations of the
country of origin.

Typeset by TW Typesetting, Plymouth, Devon

Printed and bound in USA

To Chevy's Family
and
To My Family
Two loving, caring, patient, and
supportive families

CONTENTS

PRELUDE: I'M NOT CHEVY CHASE
(A WORD OF EXPLANATION)

It all began a long, long time ago. Way before I knew that Chevy Chase carried a pole around the grounds of his home to protect guests from his "attack chicken," a slightly dangerous creature that liked to poke holes in visitors' legs.

It was backstage at Carnegie Hall in 2001, in fact. Chevy looked serious and a little nervous. This was his Carnegie Hall debut as a jazz pianist. Dudley Moore had invited him to perform at a benefit concert in Dudley's honor, about a year before Dudley's death. Chevy is actually a very talented pianist and had worked hard to play his jazz rendition of "Alice in Wonderland," a beautiful and respectful tribute to his old friend.

A couple of years later I was working on a book about Dudley, and I had occasion to interview Chevy for my book *Dudley Moore: An Intimate Portrait.* Chevy was witty and funny, as anticipated, but I was very impressed that after three decades he was still astonished by the strange state of celebrity—the wonderful and dreadful aspects of his status. I had absolutely no intention of writing another biography and was in the middle of preparations for a murder mystery in which—I was both pleased and disturbed to note—I had thought of at least three innovative ways to commit murder. Thankfully, this didn't seem to bother Chevy at all.

I couldn't shake off the thought that Chevy's captivating story ought to be told. In a casual conversation, Chevy confessed he thought that at sixty-one he was entirely too young for a biography. He had so far turned down all such offers. Yet, somehow, we began working on this one. The entire first session was devoted to discussing all the pros and cons and we shook hands at the end and agreed to try. For the second session, I turned up with a small tape recorder, which amused Chevy, and we agreed that since Chevy was apparently uninspired to write his autobiography, and was sure he wouldn't know the best questions to ask himself, I would be given the task.

One might assume that spending two years interviewing one of the world's top comedians might be a barrel of laughs, but it was only half a barrel. Chevy is complex. He's hilarious. He's long-winded. He's a bit of a depressive. And, seemingly contradictory, he's extremely well balanced. He's a talented musician. He's a worrier. He's a brilliant intellect. A fine writer. A political liberal. He's very thoughtful and sensitive, and extremely generous to his family and friends. In contrast to many of his Hollywood colleagues he is in a stable marriage to a wonderful wife and is an extraordinary father to three charming daughters.

Chevy has been an enthusiastic participant in this biography. If Chevy had written his autobiography, I would have been saved horrendous journeys over the Tappan Zee Bridge to Route 684 in New York. I would also have been spared talking to some of his crazy friends. Chevy said that Bill Murray would have some good insights and I should call him. He gave me his phone number but forgot to warn me that Bill is not always "nice," and that Chevy and Bill had once had a near fistfight in which both had to be restrained, leaving them with something closer to a relationship of cool tolerance than the love/hate relationship they had once had.

Cautiously, I dialed the number and introduced myself.

"Hello, Mr. Murray. I'm Rena Fruchter. I'm writing the authorized biography of Chevy Chase and I'd like to speak with you."

"What a *stupid* thing to do!" he yelled. "Why on *earth* would you want to write a biography of Chevy?"

"Well, he's got an interesting story to tell. A great career. A difficult childhood—"

"Stop right there," Bill said. "That's still the dumbest thing I've ever heard. He should write it himself."

"Well, actually, he doesn't really *want* to write it himself. He's cooperating. I ask him a lot of provocative questions. Look, will you talk to me or not?"

"I'm a very busy person. I don't know much about Chevy."

"You've worked with him."

"Who told you that?"

"If you don't want to speak with me, that's okay. I just assumed you would enjoy talking about Chevy."

"Now you're manipulating me," he snapped. "Fuck you!" he added and slammed down the receiver.

So began my attempts to speak to Chevy's friends and admirers, although thankfully it was uphill after Bill. I ignored Chevy's serious suggestion that I borrow a gun, turn up on Bill Murray's doorstep, and hold the gun to his head until the end of the interview. Chevy said Bill would respect me for that. I thought I could live without Bill.

Chevy certainly can write. That's where his career began. He's simply not egotistical enough to devote a complete volume to himself, however. He knew it wouldn't get done. He wouldn't find the time, or the discipline, or the right stories to tell. He was too busy, too tired, too hungry, too occupied. His daughters needed his attention.

One day, while at his house, he suggested we take a walk to the barn to look at a small doe that had been abandoned by its mother. He was personally caring for the tiny animal, feeding it from a bottle. On the way back to the house, he captured some flies with a small vacuum device specially designed to catch insects. He deposited them in a lantern where a few "pet" spiders were awaiting their dinner. In the house, two hired workers were cooking a huge pot of something that smelled quite good. I was ready for a taste until informed that it was food for the five family dogs that roamed the twelve-acre property in New York.

Then I recalled that first meeting and the attack chicken.

I felt reassured about writing this biography. If Chevy were writing, he probably would have left out the spiders, and the flies, and the chickens, and possibly even the dog food.

Part I

Formative Years

1. THE PAIN OF A CHILD

The year was 1975. A handsome young actor with a quizzical expression was seated at a news desk on the set of *Saturday Night Live*. This confident young man had only to say, "Good evening. I'm Chevy Chase ... and you're not," and the crowd cheered. He was beloved. For ninety minutes every Saturday night, he felt like he was sitting on top of the world.

Once the lights dimmed, and the performance was over, Chevy Chase returned to that place in his mind where he so often found himself. Was he really a famous comedian, enjoying the limelight? Or was he still a frightened young boy, sitting in a dark room?

When the applause finished, Chevy turned his attention back to the small boy, who was trying to figure out what he had done wrong, why he had been hit so hard with a belt. The welts on the backs of his legs still hurt. He was only nine, and he knew he had been a little mischievous. He liked to play tricks and sometimes would come home a little late. The time passed quickly while he was playing—he always felt happier when he was with his friends. At home, he could never predict when the explosions might take place, and what would trigger the next inevitable punishment. He knew when he saw *that look* in his mother's eyes that something bad was going to happen.

He wondered if his friends were also in pain, but he was too scared to ask them. He didn't think they were locked in the basement for days at a time or shut in the closet for hours as punishment for a small offense. He wondered if they too had to think about whether it was better to be hit or locked in the closet.

Chevy didn't dare try to escape for fear of the physical punishment that would follow. He knew he could never breathe a word of this to anyone. That was the unwritten law, the arrangement in his family. But he wondered why it was happening to him. When his mother dressed him up and paraded him over to Grandma Cattie's, sometimes he wondered if *she* knew, or if the others could see it in his eyes. Yet he never said a word.

The treatment Chevy suffered as a child would affect him throughout his adult life, into his sixties, and although he rose to a position of prominence and fame—becoming an American comedy icon beloved by millions—he would never fully recover from being that young boy beaten and locked in the basement. The abuse would affect how he saw the world and everything he did in his life.

Though Chevy Chase's family roots were in wealthy New York society, the treatment he experienced during his childhood did not reflect the advantages of that background. His mother, Cathalene Parker Browning, came from an extremely rich family, but as an adult she did not inherit the significant family wealth.

As a child, Cathalene was adopted by Cornelius Vanderbilt Crane when he married her mother, and she took the name Cathalene Crane. Cornelius's father was one of the founders of the Crane Valve Company, and Catharine and Cornelius traveled around the world on a two-hundred-foot yacht while Cathalene was "taken care of by the dormouse or nuns here and there," as Chevy explains it. She was a lonely child, left at home in the care of nannies, while her mother and stepfather were away much of the time. During the Depression, Cathalene looked out of her bedroom window and saw five Rolls-Royces parked in their driveway. She grew up in the mansion seen in the 1987 film *The Witches of Eastwick.*

Chevy is a fourteenth-generation New Yorker. Through his mother, he descends from the earliest Dutch settlers of New Amsterdam. Generations earlier, according to Chevy's brother John, who has taken on the role of the family's historian, they also descend from upstate New York Kanienkehaka, the Native Americans known as the Mohawks. "Chevy never cared about such stuff," says John. "He once told me that people who defined themselves in terms of their ancestry were like potatoes—the best parts of them were underground. He disdained the pretension of my mother's side of the family, as embodied by her mother, Cattie. Ironically, Chevy has at times been accused of pretentiousness by people unable to read him."

Chevy's mother married her first husband, Edward (Ned) Chase, when she was only eighteen. He came from an intellectual, artistic, and middle-class family and was a scholar, writer, and editor with a wonderful sense of humor. His own father, Edward Leigh Chase, had been a painter and illustrator, and an early member of the Byrdcliffe experiment that gave rise to the artists' colony at Woodstock, New York.

There were tensions in the marriage almost from the start. Their first child, Ned Jr., was followed closely by the birth of Chevy less than a year and a half later. Chevy was born October 8, 1943, and was given the name Cornelius Crane Chase. He has no memory of why his paternal grandmother gave him the nickname of "Chevy," although several theories have been presented to him. One such theory had to do with the Battle of Cheviot Hills, an English invasion repelled by the Scottish clan Douglas in 1436. However, Chevy was not totally convinced this was a legitimate theory. "She may have nicknamed me after Chevy Chase,

Maryland," he says. Chevy is not sure which is the true source of his nickname. He has searched for, but has never come across, anyone else with his name.

Cathalene named Chevy after her adoptive father, in the hope that he would leave part of his fortune to her or to Chevy. That never happened. The story known in the family is that Ned had an affair with Cathalene's close friend, who confessed it to Cathalene. That had not been Ned's first affair, and the marriage ended quickly after that, leaving Chevy's mother in a vulnerable state and struggling to care for two small boys. This was not made easier by the fact that she was prone to panic attacks, which had begun during her pregnancy with Chevy.

Cathalene maintained a strained relationship with her own mother, who had by this time divorced Cornelius Crane and received a substantial settlement—millions, in fact—which enabled her to live a life of luxury. Crane later married a woman who encouraged him to disown his former family and friends. When he died he left most of his money to a Zen Buddhist foundation.

When her first marriage failed, Chevy's mother went into a deep depression. Chevy was a baby when his aunt Nancy, his father's sister, discovered Cathalene rocking back and forth on the floor of her home. Baby Chevy, filthy and neglected, was in his crib. The conditions were shocking. She had clearly been suffering from serious postpartum depression, bordering on a nervous breakdown, and spent the remaining months of the first year of Chevy's life in an institution.

Chevy and his brother Ned were raised for the next year by their paternal grandparents, the Chases, who lived in Woodstock. Their father, Ned, was in the picture during that time and indeed remained an important figure in their lives. Chevy's relationship with his father was strong, although his parents' divorce when he was a small boy did nothing to provide him with the stability he needed. Chevy remembers his paternal grandparents as loving, caring people, whose kindness is probably what saved his life in many respects. But after the first year, when his mother regained custody of the two small boys, not enough time was spent with his grandparents to counteract the horror that was to come.

Chevy remembers the Woodstock of his childhood as filled with painters, singers, and musicians—a true artists' colony. This memory of pleasant, cultured surroundings contrasts strongly with the abuse that began at the hands of his disturbed mother, well before she married her second husband, Dr. John Cederquist, on Valentine's Day in 1951. Chevy's paternal grandfather later called Chevy's mother "the only truly evil person he ever knew in his life." Chevy still recalls his frequent abuse, and the lesser abuse of his brother, and he has vivid memories of certain incidents. "I can remember my brother having a high heel stuck in his head by our mother."

With her second marriage, their mother married someone as imbalanced as she was. Chevy was eight at the time. At the hands of his stepfather, Chevy suffered emotional and physical abuse that, at times, bordered on torture.

Chevy's mother was actually a young woman of great intelligence, beauty, and potential. She could be affectionate with her children, and Chevy remembers her sometimes hugging and kissing him. John says, "She was capable of affecting a posture of sublime calm and control. When not in the throes of whatever psychological demons twisted her, our mother was extremely loving and, paradoxically, protective." She spoke French and Spanish fluently as a child and was a talented pianist and sketch artist. She didn't have a career and spent a lot of time at home. Chevy recalled there was household help, and that during the summers in Woodstock there was a lot of socializing with friends. "It seemed to me she was raising puppies—poodles—or visiting with various friends, mothers of my peers."

Yet she was a very unhappy woman whose moods were totally unpredictable and Chevy never knew what would set her off. He had a good sense of humor but spent a lot of time depressed and frightened. "I knew I was a 'bad boy' but I didn't know that everybody else wasn't punished the same way I was." Chevy also feared his brother Ned, who until their teens played tricks on him just to get him into trouble. There was vicious sibling rivalry, which might not have been so bad in a less dysfunctional household, but Ned's "pranks" served to get Chevy punished.

Their mother and stepfather intentionally waited a few years after their marriage and then had three more children, continuing the pattern of abuse. Although she came along many years later, Chevy's half sister Pamela recalls their mother's habit of sending the children outside to select branches of a tree with which they would be hit for their "infractions."

"I lived in fear all the time, deathly fear," Chevy recalls. He remembers being awakened in the middle of the night and slapped, continually and hard, across the face. "I don't remember what it was for, or what I had done." This was not unusual. Being locked in the bedroom closet for hours was also a standard punishment in the household. To this day, Pamela says, she cannot keep a hairbrush in her home. Her mother would hit her with a hairbrush when she became enraged. "A hairbrush doesn't feel safe to me."

It was hard work for Chevy just to survive as a child. He was a sensitive boy, filled with fear, and thoughts of his home life while he was at school made studying hard. His grades were low yet when tested his IQ was extremely high. This made the problem worse because his stepfather, hearing this news, claimed there was no excuse for the low grades and would hit him, making his nose bleed, or would lock him in a dark closet.

Chevy felt that he was working as hard as, or harder than, his classmates, but working at "just being accepted as a person, or at understanding how to survive such fear and despair and still be a 'good' child." Chevy never told anyone what was going on at home, although he imagined some family friends must have known or suspected things were not right. He never felt that he could tell his father, Ned. By that time, Ned had remarried and had a second family. Chevy didn't want him to know, didn't want him to worry. "I was afraid if Dad would face off against John Cederquist he would lose a fight. John Cederquist was a bigger, angrier, strong man. I also didn't know I would be *allowed* to say anything."

Friends and the extended family "just knew I was a confused and sad kid." Chevy received the worst treatment of the five children. Chevy's older brother, Ned Jr., toed the line more than Chevy and suffered fewer harsh punishments. "I was fraught with fear and low self-esteem," remembers Chevy. "You're inundated with those thoughts and those fears, and you learn nothing about how to organize your time and do your homework."

Chevy's younger half brother John explained that Ned was "a model student and high school athlete. In my parents' estimation, there was no need to hammer on him, since he already 'fit the mold.' In contrast, Chever ["Clever Chever" is his nickname for Chevy] was moody and troublesome, and worse yet he responded to the poundings he received—be they physical or, worse, psychological and emotional—with sullen obstinacy, which I can tell you from my own experience was the quickest route to painful reprisal from my parents. Ned was always Mommy's golden boy, while Chevy was ever the 'pain in the butt.' It was a daily ordeal for all concerned, but a particularly vicious cycle for Chevy.

"My parents also compartmentalized their abuse and neglect of us, especially our mother. Everything was a dirty secret, to be kept hidden from my father. She didn't want her shrink husband to know anything about her bizarre conduct, and for his part my father's whole life was a secret, as he spent all day locked in the sanctum of his psychoanalytic office, poking around inside other people's heads.

"My mother, at her worst, was like an unleashed animal. It was at her hands, in her feral altered states, that Chevy suffered the darkest of his secret torments."

Chevy's brother Ned did not see a lot of the abuse but remembers that his mother and stepfather were worried that Chevy seemed more concerned with socializing than with schoolwork. Ned excuses his mother's actions because of her own difficult childhood. "I think every person has their own version of their childhood, and it becomes difficult to unravel what we might call objective fact from subjective narrative.

"My mother and stepfather had enormous difficulty getting him to do his homework. He may have been locked in the basement, but that was their effort to get him to buckle down to work.

"I had my strategy for successfully dealing with my mother and stepfather, essentially doing things which would avoid punishment or displeasure, but I nevertheless elicited those responses. I made a better show of completing my homework. I don't think of Chevy as a rebel—he was less compliant. Not loudly, he just did it."

Ned remembers occasions when the punishments were too harsh. "On one occasion, I gave her [their mother] the cold shoulder [for her treatment of Chevy]. I wasn't sure she would 'get it.' But she immediately got it."

Although his childhood perspective was a decade later than Chevy's, his brother John says, "Our mother was a piece of work. My parents were as odd a couple as I've ever known. They looked great together in old photographs, but there the compatibility ended. He was a stoic naval commander of pure Swedish blood—silent, brooding, and cold as a stone. He was brilliant—took his M.D. at Harvard Medical and after the war went back to school and took his psychoanalytic degree at Columbia. Having escaped the poverty of his childhood through school, he held a stern conviction that formal education was the only route to success.

"He was a strict disciplinarian but, far worse, he had an explosive temper and could be brutal. If crossed, he did not hesitate to take his fists to us boys. What I always found demeaning about my father's brief yet violent explosions was that he always went for the head. He was a doctor, a fucking head doctor, but he always hit me in the head."

Their mother, John added, "was as fiery as he was dark. Anything at all could pop a fuse in her, and when she blew things got ugly fast. My lay diagnosis is that she was schizoaffective—in an agitated emotional state, she lost touch with reality. Truly. She beat the crap out of us with belts and brushes."

The family lived in several houses in Manhattan. Cathalene and John Cederquist lived together for a couple of years before their marriage, on Park Avenue, later moving to a house on the edge of East Harlem. They lived in a brownstone, a four-story walk-up on a block that had some notable residents, including Vincent Sardi, John Lindsay, who later became mayor, and, next door to Chevy, caricaturist Al Hirschfeld. Chevy used to watch Hirschfeld work and would see him insert the "Nina"'s into the drawings, but he "would never tell where they were." Chevy knew Nina Hirschfeld, who was a few years younger: "A bright redheaded girl, not particularly attractive, but I loved that red hair. Her mom had it also." Maria Riva, Marlene Dietrich's daughter, also lived on the street with her two sons. They were younger than Chevy but they still played together. Chevy often saw Dietrich walking with her grandchildren. "She wore a white nurse's uniform and white hose."

Their neighborhood was also shared by people of poverty. The rough teens and gangs consistently taunted Chevy, threatening him with knives. Eventually he learned to defend himself and carried a knife in his pocket, "which I would never have used in a million years." But when the school bully threatened him one time too many, fourteen-year-old Chevy pulled his knife on him.

Nobody heard his side of the story. No one even asked for his side; he had simply broken a rule. From the years of abuse at home, Chevy had learned not to speak up, or things got worse. He didn't have a chance to explain that the bully had been beating him up at school. When his mother and stepfather heard what happened, and that Chevy was suspended from school, he was put in the cellar for several days. "I was given a mattress and a pitcher to pee in. A desk and a small lamp. The rest of the cellar was rock. There were two little windows a foot and a half in height, with bars on them." Chevy recalls seeing legs out of the windows—Marlene Dietrich's legs when she was visiting her daughter, and the legs of his best buddy on his way to school—although his shouts couldn't be heard outside.

Many years later, in 2006, Chevy received a package of letters that had been sent to his mother by his father years after their divorce. Although they lived near each other, Chevy's parents exchanged frequent letters discussing their sons. Chevy's dad posted the letters from his work address at Cunningham & Walsh, a public relations firm in New York where he was for a time employed as a writer and editor.

In the letters, it was clear that Ned was the favored son. His father expressed concern that Ned was achieving and Chevy was not. He made many comparisons between the two boys, Ned coming off more favorably in all matters academic, social skills being the only area in which Ned Senior spoke more highly of Chevy. The knife incident and subsequent suspension from school were discussed. Quite startling was the fact that Chevy's father had been told that during Chevy's suspension week he was being sent to stay with his maternal grandmother. During that time, Ned was apparently unaware that his son had actually been confined to the basement.

Chevy's dad was aware that Chevy had "one of those straight-bladed knives called gravity knives that he borrowed from a kid on the block. I raised hell about his having it, told him to get rid of it." Chevy had not disposed of it. On February 16, 1958, he wrote to his ex-wife: "Dear Cathy, The underlying reason for his having the damn knife is to impress some of his schoolmates. The reason he goes to such an absurd and pathological length is that he is without any social assurance and feels unrespected and unliked and unloved, which is exacerbated by the eternal competition of Neddy, a big brother who is a school hotshot and the darling of his mother's eye. I feel very sorry for him but that's how it is."

Again writing about Chevy, his dad said: "The truth is that he is an emotionally upset boy whose home life is not all roses and he feels he has, to quote him, a very bad relationship with you and that you do not like him."

It's not surprising that Chevy was unaffected by his mother's death in 2005. However, he had supported her, paid her living expenses, fulfilled his obligation, and taken care of her to the best of his ability for thirty years, "twice as long as she took care of me," and he spoke well of her at her funeral.

"Frankly I owed her nothing but anger and distance, but that's not me. My way is generally much more forgiving." Only once did Chevy actually confront his mother. When he was twenty-six, he took a long walk with her in Woodstock. He spoke directly about his childhood—being beaten and imprisoned. She had also been beaten by Cederquist, but did nothing to stop the abuse of Chevy. She cried about Chevy's childhood, and several times when she was elderly and suffering from dementia Chevy told her he had forgiven her. He said it to her, for her benefit, but could not feel it in his heart. Years later, he knew that, despite trying, he could never forgive her.

Chevy's parents and stepfather were all highly intelligent and well-educated people. His mother was a classically trained pianist and, Ned said, "one of the youngest to enter Bryn Mawr College, at sixteen. Twice she had the highest College Board score in the United States in French.

"Our father was a kind of charismatic fellow," says Ned. "A very bright man, especially verbally, expressing himself both orally and in writing. He was a very successful English student at Princeton, a Phi Beta Kappa." Ned Chase Senior's first job was teaching English at Stanford University. Later he was an editor in chief for several major publishing houses, including Putnam, New American Library, New York Times Books, and Macmillan.

According to Ned, there were many similarities between John Cederquist and Ned Chase Senior, although their handling of children was not one of them. Both men were World War II veterans and good athletes. Both came from modest backgrounds. Both were bright, Cederquist attending Harvard Medical School on a full scholarship. During the war he was a flight surgeon, dealing with injured fliers and sailors. Subsequently, he became interested in psychiatry. Their characters, however, were very different. "Our father was loving and devoted," Ned said. "He always made sure to live within walking distance, generally on the east side of Manhattan. I believe our parents deserve praise for their agreement to make sure my father's access to us was totally unimpeded." While Ned Senior was gentle and kind to the boys, Cederquist "could get angry enough so he could hit you. Certainly he hit me repeatedly on one occasion. I tend to think I deserved it."

Chevy's younger siblings, Pamela, John, and Catherine Anne, faced the same turbulent and dysfunctional childhood as Chevy. Pamela, like Chevy, has struggled all her life with the effects of her frightening childhood. Pamela is a highly respected and accomplished assistant director in film and television and has spent years in therapy trying to come to terms with her upbringing. Her younger siblings have struggled with drug addiction and depression. With Chevy's help, John completed a rehab program twenty years ago, and Catherine more recently completed a program and has been clean for two years.

"My father was way more physically abusive with my brothers than with me," recalls Pamela. "John used to get hit so hard that he'd go flying into walls, Chev got locked in closets. With me, Dad only backhanded me out of a chair once. Most of the abuse was spiritual, mental, emotional, physical, sexual boundary crossing [inappropriate discussions or touching]. Neither of my parents was equipped to do the job, in any way, shape, or form. They should never have been given the role of parents. It looked good from the outside, but it developed into a world of neglect, a world of abuse, a world of mismanagement. My mother hated being a mother. She hated having children."

Chevy remembers hearing his mother tell Pamela, when she was a child, "Whatever you do, don't have children." Even then he was shocked and angry that any mother would say that to her own child.

"One of the things about Chev is that he tries to come to the world innocent," Pamela said. "He tries to trust first. It makes him an amazing person, but in the shark-infested waters of Hollywood it probably didn't serve him as well as it could. We are all broken, all five of us. Fame makes it way more difficult. At the top of his game, who's he gonna talk to? That whole world is very, very isolating. Fame is not a great place," she adds.

Chevy's experience has shaped how he acts as a father. Chevy and his wife Jayni both believe strongly that children learn by example, and have "never laid a hand on them, nor have we been overly permissive. We've been as balanced as we can be." Their daughters are fully aware of Chevy's childhood and have high praise for his parenting skills.

As a youngster, it took some time for Chevy to learn that his childhood was unusual, that not every child lives in fear. This realization came at the age of twelve, when Chevy saw his friend Jon Tabori talk to his own mother in an impertinent way. "I immediately thought to myself, 'Uh-oh, I'm about to witness him getting the shit kicked out of him.'

But her response was the normal one. I thought, how strange, how much I could love this woman, this family."

Chevy had some respite on the occasional weekends spent in Woodstock. Chevy's grandparents continued to be a positive influence whenever he saw them. Chevy would walk to their house through the woods, whistling "Be Kind to Your Web-footed Friends," and his grandparents could hear him a mile away. Much later, when Chevy was in his twenties, both of his mother's closest friends admitted to Chevy that they knew of the problems he'd had as a child. "My aunt Nancy and my father's parents knew as well. I was so often at their house. It wasn't appropriate to meddle. They knew me to be a sensitive boy, always a tear in my eye."

Chevy's education is a blur, with Chevy struggling to maintain his grades and keeping the details of his life a secret from everyone. He went to two high schools—Riverdale, a prep school, "where my brother was an athlete and I was kicked out," and then to a more nurturing high school, Stockbridge. He then went to an "Ivy League-ish college, Haverford College in Pennsylvania," and finally to Bard, which during the 1930s Walter Winchell had called "the little red whorehouse on the Hudson."

At the end of one marking period, his grades were four D's and an F. He had been taught by his dad and granddad that the mark of honesty was looking directly in a person's eyes. His father lectured him about his grades and he went back home. His stepfather was waiting for him, sitting at the dining room table, ready to talk to him. Having just come from his father's home, where he had been reminded to look in his eyes, Chevy was now faced with Cederquist, who took that to be "a threatening kind of thing. So every time I stared, he would slap me in the face. 'Don't try to stare me down,' he said. I kept thinking of my father, honesty in the eyes. But it was like electric shock treatment. I learned not to look in the eyes.

"My life is a story about a person living in darkness and fear, with no self-esteem, who did so poorly in school that he was kicked out but was consistently told he was so intelligent and could do so much better—and was loved by the teachers.

"I was just working to survive a life where if I got home at six-thirty and dinner was at six, I got beaten for that." Recalling his war experiences, his stepfather would say to him, "I've seen men get back to their posts on time with both legs shot off."

Chevy was sent to a therapist as a child to find out why his grades were so low when his IQ was so high. It would have been a chance to speak up about what was really going on in his life, but his mother attended every session (not the usual practice now). He never breathed a word of the abuse.

Chevy's punishments were sometimes doled out over a period of days. If his mother was angry she would lash out, but she could also measure the abuse carefully. "She would say to me, 'Ten lashes on the backs of your legs every day for a week at five p.m.' How can you hold on to that kind of anger against your kid?" Finally, a gym teacher in the high school locker room noticed his legs. He sensed that something was going on. But that was the 1950s, and abuse wasn't dealt with by the authorities the way it is today. In fact, nothing was done about it. If this abuse were to take place now, Chevy's mother and stepfather would go to prison. Then, if he had told anyone, his mother would have denied it. "She would have said it was a lie."

The abuse of Chevy stopped when he was fifteen. He was eating breakfast one Saturday and John Cederquist came in the room and began hitting him in the head, telling Chevy to go to the library and do his homework. At that moment, his brother Ned, then seventeen, stood up and knocked his chair over. "He stared in the eyes of Cederquist, not saying anything. Then I stood up," says Chevy. "I saw him look at my brother, then at me. He never hit me again." Ned was surprised to learn much later that Cederquist never physically abused Chevy again after that confrontation.

Although their sibling rivalry had been strong, Chevy and Ned's relationship grew in that one instant. There had been one earlier occasion when Ned had been Chevy's protector when they were on a school bus going to Riverdale. "A bully named 'Greg' was always beating me, making fun of me," says Chevy. One day, Ned waited for him to step off the bus "and beat the crap out of him." Chevy thought Ned might have been "narcissistic, protecting his younger brother," but it didn't matter. Ned had noticed that his friends liked Chevy and admired his sense of humor.

Once Chevy left home he had little to do with his stepfather, but he continued to have contact with his mother and later helped to support her. Eventually she divorced Cederquist and married Lawrence Widdoes, a musician and composer who was on the faculty of Juilliard. It was a much better relationship for his mother, and for the family as a whole.

Chevy never lost his anger toward either of the abusers and has always carried the portrait of abuse with him. "I always turn to it in my mind. How dare that man. I did see him when he was very old, at my half brother's wedding. He was remarried, and he was an old man, with Parkinson's. I was tall and he had shrunk. I looked him in the eye, and still that look of meanness . . . and that voice.

"I'll never forgive them. At their graves I didn't. It was too hard for me. You would think a grown man could shake it off, as the coffin is being lowered, to say, 'I forgive you.' I don't forgive them."

2. ROLLER-COASTER EDUCATION

Rumor has it that Chevy's Haverford College career ended abruptly when officials had to deal with the slightly unorthodox issue of a cow on the second floor of a dormitory building. Chevy is careful not to fully deny the accusation but does say that it wasn't entirely his idea to bring the cow upstairs.

Chevy's early education had been spotty, and the discrepancy between the brilliance of his mind and the quality of his schoolwork continued for many years. Most of his early education, along with his brother Ned's, took place at PS 6, a public school on New York's Upper East Side. Chevy stood out from the crowd and was often the target of bullies until he was in his mid-teens. He did not always handle his frustration well and this was clearly the case at PS 6. It was a solidly middle- to upper-middle-class school with a good reputation. Chevy's first encounter was in the boys' bathroom, when he was approached by 'Alan', "a fat kid whom nobody liked. I'd gone inside during recess, and I was alone in the bathroom taking a leak at these big, huge urinals." Along came the boy, "pulling my hair while I was peeing, so I bit him."

Now it is very important to note that Chevy was not a biter. "I don't remember knowing any biters, I never hung out with the biters, and I'm against it!" Nevertheless, with his hands otherwise occupied, Chevy apparently had no choice. He bit hard. "Apparently I bit him hard enough so that when I saw him twenty years later, at a cocktail party or something, he showed me the scar." Chevy had bitten right through his skin and taken a chunk off. "There was clear-cut evidence I had bitten him."

The school called Chevy's mother and he was suspended for a day. On that occasion, Chevy said, the punishment doled out to him by his mother seemed appropriate. She made him spend an entire day writing in a loose-leaf binder, "I will never bite anyone again." He never did.

Chevy's and Ned's education in grades three through eight took place at the Dalton School, a well-known private school in New York City. The cost of the two brothers' education was shared by their parents. Letters from around that time indicate that after Ned's graduation from Dalton, Chevy's mother needed some persuading to let Chevy complete eighth grade there. Ned Senior wrote several letters stating that Chevy deserved the chance to finish there rather than return to public school.

In a handwritten letter from Ned Senior to Chevy's mother before Chevy's final year at Dalton, he wrote (the first sentence underlined twice): "It's vital you put in Chev's Dalton application right away ... Chev has only one year to go and of course he must go somehow; it would be tragic to cut him off now. We'll have to manage some way, with the Chases and Cattie helping out as is necessary. Would be unfair for Neddy to get full support and Chev (who needs it even more) to be cut off his final year."

Chevy finished the eighth grade at Dalton and followed his brother to the Riverdale school, a private school in the Bronx. After a while it was clear that the school was "not working to Chevy's best interest," his brother says. "I was kind of a semi big shot at Riverdale. I was quarterback of the football team, captain of the track team, played tennis, basketball. I was a sort of 'big man on campus,' if you will.

"To some degree, in the eyes of some, most importantly my mother's, I was precocious in a lot of ways. But Chevy was more of what one might call a late bloomer. My mother felt the rivalry was not good. I was a hotshot; he was a minor lunar moon. She thought, correctly, it was time for him to forge his own identity unimpeded by his big brother's luggage," Ned said, adding, "Chevy was obviously a bright and gifted guy."

Chevy had problems at Riverdale, attending summer school more than once to make up classes he had failed during the school year. Quite a feat, he also managed to get kicked out of summer school. One summer, he was repeating a year of French class with the only other funny kid in the class. "It was Mr. Schultz, my friend John, and I." Chevy and John had flunked French, because "neither of us gave a shit." The three of them shared a room that during the year was used as a study hall for two hundred people. In the summer, however, most of the desks had been removed so the floor could be refinished. There was nothing French about Mr. Schultz, which was an endless source of amusement for the two fourteen-year-old boys.

Though there were only the two boys in the class Mr. Schultz was easily rattled. Chevy and John found endless ways to catch him off guard. Their favorite was to very slowly lift their shared desk with their knees. While attempting to meet the demands of the French grammar they found so boring, the boys would lift the table, imperceptibly, over a five-minute period. When their teacher seemed to be completely absorbed in the lesson, they would let the heavy table drop. Every time, Mr. Schultz would shake. "I think he may have had a heart problem, but we got a big kick out of scaring him. Ultimately we got kicked out!"

When it became clear that Chevy was never going to graduate from Riverdale, Chevy's mother began the process of finding a boarding school for him. Cederquist had stopped abusing him by this point, and the final incident with his mother also took place around this time. Chevy was talking to his mother and she was in bed at the time. She was upset about something and reached up to slap him but he grabbed her wrist, stopping her. "I ought to kill you," he said, shocking her by the strength of his reaction. Later, his stepfather gave him a Freudian lecture on a boy saying that to his mother and "on how close to a real threat that was," Chevy recalls.

Chevy's mother took him to look at several boarding schools, including Stockbridge in Massachusetts and the Woodstock School in Vermont. He was accepted at Stockbridge, a small private boarding school. He lost a year in the transfer, starting as a sophomore when he should have been a junior, but it was a positive move for him. He not only was able to shine but was living in an environment away from abuse where he felt very comfortable. In this more appealing situation Chevy finally made his mark; he had decided to turn things around and was salutatorian of his graduating class.

His commencement address was a very serious message to his fellow students. "The last couple of years, we had all been involved in sit-ins and demonstrations. I was always the voice of reason," Chevy explains, unable to resist a chuckle. "The speech was about . . . when you leave this place, take what we've been given from this place—a good, honest communal sense of our peers in the world as a village. Be sure you understand what it is you demonstrate for, march against." Chevy, always a crammer, remembers writing it at four in the morning.

In Stockbridge, he was older than his classmates yet found himself socially shy and awkward. Both Dalton and Riverdale had been boys' schools at the time, and he now had trouble figuring out how to relate to girls. He went to the coeducational Stockbridge school knowing nothing about sex. His male class mates seemed to know a lot more than he did, and they all sounded like they were experienced. Only years later did Chevy realize that some of them "were braggarts and were making up their experiences."

He heard all about first, second, and third base and quickly learned what it all meant. "I was way behind as far as all the guys were concerned." He became good friends with Steve Rivers, son of the painter and jazz saxophonist Larry Rivers. Steve influenced Chevy's actions and his appearance. Until then, his hair had been kept very short, according to the clean-cut, sometimes even crew-cut, standards of appearance set by his mother and stepfather. Steve persuaded him to grow his hair. Steve was experienced and ready to guide Chevy through all of it—socializing, sex, and life in general—and as Chevy's good friend he never made him feel inadequate for his lack of experience.

Chevy fell in love with "Melissa," whom he considered "the most beautiful girl I'd ever seen." She was the daughter of an actress and had spent her childhood and early teens in Los Angeles. Melissa was fifteen and Chevy was sixteen. She was sexy and all the boys wanted her. But Chevy, shy as he was, approached her. On weekends at Stockbridge, "you could take a girl on a picnic, make out." Chevy remembered holding hands with Melissa, walking with a picnic basket, having their picnic, and kissing.

When he went back to the dormitory and shared the experience with Steve, he told him all about the strange type of kissing—"with teeth and tongues and her mouth wide open." He had not known about this. "I learned apparently that's the way you kissed. For me it was a big thing to hold hands with Melissa. I was so scared of it all, that's why I was behind everybody else. I was embarrassed about myself having an erection, and it was all a mystery to me."

The next weekend they went on another picnic, "and kissed again in the sunlight. It was delightful." Steve had told him he was now supposed to go to second base. "I had specific instructions from Steve—put my hand on her breast, feel her up. I had no idea how to do it, but my whole body couldn't wait to have sex with a girl." Chevy, still very shy, tried to remember the instructions, but he became nervous, flustered, and couldn't figure out how to get to her breasts.

"She was wearing a blue dress with a boat-neck collar. There would have been plenty of room—and there was a zipper in the back—to do what any normal guy would do."

After he kissed her, he knew she wanted to go further. "She had all this experience, and I had to live up to that as a man." The only thing he could think of was to pull her collar forward and peer down her dress. "I saw her bra and she was developed, but I wasn't quite making it to second base." After that, she broke up with him, and Chevy had to endure watching her going out with one of his good friends. "I had made an ass of myself, but that's how shy I was." Chevy never learned if she talked, although nobody ever mentioned his disgrace.

It took until Chevy was a junior in high school for him to have the courage to try again. Despite his difficulties learning the French language a couple of years earlier, he met another girl at Stockbridge—one from a French background whose mother spoke more French than English. Chevy and "Julie" were both virgins. "As would be typical, I was six-four and she was five-two. We were an item for the last two years of high school."

Julie lived with her mother in a small apartment in the Bronx when not in school. During those times, Chevy could visit her when her mother was at work. But it was always a problem for him. "Boys at that age, they have an erection at the thought of a girl. Whenever her mother would walk in after work—we knew she was coming at five—I would always have an erection from making out."

One evening around this time, Julie's mother came home a few minutes early. They weren't supposed to be in the bedroom, and there was no time to change rooms. Julie assured Chevy that her mother always went to the bathroom when she arrived home. As soon as she closed the door he could make his escape. Chevy was expected for a formal dinner at Grandma Cattie's, and he would have just enough time to go home, get ready, put on his jacket and tie, and accompany his family there. "My mother wanted us to be on time, dressed up with nice ties and jackets going to Grandma Cattie's, and in the end there would be money in it for my mother." They didn't see their grandmother often and this was a major dinner. Chevy's grandmother was married to her third husband, Rudolf Anton Bernatschke, by this time, and away traveling a lot.

Julie's apartment was laid out so that you would go through the kitchen and living room and down a long corridor, at the end of which was Julie's bedroom, a bathroom to the right, and her mother's bedroom to the left, opposite the bathroom. When Julie's mother came home, Julie whispered that it would be only a few minutes. Chevy put on his winter coat, threw his sweater around his neck, and stepped into Julie's bedroom closet, which was filled with dresses. He tried to hide but there he was, "a big hulking awkward six-foot-four," squashed into a closet. He did his best to blend in among the dresses, but nevertheless his head was jammed up against the metal clothing rod. He was nervous and wasn't thinking so much of his discomfort as the consequences if her mother discovered him.

Breaking her usual pattern, Julie's mother did not go to the bathroom. After three hours in the closet, with periodic visits from Julie checking on him, her mother became suspicious. He heard the two voices, speaking in French, getting louder. Chevy then heard Julie's mother coming down the hall, followed by her daughter.

She turned on the light in the bedroom and Chevy could see what was going on through a crack in the closet door. A tiny woman, she got down on the floor and looked under the bed. Chevy didn't breathe; he was now soaked with sweat from wearing his winter coat and from the sweater he had tied hastily around his neck.

Finally she came to the closet and opened the door. He didn't move—he was frozen in place, staring ahead, eyes wide open, not even looking down when he was discovered. The woman let out a bloodcurdling scream and raced out of the room, followed quickly by Julie, shouting in French.

Then, a few moments later, he couldn't believe what he was hearing: laughter from both of them.

Chevy couldn't stand the suspense any longer. He stepped out of the closet, walked down the long hallway, and asked what could possibly be so funny.

He had already missed the dinner and knew there would be hell to pay. Julie explained. When her mother saw Chevy frozen in place, eyes wide open, his head against the clothing rod, and something tied around his neck, she believed he was dead. She thought her daughter had killed him. The crisis was over, they all laughed, and the pair continued their relationship until graduation.

Chevy was well liked at Stockbridge, confirmed Benno Friedman, whose close friendship with Chevy began at the school and continues today. "He was popular and good looking," Benno says. He was not aware of Chevy's abusive childhood, and during their school years Benno only visited him once or twice at home. Benno had no particular expectations of how Chevy's career might develop, but Stockbridge was a school whose students came from high-profile families. "Some of them were making the movies—some were in the movies. Their futures seemed unlimited," he says. The school had 120 kids, and 30 in a class. "These kids came from celebrity parents, and some became celebrities. His fame wasn't far-fetched. Some kids see doors closed to them, but we thought anything was possible." The two related through music, participating in a student jazz ensemble in which Chevy played drums and Benno played the piano. Chevy's later progress as a pianist surprised Benno. "He went way beyond what I expected him to do. Chevy was a natural—he had a great ear; he still does."

After graduation, Chevy and some of his friends spent the summer working at Tanglewood Music Center. They were busboys and waiters, wearing white coats and white pants, and did whatever jobs they could to enable them to attend all the concerts, folk and jazz and classical, that took place there. It was a wonderful summer of music. Chevy was in charge of the morning coffee and remembered "spilling hot coffee on Pete Seeger's left hand," not the high point of his summer job.

At Dalton, Pete Seeger's brother John had been a teacher. "He looked exactly like Pete, but younger." At the morning assembly they heard John Seeger sing, and he sounded just like Pete. He taught geography and guitar, and Chevy to this day is grateful for the geography lessons. "Most schools don't teach that in this country. I can draw a map of the world, and the US and all the states."

Chevy was involved in a lot of pranks and jokes then that his friends would later see on *Saturday Night Live*. Chevy's friend Benno recalls, "I have one great memory of dinner in New York after high school. We went to a Tad's steakhouse and decided to be silly. Chevy would knock something off the table. We would both crawl around under the table, get up, eat from somebody else's plate, creating a scene, and being stupid. I had an old Buick and I remember driving down Park Avenue, spontaneously deciding to drop something out the window. We would open both doors, looking for something, and holding up traffic. [A few years later] I recognized this same humor in his *Saturday Night Live* stuff!"

By the time Chevy got to college he was already a strong political liberal. His father had always engaged Chevy in intellectual discussions as it was his mission to educate his children to know what was going on in the world, and to make them question, and understand, and to think for themselves.

His college years showed Chevy as a procrastinator, with grades not as high as they should have been for someone of his intelligence. Haverford College is among the toughest schools to get into, one of the top small elite liberal arts colleges. Chevy said he was "unprepared for the amount to be read and understood. It was hard to get through. I was overwhelmed, shell-shocked from my upbringing, and I'm glad I ended up not liking it. I wasn't prepared academically or emotionally." Chevy entered the all-male college as a premed student. He had long been interested in biology and was both fascinated and excited by the means of healing illness. He wasn't happy about the environment at Haverford, and found the honor system a little weird. "If a guy cheated he was supposed to report himself." Indeed, someone he knew who cheated had reported himself and been kicked out!

After completing one year, Chevy was encouraged by the school administration to take a year off and get some therapy or go to another school. The dean of the college was very straightlaced and, according to Chevy, believed that Chevy had "disciplinary issues, acted out by being funny, and was over the line." He was not encouraged to return to Haverford, although he probably would have won an appeal if he'd wanted to go back. Instead he transferred to a school more suitable to his highly creative nature: Bard College, in Annandale-on-Hudson, New York. During his time at Bard, Chevy began a relationship with the actress Blythe Danner that was to last several years, on and off, through college and after. Their relationship was stormy and both struggled with the end for a long time.

They were drawn together by their intelligence and love of music, "particularly jazz," Chevy said. He recalls that he and Blythe brought jazz great Bill Evans to Bard for a concert. Chevy had established a friendship with him in high school and had arranged for Evans to play a concert at Haverford.

Bard was a much better atmosphere for Chevy, but it meant abandoning his thoughts of medical school, as there was not much of a science program at the college. He was part of a more creative, interesting group than he had met at Haverford. He got through, with a B.A., majoring in American literature, and was very impressed many years later to be awarded an honorary master of arts degree from Bard.

Some important personal bonds date from Chevy's Bard years. Chevy and John Clements were both transfer students into Bard. John had come from Swarthmore and the two established a friendship that continues today. Clements recalls that the real Chevy was very close to the character later seen on *Saturday Night Live*, but he was even funnier in person than on television. Chevy told few people about his childhood, and John was one of those who knew about his difficult past during their college years. Peter Aaron, another friend who is still in touch with Chevy today, also met Chevy at Bard, where they forged a friendship that included Peter's younger brother Andy, who attended Bard a few years later.

An important part of Chevy's mission in those years was to stay out of the army and the Vietnam War. While a junior at Bard, Chevy was called in to the recruiting office on Whitehall Street for his preinduction physical. "That required getting naked, going through a line having various things done, coughing, looking up your fanny." Then there was the written portion, in which Chevy was fairly honest with his answers, denying "headaches, bedwetting, liver disease, kidney problems, etc.," and coming away with a 1-A classification, which to his horror meant that he would be inductable after finishing the next year of college.

After his senior year, Chevy was called back for the induction physical, truly concerned not just that he might be drafted into the army but even more, in violation of all his principles and beliefs, that he might be sent to Vietnam. He would have fought for his country, but like many liberal intellectuals in the 1960s he wouldn't go to war for a cause that violated his moral beliefs. Chevy was about to play one of his best life-saving roles. Copying a college friend who was a certified schizophrenic, Chevy prepared for his physical by staying up for two nights in a row. He didn't shower for several days, until he stank, and he smeared VO5 all over his hair. He tried to make needle marks on his arm but was obviously not expert enough to do this effectively because nobody noticed them during his exam. Back in the naked line, Chevy covered his genitals with his wallet and, following the example of his nameless schizophrenic friend, let his tongue hang out of his mouth.

The year before, he had denied problems on the written test, but now, in a desperate fight for his life, he checked off yes for everything. Yes, he had headaches. Yes, he had wet his bed. Yes, he had homosexual tendencies. Being a very honest person, he justified it all by noting that the form had queried "Do you now or have you ever had . . . ?" Well, Chevy said, everyone has had a headache; every child has wet his bed on occasion; every adolescent boy, wrestling on the mat, has had that fleeting homosexual thought. It's normal.

After the physical exam Chevy was called into the psychiatrist's office—a stereotypical doctor with a German accent who might well have been featured in any Hollywood movie as the caricature of a psychiatrist. Immediately, the doctor asked why Chevy's answers had changed so much in just one year. His answer: "I didn't know it said *have you ever had . . .*" Then the doctor asked, "Do you like boys?" to which Chevy replied, "Why, yes."

"Do you like girls?" the doctor continued.

"Yes, I do," Chevy replied.

With Chevy's fine performance, he expected to get a 1-Y Section 8, signifying that he was psychologically unfit for the army. Much to his surprise, he was designated a 4-F, which is given to those who have physical problems. A very lucky break. After his evaluation, however, he was treated as if he was a Section 8: "I was helped by two soldiers. Very gently taken by both arms. They helped me to dress and took me gently to an area with a counter, where I signed a couple of things, and said, 'Take it easy.'" They let Chevy go, giving him a card that stated he was 4-F. Chevy was then free to begin writing.

3. SEARCHING FOR A PATH

It was 1967, and Chevy had just graduated from Bard College. It was a turbulent time politically and socially—good fodder for someone with Chevy's astute political mind and satirical sense of humor.

It was a time of continuing protest against the Vietnam War, as the troop level reached half a million. Antiwar protesters marched on the Pentagon.

Communist China announced it had the H-bomb.

Dr. Christiaan Barnard performed the first heart transplant in Cape Town, South Africa. Dr. René Favaloro, an Argentine cardiac surgeon practicing at the Cleveland Clinic, developed the first coronary bypass operation. Stalin's daughter Svetlana defected to the West. Jayne Mansfield died in a car crash.

Three Apollo astronauts died in a fire on the launch pad. There were deadly race riots in Newark and Detroit.

A military coup overthrew the government of Greece. Americans had their first Super Bowl on January 15, 1967 (Green Bay Packers 35; Kansas City Chiefs 10).

All that was going on was not lost on Chevy. The next few years were a time of searching for direction. After graduating, he was writing, he was playing jazz and rock, he was acting, he was doing a variety of odd jobs to earn a living, yet no particular direction had become clear. He had graduated college as an American literature major but spent about a year and a half studying sound engineering in New York. He took a variety of jobs to make ends meet, which they barely did. He was a motorcycle messenger. He drove cabs; fast driving has always been a favorite activity for him.

Chevy's friend Peter Aaron remembers spending a lot of time "hanging out and being silly" with Chevy after college. One incident upset Peter's father. Chevy, Peter, and other friends were, by chance, interviewed by an NBC reporter while playing Frisbee. "Our main pastime was playing Frisbee on the streets of New York—under buses and across the windscreens of taxis," Peter explains. At that time, there was little security, and the young men would often go to the Central Park Zoo at night, "right up to the seals and throw a Frisbee across their enclosure. The Upper East Side belonged to us," Peter says. That particular evening, however, they were in front of the Seagram building when a reporter for the NBC segment called *New York Illustrated* approached them to discuss drug use among young people. They gave a very candid interview. Too candid. At the time, Chevy had two jobs—working as a motorcycle messenger and driving a truck for Peter's father's company, Sherry-Lehmann. When Peter's dad heard about the interview, "he went berserk," says Peter. The state liquor commission was tough on liquor-store owners, and having both his son and one of his employees talking about their drug use was, as Peter puts it, "not a good thing." Peter's father used one of his NBC connections to have the piece pulled before it aired.

From 1966 through the early 1970s, Chevy became completely preoccupied with Channel One underground television, an innovative form of entertainment including parodies and improvisation. Chevy was writing and performing in a building at 62 East Fourth Street, where Ken Shapiro and Lane Sarasohn, his old friends from Bard, were also experimenting with innovative forms of entertainment. Peter Aaron's younger brother Andy was also close to Chevy at the time. He was in high school and would visit Peter at Bard, which he later attended. Andy recalls his brother taking him to see Channel One when he was about sixteen. "It was underground, weird, outrageous. The coolest thing I had ever experienced. I went several times, and eventually Chevy gave me a ticket, writing on it, 'Let Andy in whenever he wants, Chevy.'"

Andy knew Chevy well before going to Bard. As a budding filmmaker who would work with Chevy professionally many years later, Andy showed a couple of his Super-8 movies to Chevy, and Chevy helped him film some more. At Bard, Andy's status as a freshman was immediately improved when Chevy, Rick Belzer, and Ken Shapiro showed up to film a *Groove Tube* skit and put Andy in the film, which was aired at the East Fourth Street theater. "Belzer was the foul-mouthed president of the US, and I was the reporter, with the cameras behind my head. Ken Shapiro had a gun in the skit, and Belzer subdued him. The main joke was that the President was so foul-mouthed," Andy says. The visits started with film shoots, and Chevy sometimes stayed over at Bard, where he seemed very comfortable. "He liked going up there, spending a weekend, meeting cute girls—even though he seemed a little bit too old. He was wistful, wanting to hang out at Bard," says Andy.

Robert Taylor, writing in the *Village Voice*, described Channel One as "a combination of forms: parodies of programs and commercials recorded on videotape, shown in a theater on television sets suspended above the audience . . . The audience on the hot Sunday night when I caught the show included a number of hip types, many girls in pants, about two dozen people and a tiger-striped cat."

It was here that Chevy laid the groundwork that took him eventually to *Saturday Night Live*. The article continued: "The studio is on the second floor of the building, in what must have been an elegant ballroom. It is a huge room with grimy gilt trim, dirty crystal chandeliers and faded wall panel paintings."

Taylor went on to interview Chevy, one of the latter's first interviews with a New York newspaper. He described Chevy as "a lanky 24-year-old who writes and acts in the show, takes tickets, answers the phone and works in a rock band on the side, sat at a round table covered with a paisley bedspread and talked about how Channel One got started." Chevy credited Ken Shapiro, "who was a child star on Milton Berle's old TV show," with providing the videotape machine to get things rolling.

"We got ideas," Chevy continued in the interview, "working together, wrote them down. Our first show was predominantly satire, and got good reviews, but we weren't an overnight success." It was experimental theater, taped for TV. "It's like we're saying we're bored with TV and we want something different. And one way people can find something different is to go to the theater. The main thing about our show is that it's a great hour and a half with a lot of laughs."

All the sketches involved humor. One of the early sketches was an interview with the "Maharishi Mishimashi Yogi," who giggles through questions about moneymaking, seated in a lotus position with a lap full of flowers. There's another sketch of a man shaving who discovers he has four hands, and a karate demonstrator whose (plaster) hand smashes to pieces. Much of it was juvenile in nature but the audience was stoned most of the time and found it hilarious.

Their best sketches became the *Groove Tube* film, produced in 1974, many of them clearly the precursors of *SNL*, with fake commercials, news items that pushed the envelope, and public service announcements such as a venereal disease "commercial" narrated by a penis and testicles. Not to mention a report on the first-ever "International Sex Games," televised in the same manner as any sports event, with running commentary describing the contestants' every move, and featuring instant replay and background on the event and the teams. "The West Germans," it was reported, "were practicing six hours a day."

"Nothing in my life has been mainstream," Chevy says. Somehow, without intending it, he has always been on the cutting edge.

He couldn't have predicted, however, that he would ultimately gain fame and acclaim as a comedic writer and actor. Strangely, he recalls one prophetic comment he made. In the summer of 1971, Chevy was a counselor at Camp Tamakwa (in Ontario, Canada), running the boys' part of the camp. At the end of the summer, the campers asked if he would be back next year. "No," he joked. "I have to go be famous."

It was not surprising that Chevy rushed into his first marriage without really knowing enough about his bride-to-be. His childhood had set him up to search for the love and kindness he had been missing. But somehow he was repeatedly drawn to women who hurt him. Later he would understand that his turbulent relationship with his mother had caused him to be all too comfortable with difficult or abusive women.

It took three tries and years of gaining perspective and maturity for Chevy to get it right. The first of Chevy's three marriages took place in 1969. Chevy met Susan Hewitt, a pretty and lively young woman, whom he described as a "groupie," at one of the rock concerts he was playing, with the group Chameleon Church, at Wesleyan. Chevy was playing drums. He was twenty-five and she was nineteen.

The romance blossomed, and Chevy was too naive at the time to know that Susan was not only unstable but using a variety of drugs. Susan also thought he might become a big rock star, Chevy says, even though he was earning only about $25 a week at Channel One at the time. A few months into his relationship with Susan, he ran into Blythe Danner and both thought of rekindling their romance.

Chevy had been unhappy about elements of their previous relationship but was willing to give it another try, as their emotional bond was deep.

Chevy was not happy with Susan and still drawn to Blythe. He made the decision to break up with her, intending to marry Blythe. That evening, he went home and told Susan. She informed him that she was pregnant. They considered having the child but then Chevy spoke with his mother, who stood firm on ending the pregnancy and persuaded Susan that termination would be best for both of them. Susan agreed but on condition that Chevy marry her.

Chevy's brother Ned recalls this being a difficult time in Chevy's life. The family was "watching the relationship," and Chevy's mother became particularly concerned when Susan became pregnant. She saw the danger to Chevy's future. Chevy's relationship with his mother was superficially cordial at that point. Abortions were illegal in the United States, and Chevy's mother arranged a trip to Puerto Rico for Chevy and Susan, where she had an "induced miscarriage." When they came home from the trip Chevy met with Blythe, telling her that, despite his feelings, he had promised to marry Susan and had to be true to his word. In a scene replayed many times since in Chevy's mind, the relationship with Blythe ended that evening.

Susan, meanwhile, became Chevy's wife, a relationship that lasted four years, until they divorced. Nobody in Chevy's family could understand why he let Blythe go, says Chevy's younger half brother John Cederquist. "I never bore witness to the fiery side of their relationship [but] everyone in our family loved her. Of course, what I remember about Blythe was how absolutely sweet and wonderful she always was with Pamela and me. I was just a boy, and found her simply beautiful, articulate, and well mannered—a 'perfect lady' in all ways, to use our mother's language."

During Chevy's first marriage, he began working for Dan Melnick at Talent Associates as a writer for an ABC game show called *The Generation Gap*, in which opposing teams grouped by age answered questions about the pop history of each other's era. During the same period, he was working on Mayor John Lindsay's campaign. Melnick was only a few years older than Chevy, but he was established in the entertainment business. Chevy said they were friends, but Chevy had trouble respecting him. "He fired me when I asked for a raise, for more than a hundred a week after working my balls off. He said, 'Are you kidding me? You're hanging on by your fingernails.'"

Chevy's goal was to be a comedy writer. "I felt I was naturally funny, and my father was my inspiration to some degree," Chevy said. He was constantly producing informal audiotapes and videotapes with his friends, and doing collaborative improvisations. He wasn't intending to be onstage as an actor, except for musical performances and perhaps occasionally to demonstrate material he had written. For about four years, he added rock 'n' roll bands to his various activities, playing as a drummer, pianist, and vocalist. He was fascinated by the jazz musicianship of pianist Bill Evans and began teaching himself to play the piano. He had perfect pitch (the ability to accurately identify any note by ear), considerable musical talent, and a flair for the keyboard, but learning to master the instrument was an uphill battle for him.

Chevy came home from one rock 'n' roll tour to discover that Susan had run away with an employee of Max's Kansas City (a Chelsea hangout and favorite watering hole for the Andy Warhol crowd), where she spent a lot of time. Chevy was miserable in the marriage. "I came back to a cockroach-ridden one-room apartment," remembers Chevy, "a place where the cockroaches opened the door, and discovered our bed unmade, and an ashtray filled with cigarettes that were not her brand. A couple of long ashes. She had an affair, and simply left. That was the end of that."

Life didn't get much better after the marriage ended. Chevy continued living in the one-room apartment in New

York. For a time, on the rebound, he was involved with another young woman, "Linda," whom John describes as "a bright, lively, and very engaging young woman. She was into roller-skating and disco dancing and would skate next to Chever while he ran in Central Park, which he did pretty religiously. Linda had an Irish Setter named Shanti, and Chevy had a tabby cat named Swipe—short for 'Asswipe', according to him."

This pair of pets "got along famously," John adds. "Whenever Chev and Linda visited, the dog and cat would settle down in the middle of whatever room people were hanging around, and Shanti would take Swipe's entire head in her mouth and gnaw on it loudly. Swipe seemed perfectly content with this arrangement; Chevy said that he [the cat] had never come back from an LSD trip, but we all figured he was just kidding."

According to John's sources, Linda later did a considerable stretch in prison for cocaine trafficking. John, now twenty years' clean, is a New York City-based graphic artist and a writer. Then, he says, he was "a highly impressionable gun-toting drug addict, who cut school to sleep in the wisteria pergola behind the [Central Park] bandshell during the daytime and spent my wee hours spray-painting subway trains."

One of his works is on the cover of *Subway Art*, "Henry Chalfant's seminal photo book on New York City graffiti and graffiti artists. Chevy was the only one in my family who thought that was cool—my parents wrote me off as a loss by the time I was sixteen." Chevy was on the road with a rock group, and doing other jobs, but still not making much of a living. He was subletting his apartment from an older friend of Susan's and had left his possessions in the apartment while he was away. Chevy came home from one tour to discover his belongings in the street, homeless people in the area wearing his clothing, and all his slides, photos, and records from four years of his life simply gone.

Chevy kept in touch with college friends and established performing partnerships, and, like many of the time, remained politically active, protesting the Vietnam War and smoking pot. Not long after graduating from Bard, Chevy and a bunch of friends from college, "including a number of potheads," went to march on Washington. Before the march began, Chevy and his friends played some touch football, and somebody came along with hashish. "We all ate about a dime's worth, a block of chocolate or sticky stuff—you just chew and swallow it, and you get high, as if you were smoking pot."

They attempted to play their game. "Very simple stuff. The defensive side is required to count to ten while the quarterback is looking for somebody to get the ball to." After about half an hour, the plays were becoming increasingly complex and there was a lot of giggling from the young men. "There was the Statue of Liberty play, where I pull my arm back to throw, somebody grabs the ball, just crazy nuts stuff. A direct result of the hash. I have nice memories of the relatively benign drugs," Chevy said. "Thank goodness, because what things turned into later was just hideous."

National Lampoon was a humor magazine that began in 1970 as an outgrowth of the *Harvard Lampoon*. Harvard alums Doug Kenney, Henry Beard, and Robert Hoffman managed to license the "Lampoon" title for a national publication, which took a while to catch on but made a strong satirical statement. Some of the magazine's contributors, including Michael O'Donoghue and Anne Beatts, later left to join *Saturday Night Live*.

The magazine inspired various spin-offs, including *Lemmings*, a satirical music and theater revue and Woodstock parody, the *National Lampoon Radio Hour*, several record albums, and a series of movies that began with *Animal House*, in 1978, and was followed by the *Vacation* series, in which Chevy starred, and a large number of other *National Lampoon* feature films not connected to Chevy, including *Men in White*, *Golf Punks*, and *Gold Diggers*.

The magazine declined during the 1990s and was last printed in 1998. The name and logo still exist and, in 2006, three *National Lampoon* movies began production.

Chevy was writing for the *National Lampoon*, and occasionally for *Mad* magazine, when he received a phone call from Christopher Guest, whom he had known at Bard, although not well. Chris had been hired for *National Lampoon*'s *Lemmings*, aptly described by the show's CD liner notes as "a satirical joke-rock mock-concert musical-comedy semi-revue theatrical presentation, or none of the above."

The call from Guest came about after Peter Aaron bumped into him walking on the street in New York. "Chris asked me if I knew a comedian and musician," Peter recalls. Peter suggested that Chevy apply for the role in *Lemmings*, and had to talk him into doing it. Peter recalls that Chris was at first "not keen" about the idea of working with Chevy, although ultimately Chevy and Chris became close friends. "They had the perfect mix of people for *Lemmings*," Peter adds. "I had the notion that Chevy could be internationally famous. He was good looking and funny. It seemed ironic that he was living like a bum for a long time. I couldn't understand why nothing was happening. I had no notion of money in the family. I was encouraging him to find a mission." Peter doesn't remember Chevy wallowing in depression—just not doing much at that point.

Guest asked Chevy to join him and John Belushi, a "ringer from Chicago," who became the star of the show. Belushi came from the famed improvisational comedy theater Second City, which had actually blossomed from the Compass players, a 1950s cabaret revue launched by University of Chicago undergraduates. Second City alumni were all over the comedy scene at that time. There was an influx of Second City comedians from Chicago and Toronto (which had its own troupe) into New York, and it served as a breeding ground for *Saturday Night Live*, which would be created a couple of years later. The name was drawn from derogatory comments made by A. J. Liebling in a 1952 *New Yorker* magazine article that called Chicago second best, second in size and quality to New York City.

In 1959 the first revue show premiered outside of the university, and it continues to include a mix of improvisational and scripted scenes to this day. Improvised musical performances are also a part of the Second City philosophy, and its influence was clearly felt in the *Lemmings* parodies of Woodstock.

Chris Guest and Chevy were on the soccer team together at Bard but were not friends at that time. "I was a freshman, he was a senior," Chris recalls. He knew Ken Shapiro from Bard and saw a tape of Channel One at the time he was preparing for *Lemmings*. "We were looking for people who were funny and played music. I suggested Chevy come in. He fit in the show, and it was the beginning of his professional career."

Before Chevy joined the team of *Lemmings*, Guest had made it clear the second half of the show would be a musical parody of Woodstock. "I played the drums and I also played a Hell's Angel who had Tourette's syndrome and whose Hog had been touched by somebody, 'some fuckin' peace freak,'" Chevy said. His character could not control his language. In the meantime, John Belushi came out as the Woodstock leader, making all the bizarre parody announcements.

Completely unannounced, Chevy would come out onstage wearing a Hell's Angels leather jacket and saying "fuck this and fuck that." "I came up with this phrase that I shouted loud, angrily." Pretending an audience member had hit him, and falling hard, the Hell's Angel with Tourette's shouted, "I fuckyoushitfuckpissprickpussycockfart," right at the audience. That began eight shows a week of Chevy's "falling" career. Chevy had learned how to take a tumble without hurting himself. Later, he would open every *Saturday Night Live* show with a fall. "I was very athletic, a pretty good drummer, later a good singer. I learned about improvising." Chevy got a good review from the *New York Times* for that performance, he recalls.

After watching no success or progress in Chevy's life for what seemed like a long time, Peter Aaron was very encouraged when Chevy joined the cast of *Lemmings*. "I must have gone to see it five times," he recalls. John, Chevy's brother, recalls going to see *Lemmings* for the first time down at the Village Gate. Now, he says, the building is "a CVS drugstore—there's irony. That's where I first met John Belushi. My first time there, I followed Chevy into his dressing room just before the show, and there was this hairy mess of a guy collapsed over the sink with a needle hanging out of his arm."

" 'Never mind him,' Chevy advised. 'That's just my friend John.' It turned out that John and I had the same birthday, January twenty-fourth, but nine years apart."

Around this time Chevy first met Harold Ramis, who would later become the director of two of Chevy's films, *Caddyshack* and *National Lampoon's Vacation*. He also became a good friend and someone Chevy respects and admires. Harold and John Belushi were friends from Second City, and Harold went to see *Lemmings*. "I was so impressed with everyone," Harold said. "Chevy and Chris Guest were brilliant, cool, and charismatic. Coming from Second City"—which is where Harold assumed all the good improvisational comedians originated—"I thought, 'Who are these guys?' I felt competitive. When *Saturday Night Live* started, I knew Chevy to say hello."

After *Lemmings* closed, Chevy spent the next three years writing and was eventually accepted by the William Morris Agency, a big step for a young writer. Chevy's "first real union gig" was writing for an Alan King television special called *Energy Crisis, Rising Prices and Assorted Vices*. He also played a streaker in Central Park. Through his work on the show, Chevy received his first Writers Guild Award in 1973.

After the Alan King special, Lou Weiss, a top executive at William Morris Agency, advised Chevy to go to California, where he said all the work was. Chris Guest was leaving, and Chris and Chevy assumed that between the two of them, they could afford a small place in Laurel Canyon. They actually shared a large house there for a few months, and had a lot of fun, according to Chris. Guest was hired to write for a Lily Tomlin special, and Chevy thought he might do the same, but there wasn't a spot open when he arrived. Chevy once again accepted many odd jobs—everything from mowing lawns to working in a gas station to building houses—in order to pay the rent.

Chevy credits Chris Guest with giving him the confidence to push forward as a performer. "Chris figures prominently in my life. He was behind me all the way. When I wasn't sure if I could do *Lemmings*, he said, 'Yes, you can!' He embraced me and taught me things and brought me under his wing. Chris was an amazing influence, but his manner could be aloof and intimidating to some."

When Chevy and Chris went to Los Angeles, they were "poor but happy. We loved living together. Chris and I were very close, good friends." Chevy admits he was jealous of Chris's abilities. But he could also make Chris laugh, which was not easy to do. They had the same sense of humor.

Chevy was pounding the pavement, with the help of the William Morris Agency, and he eventually managed to land a job as a writer for *The Smothers Brothers Show* during the 1974–'75 season. The music and comedy variety show by Tom and Dick Smothers had been on and off the air since the 1960s, and this attempt to recapture their act on air lasted about a year.

Chevy's brother Ned says, "In the past, Chevy had struggled. He'd been unemployed out in California, he'd worked for the Smothers Brothers, and won a Writers Guild Award for that. He'd worked for Alan King. And there were also times he wasn't working at all. The situation was checkered prior to *Saturday Night Live*."

In the spring of 1975 Chevy met Lorne Michaels. In the summer, he was hired as a writer for NBC's *Saturday Night*

Live and moved back to New York. He was sad when his Laurel Canyon time with Chris ended, but excited about the new opportunity. Interestingly, while Chevy joined the team on *Saturday Night Live*, Chris was one of the "ABC Primetime Players" on the competing and short-lived show *Saturday Night Live with Howard Cosell.*

Chevy says, "Chris had the integrity to believe, 'This is what I do best. If you like it, take it. If you don't, then you don't get it.' We don't see much of each other now, but he was a very important influence in my life."

4. SETTING THE RECORD STRAIGHT: *SATURDAY NIGHT LIVE*

Chevy had been writing for the Smothers Brothers in California and trying his hand at experimental comedy writing and acting in New York City. He had been playing drums with various rock 'n' roll groups. He was not sure exactly where his life and career were headed when a chance meeting with Lorne Michaels, executive producer of *Saturday Night Live*, led him to become one of the show's writers.

Chevy recalls standing in line for a midnight showing of *Monty Python and the Holy Grail*. He ran into several friends and was funny while waiting. "One of the people near me was Rob Reiner and he was in line with Lor [Michaels]. I had met Rob once or twice. Lorne asked h, 'Who is that guy?' and Rob told him I was a writer f the Smothers Brothers." Nothing was said then, but s ong after Chevy's agent called him, asking him to r with Lorne.

Lorne clearly remembers meeting Chevy for rst time and inviting him to be a writer on the show their first official meeting at the Chateau M at in Los

Angeles and, Chevy recalls, "This attachment formed immediately upon meeting." The first day they became like blood brothers, laughing at the same things, connecting on a deep level. Lorne invited Chevy to sit in on all his meetings the rest of that day.

Regarding Chevy joining the team, Lorne says, "People—management, agents—were talking for him at that point and wanted a guarantee that Chevy would be a performer as well. I couldn't give it as a guarantee. They said no, and I began assembling part of the New York team. Michael O'Donoghue and people that he had worked with in the past." Chevy wasn't sure about accepting the offer and said no. He took the summer to try acting in a play, but he found himself continuing to think about Lorne's offer.

Despite his earlier success with Channel One and in *Lemmings*, however, Chevy felt he couldn't act. "I was very frightened. Tried a commercial and didn't get it. The same with a play." He wasn't ready, he says now. His part in Paul Lynde's stock ensemble in Hollywood was the inadvertent catalyst for Chevy to join *Saturday Night Live*. He began rehearsals but it wasn't the right role for him. He was planning to quit. "I called Lorne over the pay phone in the theater lobby to ask if the writing job was still open." Fortunately only two weeks had passed and Lorne was not finished assembling his group. Before Chevy could say "I quit" to Lynde, he was fired. How fortuitous, Chevy thought.

Lorne Michaels offered him $800 a week as a writer (he got paid extra, AFTRA scale, for acting) and also allowed Chevy the option to leave after a year, when most of the other writers had five-year contracts with NBC. Chevy was not intending to leave after the first year but needed to know that he could. Chevy was thirty-two, and the creative team of SNL was populated by a bunch of smart, wacky kids, with various degrees of acting experience, doing an hour and half of skits, and the programs featured musical acts on catch of day. Nobody had a clue at first that it would way it ultimately did.

Many of the trademark elements of the show were Chevy's—the phony ads, the politically satirical Weekend Update, the on-screen captions taking audience members by surprise. Originally it was Lorne's idea to use midnight as the spot for Weekend Update. After midnight, the sponsors turned their backs and the *SNL* writers could get away with slightly more outrageous material. Chevy brought to it some of the material he had written for Channel One and *The Smothers Brothers Show*.

The idea of news for the hard of hearing, for example, featuring Garrett Morris as headmaster of the New York School for the Hard-of-Hearing simply repeating the top story of the day by shouting it, was proposed originally for *The Smothers Brothers Show*. The Smothers Brothers believed that the New York School for the Deaf would be offended.

"I was an all-purpose writer and the only guy who had worked on television shows, besides Herb [Sargent] and Lorne. I was the go-to guy when it came to putting the show together." Many of the first year's shows were written jointly by Lorne, who had been a comedy writer and performer in Canada, and Chevy, who had completed a dozen years of writing parody for television.

The *Saturday Night Live* team simply clicked, and they were shocked to discover their own success. For Chevy, the shock was twofold. First, it was a great pleasure to see his writing, and the efforts of his colleagues, receive such unexpected acclaim. The second, and bigger, surprise was Chevy's own success on-screen. His presence increased with each successive show, and his "I'm Chevy Chase, and You're Not"—simply a throwaway line at first—became legendary, along with his bizarre and imaginative falls, one of them opening each show. He had become very experienced at falling in a relaxed way during the year and a half run of *Lemmings*.

One friendship that formed early on was with the musician and actor Paul Shaffer. Paul was hired by the show's musical director, Howard Shore, a friend of Lorne's from Canada. Paul knew many of the cast, including Gilda Radner and John Belushi: "I loved funny people. I thought Chevy was incredibly talented and very musical. When there would be a break in the blocking, Chevy would always come over and noodle around on the keyboard."

Watching his falls, it is impossible to believe that Chevy did not hurt himself every week, although he tells the story of one horrible incident when he was set to fall forward. The property man, who was then in his eighties, forgot to line the inside of the lectern with padding under the spot where Chevy was to fall. He fell forward onto solid wood, did the rest of the show even though he was peeing blood, and spent the next week in the hospital. "The girls"— Radner, Jane Curtin, and Laraine Newman—sang a song for him on the air the week he spent in his hospital bed and not on the show.

The chorus was "Chevy, I love when you fall down each Saturday night on my TV. Oh, but Chevy, every time you take that fall, I wish that you were falling . . . falling for me."

Chevy's fame felt like "a gradual development" to him, but in reality it was condensed into a short period of time. He became aware of it walking to work, carrying his briefcase, from Sixty-first and Lexington to the Rockefeller Center. "That was remarkable to me. A lot of looks. But people left me alone." The feeling became even more bizarre when he was on the cover of *New York* magazine for the first time in 1975. "Seeing that on the stands. People would see me and it, a strange and fun moment. I remember buying it off one of those stands on Sixty-first Street and saying to the guy, 'Look.' And he said, 'Yeah, that's you—you're famous.' I remember liking that."

Nothing stopped Chevy from walking around. He was asked for autographs but people were respectful. Chevy's sister Pamela was away at school when Chevy began *Saturday Night Live*. In December, she left with her school choir to tour England and came back in January. "Before I left, I had known Chev as 'He's my big brother, he's been in a movie [*Groove Tube*], at the Village Gate in *Lemmings*, trying to do this thing . . .' He got a job writing for this TV show—it was on late at night."

Pamela would watch the show in an empty room downstairs in the dormitory. While on her trip, the *New York* magazine article had come out but she had no idea that had happened. The first Saturday night back in the States, she realized, "I can watch my brother's show because it hasn't been canceled yet. I was so excited, went down to the common room, which was always empty, but it was packed wall to wall with people." She thought there was a game on, but at eleven-thirty, the television stayed on NBC. "The entire room of people watched, raptly, completely latched on, laughing so hard. I just stayed in the back of the room. I had this moment of, 'Wow, he's on the road. He's going to be just fine.'"

Chevy's brother Ned also remembers his surprise when Chevy first hit the public in a big way. Ned recalls an old school friend of his and Chevy's from their Dalton days seeing the *New York* magazine cover on an airplane. Ned learned about the story from this friend. "It was the beginning, a great thing!" Chevy's brother John also recalls the moment. "At first we were stunned. But he wore it well, so we took it in our stride. I remember when it first struck me that he was famous. I was seventeen, roller-skating on the Lower East Side. I looked down to see my brother's mug staring at me from the cover of *New York* magazine. I still have that copy, dated December 22, 1975.

"Chevy was an overnight hit coast to coast, featured on cover after cover of all the top magazines over the next few months. Truth be told, after my initial shock I didn't find it so surprising. Chevy was—always had been—a very funny guy."

Chevy was always a political liberal, and although he knew and liked Gerald Ford, the president became an endless target of Chevy's physical humor. Some of Chevy's all-time favorite sketches were mercilessly at his expense.

The Christmas 1975 *SNL* show, hosted by Candice Bergen, was a perfect example.

"Christmas Eve at the White House"

Gerald Ford . . . Chevy Chase
Frank . . . Garrett Morris
Director . . . Joe Dicso

[Fade in on a shot of Gerald Ford sitting in a chair in a comfy room with a fireplace and a Christmas tree. Superimpose caption: "Christmas Eve At The White House." Dissolve closer to Ford, who clumsily puts a record in the record player on the table next to him.]

Gerald Ford [singing along]: In your Easter bonnet, with all the frills upon it/La la la . . .

[Frank, the butler, enters. He is dressed in a tuxedo and is carrying a drink on a coaster. He stumbles on one of the presents under the tree as he walks in.]

Frank: Here is your cognac, Mr. President.

[Ford rises from his chair and puts his hand on Frank's shoulder.]

Gerald Ford: Fred, you've been with me a long time now. I don't think that on Christmas Eve you have to call me "Mr. President."

Frank: Uh, Mr. President, my name is Frank.

Gerald Ford: Frank . . .

Frank: And what should I call you?

Gerald Ford: Well, how about "Dr. President"?

Frank: OK, Dr. President, the First Lady says you should turn up the Christmas carols so that everyone can hear them.

Gerald Ford: No problem there.

[Ford goes over to the record player and turns the volume all the way down.]

Gerald Ford: Would you ask Betty in here to help me trim the tree, please?

Frank: Uh, yes, sir.

[Ford takes the coaster from under his cognac and places it on the mantelpiece. Frank quickly drinks the cognac when Ford's back is turned, then exits. Ford starts to literally trim the tree, using a barber's comb and scissors, before Frank enters again.]

Frank: Uh, Mr. President, it is time for the Christmas Eve White House Fireside Chat with the nation.

Gerald Ford: Oh yes. Fine, thank you.

[Ford puts down the scissors as Frank exits. The director enters as Ford takes a seat in his chair.]

Director: Ten seconds, Mr. President.

Gerald Ford: All right.

Director: 5, 4, 3, 2, 1.

[Ford has already started talking since the beginning of the countdown.]

Gerald Ford: . . . Merry Christmas to all of you and good evening.

Announcer (V/O): Ladies and gentlemen, the President of the United States.

Gerald Ford: . . . join me for this Christmas Eve. Perhaps sit with me by the fireside and spend this time together as I put up Jack and Susan's stockings, and put the final ornament on the tree.

[Ford gets up to the fireplace, where there are two Christmas stockings.]

Gerald Ford: This will be a Merry Christmas for the entire nation, I hope.

[Ford hangs up the stockings upside down, spilling the gifts inside.]

Gerald Ford: Peace and goodwill . . .

[Ford picks up a handful of presents and tries to put them back in the stockings, but they fall to the floor again]

Gerald Ford: . . . toward all men.

[Ford walks over to a ladder perched next to the Christmas tree.]

Gerald Ford: Put the final Christmas tree ornament on the tree.
[Ford climbs the ladder and struggles to put the final ornament on top of the tree and starts tipping.]
Gerald Ford: No problem . . .
[Ford falls completely off the ladder from the top of the Christmas tree, landing headfirst on the floor. He looks into the camera and smiles.]
Gerald Ford: Live from New York, it's Saturday Night!

Ford partially blamed the *SNL* skits, and Chevy's repeated sketches painting him as a bumbler and a klutz, for his losing the next presidential election to Jimmy Carter. However, he seemed to accept it as "showbiz" and didn't hold it against Chevy, always treating him in a cordial way. Proof was Ford's personal invitation to Chevy years later for the opening of the Gerald Ford Library.

For Chevy, *Saturday Night* was in some respects a dream come true—working with colleagues who thought and felt the same way about comedy, partnership with Lorne, and, as it turned out, performing on camera and quickly becoming the darling of the public.

The concept for the show came in stages. "Chevy and I wrote a lot together—he, Michael [O'Donoghue], and I," remembers Lorne. "Chevy and I had the most TV experience. He was one of the creators of the show—over many dinners, many conversations—not a full-blown-from-Zeus kind of thing."

Lorne intended to be the newscaster on Weekend Update; he had done something similar in Canada. "But the closer we were to going on air, the more it became a weird conflict for me. I realized that Chevy would be perfect for it. I didn't realize how important it would be. On the first show, I insisted Chevy should use his real name." More and more, Chevy wrote the Weekend Update sketches, sometimes late Friday night. They became part of his *SNL* persona, linked to him even years after his departure. Often, cracks about

President Ford were not only in skits but sprinkled throughout Weekend Update.

> Don Pardo's introduction: And now, Weekend Update with Chevy Chase.
> [Chevy dials the rotary phone, waits a few seconds for an answer, then hangs up.]
> Chevy Chase: Good evening. I'm Chevy Chase, and you're not. The top story tonight: The Senate Intelligence Committee has revealed that the CIA has been involved in no less than nine assassination plots against various foreign leaders. Commented President Ford upon reading the report, quote, "Boy, I'm sure glad I'm not foreign."

"Being live, things were always in motion, which affected how the audience responded," Chevy remembers. "Most of the audience was above, looking down through various cranes, cameras, mikes, etc. They also had small monitors set thirty to fifty feet apart throughout the audience."

One danger was that the audience might be watching how it all worked, or looking on the monitors, and the cast was in danger of losing laughs: "Losing concentration on the sketch, depending on the motion and what's going on. It's a delicate process."

For the first few months the censors, knowing the show was live, were particularly vigilant. The cast had its own system for getting around the censors. "During the dress rehearsal, for instance, the censor is in there watching, looking at the script, the screen. Michael O'Donoghue or I would sometimes go and interrupt him, when he needed distracting during something we knew might not be 'in compliance,' and ask him what he thought of the previous sketch. It would be his ass on the line." Whether the offending lines would actually be in the script was questionable. Lines they knew would be troublesome were ad-libbed. The pair got a number of things passed with their "distract and conquer" method.

Carl Reiner recalls the first time he met Chevy. His son Rob had hosted one of the early shows—in fact, the third show, on Saturday, October 25, 1975. Rob took Chevy to meet his dad, along with a tape of the show, not yet broadcast. Carl remembers being very impressed by it, understanding that Chevy was a writer on the show and not intending to act regularly. "It was extraordinary," he says of the episode and the concept. They discussed Chevy's fall on the show, at the time still "a fluke" and not planned as a regular feature. "His falls were most ungainly and yet graceful. The only other person who had that same ability was Norman Lear," Carl adds.

Chevy went from unknown writer and actor to star and household name during the first year of *SNL*, although he insists this wasn't his plan. "I was not intending to be famous—that was not a goal," insists Chevy. "I wanted to be funny." The show had a star-studded first year of hosts, and there was a strong emphasis on musical performers. George Carlin hosted the first episode, on October 11, 1975, followed in the next few weeks by Paul Simon, Rob Reiner, Candice Bergen, Robert Klein, Lily Tomlin, and Richard Pryor. And it was a season whose music included Carly Simon, Gordon Lightfoot, the Preservation Hall Jazz Band, Randy Newman, and Phoebe Snow. Each new show seemed to be a whirlwind of surprises on many levels.

Chevy loved the challenge of *Saturday Night Live*, and his new experience of fame, but his personal life was a big problem. At the start of the show, Chevy was divorced from his first wife and involved with Jacqueline Carlin, who lived in California. Jackie became his fiancée during this year and saw no reason why Chevy should remain in New York when she was in LA. Chevy found it hard to resist the constant pressure from her and, once again looking for love and needing to be accepted, he began to consider putting aside his success on *SNL* for the unknown. He couldn't say no to Jackie's demands. It was complex and difficult. Other people saw it purely as the call of big bucks in Hollywood. For Chevy, there were several factors, but by far the primary one was his relationship with Jackie.

Chevy was so taken with Jackie's beauty and his desire for a wife and a family that he wasn't paying enough attention to what was happening. He didn't realize that she was thinking of herself. His career and newfound success on *SNL* meant little to her. She began threatening him, telling him she would go out with other men if he did not move to California. Chevy struggled with this for months but could not have anticipated how much of an impact his decision would have on his life.

Everyone was surprised and shocked when Chevy left *SNL* on October 30, 1976, after just one year. Only a few people knew of the personal struggle that was going on in his life, and it seemed that everyone was angry with him—the public, the cast, the press. Chevy's departure caused an outcry that in some manner continues to this day, people harking back to the good old days. Chevy insists he was maligned and misrepresented, that the record needs to be set straight. According to Lorne Michaels, Chevy's departure had to do, in part, with his sudden fame. "Everyone handles that sudden fame differently. *New York* magazine's cover story on Chevy, and Jeff Greenfield's comment that Chevy was the next Johnny Carson, meant as a compliment, put pressure on Chevy from that moment on.

"William Morris Agency was representing him; things were offered to him. He was torn," explains Lorne. "Chevy and I were very close. On the most fundamental level, he was one of the founders of the show."

Chevy was only just beginning to deal with fame, and he had no idea that his life was no longer his own. In part, he belonged to the public and was responsible to his recently earned fans. He did a number of interviews at the time of his departure and, it seemed, whenever he was interviewed later the question always arose. Sometimes his answer made colleagues and *SNL* cast members angry. In an interview with Larry King several years after the fact, he was asked the question again.

"Well, I left after a year because I was the one person who had a contract for only a year, and I never really wanted to do any show for more than a year. I felt we had done what I wanted to do, which was basically subvert television and parody it and lampoon it, and that was one reason. The other reason was a very personal one, which is really that I was in love with a girl out here in California and I hadn't been able to see much of her that year and I wanted to marry her. It was a very tough decision and I've always missed it."

"But glad you made it? No regrets, or some regrets?" asked King.

"Well, I think I've always regretted not being a part of something that comes so naturally to me. It's taken a lot of years to learn the craft of what I'm doing now and I've enjoyed it but, you know, *Saturday Night Live* is in my blood. It really was something that I was one of the founders of and it was hard, and it's always been hard."

Dan Aykroyd was, and still is, a close friend of Chevy's. Dan had arrived for his first *SNL* meeting on a Harley-Davidson, wearing an all-black biker's outfit, topped off with a black peak aviator cap with goggles and red neckerchief, "which I used when I checked the dipstick. I looked like a gay biker from Canada." Dan had heard about Chevy from Chevy's fellow *Lemmings* colleague John Belushi. "John loved and recommended Chevy. We met in New York City, and he was solidly ensconced with Lorne. I remember him kind of looking askance at the biker outfit."

During the first year of *SNL*, Chevy and Dan "clasped arms like Roman legionnaires." Like Chevy, Dan was hired as a writer and ended up acting. "I love him like a brother. It was just heartbreaking when he left," Dan says. Chevy had spoken with him about his reasons for leaving. They had conversations about Jackie, Chevy's planned move to

California, the possibilities in LA. "There were offers," Dan said. "Chevy was one of the senior members of *SNL*, not as young as everybody else. It had done all it could for him."

Lorne and Chevy were extremely close during their year on *SNL*, and for some time later, rekindling their working relationship with *Three Amigos*, which was written by Steve Martin, Randy Newman, and Lorne. In more recent years, they have maintained a more distant friendship, with Lorne saying, "I love the guy" and Chevy still feeling hurt that Lorne allowed him to make the wrong decision. In fact, Chevy wrote a letter to Lorne as late as 2004 "setting the record straight" about aspects of his departure and the circumstances surrounding it.

"I know it was an incredibly hard decision, defined badly by the audience, who really had a hard time with it," says Lorne. "But I think he'd waited his whole career for that 'Hollywood is calling, I can be a movie star, everything under the sun' that first season."

Clearly, there were hard feelings all round. Chevy wanted Lorne to help him resist Jackie's pressures. He felt hurt that Lorne told a "pull-of-Hollywood" story to the press afterward, never mentioning Chevy's personal struggle at the time. And he felt very upset that, when he returned to the set later, his photo had been removed from the large cast pictures of the first year and replaced by Bill Murray's.

Lorne, however, felt that Chevy had to make his own decision. "I didn't want to put any pressure on him. Jackie kept putting pressure on him." Lorne recalls writing sessions that were interrupted by calls from Jackie lasting an hour and a half. And Chevy coming back into the session upset: "A lot of 'I don't know what to do, I don't know what to do.'" Jackie was an aspiring actress and wanted him in LA. "The tug was real . . . and hard," Lorne said. "Maybe I could have slapped him and said, 'You owe it to America to stay.'" After Chevy, no other cast members ever left quickly, he recalled, with the exception of Eddie Murphy.

Chevy spent a long time angry and felt Lorne should have publicly told the rest of the story in the early years, when Chevy's *SNL* public was upset with him. Lorne now says, "He was in a movie. I didn't mean the Jackie thing wasn't there. I didn't think he sold anyone out. His girlfriend was on one line. He wrote me a letter saying how torn he was, upset I didn't stop him. If there was the perception that he betrayed me or the show, categorically *not!*" he adds emphatically.

Chevy's brother Ned remembers, "Lorne told me, and anyone who would listen, that he thought Chevy was leaving too soon. I will defer to Chev and people in the business as to 'whether you had to do it all over again' that was the very best choice. Certainly it got Chev started in film. [As far as] rearranging the dominoes in our life—who knows what happens if he stays. Maybe Billy Murray is flipping hamburgers somewhere. I don't know. Chevy leaving presented an opportunity for Billy."

There's only a thin scab over the open wound of Chevy's departure, and it hasn't yet fully healed. The stories continued to swirl even in the 2002 book *Live From New York*, written by Tom Shales and James Andrew Miller. Several former cast members were quoted as saying that the effect of Chevy's leaving was twofold. Everyone—Lorne, cast, public—felt abandoned, and it saved the ensemble feeling of *SNL*, which was headed in the direction of becoming "The Chevy Chase Show." Chevy, in fact, was the only cast member who had said his name on the air every week, and it had definitely made a difference. People not only recognized his face but they remembered his name. There was no way of reconciling the two elements in this rather strange equation. It was a year that shaped Chevy's direction and influenced television history.

While at *SNL*, Chevy was thirty-two, but in many ways he was still a confused kid. He was in love and couldn't resist the power of that draw, although he had jeopardized the relationship with a very brief dalliance with Candice

Bergen during one of her weeks on *Saturday Night Live*. "My wife-to-be, Jacqueline, knew her through modeling, and called her at home, and I had been in her bed. It was my first and only time cheating on Jackie. Candy and I were two infatuated people who had three days of love." But he smoothed this over and it didn't seem to affect his determination to continue with plans to marry Jackie.

When Chevy left *SNL*, he was given $2 million in an NBC agreement that specified he would not host a show on another network for a couple of years, and that he would make three comedy variety specials over the next two years. The $2 million was the total budget for the three productions, including his fee. The first two specials, he says, went over budget, and the third one was never made. Chevy says the agreement was private, and nobody would have known about it, although these things have a way of leaking out. This was another black mark against Chevy, which was interpreted by some as confirming that he had left *SNL* for big money.

At the time Bernie Brillstein was Chevy's manager, and Chevy was also with the William Morris Agency. It was standard practice for actors to have a manager and an agent, who served different functions. The manager's role was to oversee the entire career while the agency handled bookings.

When Chevy suddenly hit fame, his brother Ned suggested that he should have an attorney. He recommended Bruce Bodner, an attorney who, like Ned, had graduated from Harvard Law School. He was a corporate and securities lawyer at the major New York firm Weil, Gotshal & Manges, later leaving to form his own company. Bodner was not an entertainment lawyer but he was about Chevy's age and very smart. When they met, they hit it off. "Chevy is a very trusting and open and loyal kind of guy. He was comfortable with me and hired me." It was the beginning of a relationship that has lasted more than thirty years, Bruce acting as attorney, friend, and producer of three of Chevy's films.

When Chevy hired Bruce as his attorney, Bruce told Chevy he wasn't sure that Bernie should continue as his manager. He told Chevy that the relationship was a conflict of interest. Bruce described himself as a "belt and suspenders cautious lawyer, conscious of conflicts. Not having much experience in the entertainment industry, I didn't realize there's no such thing. And it all happened very quickly. Agents represent producers and talent on the same film. But I was concerned that if Brillstein represented Lorne and Danny, how could he also manage Chevy's interests?"

The meeting with NBC was called because NBC didn't have Chevy under contract. He had signed up for one year as a writer, but his performances were not contracted. "They'd run in the day of the performance with a 'day player' contract," Bruce recalls. "NBC woke up one day and he was on the cover of *New York* magazine, and he didn't have a contract. I'm not suggesting the others would have left but they were contracted, committed. Chevy wasn't."

Chevy wasn't sure what direction *SNL* would take the next year, and he was quoted in more than one interview as saying he wasn't sure how much more he could contribute, that he'd taken it as far as he could. "From an artistic standpoint," Bruce adds, "he wasn't saying, 'Now I'm gonna cash in and make films.' It was a very personal involvement with a woman. He sensed the show had reached a certain level, and he could continue with pushing the envelope, with different forms of sketches. But Chevy may have sensed it was time to move on."

Chevy explains, "The point is I ended up one afternoon with Bernie being fired and two million dollars from NBC for not going anywhere else for two or three years. That's what Bruce called a holding deal. In other words, NBC had no right to keep me there, but gave me two million toward three comedy specials and an agreement not to star in or host anything on another network.

"Bernie told people, 'Bullshit, he had lucrative contracts from Paramount.' People believed and consistently believe I left for greener pastures. And every book written about *SNL* claims I left for greener pastures!"

Bruce remembers: "[Chevy] was contemplating whether to stay or not. Up until the point he signed the deal, so to speak, he was struggling with whether to leave or stay. I was not really in the position of a confidant, but I think he was ambivalent to the point he decided he was going to leave."

After finally leaving *SNL*, Chevy had a difficult time. He missed his colleagues. He missed Lorne. He missed the excitement and pace of the show. "I couldn't even watch the show after I left, it was so painful. Lorne knew why I was leaving and how hard it was for me. I would get teary-eyed when Weekend Update would be coming on, because I missed it so much. I didn't know how to handle it."

5. STORMY RETURN

As much as he missed Chevy after his departure from *SNL*, Dan Aykroyd understood Chevy's reasons for leaving and felt he shouldn't have had to face such bitterness. "That one year of work was so positive and full of joy," Dan said. "It was vital to the show's history. I stayed four years. I understood why he wanted to go."

In a strange sort of way, Chevy's departure also helped to keep *SNL* on the air, Dan said. Because Chevy became such a big star in his first year, it provided strength for NBC. If *SNL* produced one major star in its first year, NBC thought, they'd keep it on the air and see what else happened. "His deal put *SNL* where it is. And Chevy's film career was worldwide currency for *SNL*."

Although Chevy was struggling with his departure from *SNL*, he was at the same time caught up in plans for his wedding to Jackie. He was "actively getting ready for a real marriage," hoping it would be different from his first marriage. He invited everyone from *SNL* to be at the wedding, and most attended. The wedding was a wild event "during which John [Belushi] got so loaded he actually started making out with my mother."

Chevy's friend Paul Shaffer left *SNL* around the same time as Chevy to film some episodes of a sitcom. The show wasn't picked up and he returned to *SNL*. Paul wasn't there for the initial repercussions of Chevy's departure but he recalls, "Lorne feeling that Chevy had deserted him." Lorne had also wanted Paul to stay but realized that the appeal of starring in a sitcom was hard to resist.

Chevy asked Paul to work on his NBC special, hiring him as a special musical consultant. "That's where we really bonded," says Paul. The first of three planned specials that were part of Chevy's agreement with NBC, this show featured ninety minutes of comedy, music, and sketches— everything from jazz and rock to a parody of a three-way boxing fight.

Tom Leopold, who would become well known as a comedy writer for *Cheers* and *Seinfeld*, was also working on it. Chevy met Tom at a party in 1975, during the first year of *SNL*. Tom didn't really know Chevy, but knew that he had roomed with Chris Guest in Los Angeles. Tom was sitting by himself and was impressed when Chevy, the big new star, came over, sat down next to him, and said, "I hear you're the funniest guy." Tom simply said, " 'Yeah.' I agreed with him and didn't try to be funny back. He burst out laughing. That's one of my favorite stories."

Tom credits Chevy with giving him his first big break, an opportunity to work on Chevy's first NBC special. The process of working with him was wonderful, Tom relates. "Chevy was the biggest star in America, and it was the most fun imaginable. His special was the biggest one going." Tom and Chevy were in the KTLA Studios one afternoon around the same time that *Liar's Club* was on air, and there was a long line of people waiting to get in. Tom went to the front of the line and said, "Who wants to meet Chevy Chase?" At that moment Chevy was in the office with his manager. "I opened the door and said to Chevy, 'Some folks from *Liar's Club* want to meet you.'" Fortunately, the office had front and back doors. "Two hundred people came through the front, shook Chevy's hand, and went out the back. He thought it was hilarious. It really made him laugh, and he *got it*. Such silly stuff. It was just a stupid thing. He got to the 50th person, the 100th person, the 200th person. The longer it went on, the harder he laughed."

Chevy, Tom, and Paul spent a lot of time together, time that was therapeutic for Chevy. One of Paul's assignments was to find a classical piece to be used as background for a mime performance by Chevy. In the performance his whitened face appeared three times on a single screen. It was an extraordinary example of his ability to mime. Set against a black backdrop, the concept of the three images was one developed originally by Chevy and Ken Shapiro at Channel One, using Bartok's *Concerto for Orchestra* as the music. The concept was repeated several times over the years and, in fact, returned as brief interludes during Chevy's 1993 talk show.

Tom was impressed that Chevy had such faith in his comedic sense. While filming the NBC special, Tom tried out some unusual ideas. "I wrote this bit called 'Beef Like Me.'" The inspiration, if you can call it that, was the movie *Black Like Me*. Tom recalls saying to Chevy, "You're gonna go through everything a cow goes through, and we'll call it 'Beef Like Me.' We went to a real slaughterhouse, and Chevy went up the ramp with the cows. [Chevy actually passed out while hanging upside down on a rack, Tom remembers.] I was a cowboy, with chaps and a Texas hat. It ends with Chevy under the cellophane wrapping in the grocery store with pricing. He knew it was hilarious— he didn't think about it, or worry about it—he just did it."

This special featured Tim Conway portraying a number of different characters. Other shorter spots featured Jack LaLanne, Chevy's wife Jackie, and as he described it while introducing the show—dogs, boxers, golfers, and cattle, and the musical group Stuff, joined by Chevy at the keyboard. Jack LaLanne offered a "physical fitness program for the dead," with "post-mortem exercises," designed to "make the most out of dying." Chevy's familiar three faces in white were a brilliant touch near the end of the evening special, each of the three faces characterizing part of the orchestral performance.

The show also portrayed a three-way boxing match among Ken Norton, Duane Bobick, and Jimmy Ellis, with Chevy and Tim as fast-talking sports commentators.

Chevy has always been fascinated by the subtle psychology of commercials, and liked doing parodies of commercials. There were several in the special—a fake car rental commercial for "Hurts," showing Chevy jogging and falling—Chevy's brand of slapstick—as he sprints toward his car. There was also a commercial for eye drops, familiar and hilarious to anyone who has ever failed to actually get the drops in their eyes.

Chevy's marital bliss didn't last long. Chevy's brother John remembers one visit when "Chevy picked me up in a brand-new silver Porsche Turbo Carrera and tried to impress me by speeding through Topanga Canyon doing a hundred and ten. He had a great place up on Mulholland Drive—the pool, the view, the whole nine—and there I had the pleasure of listening to him and Jackie arguing day in and day out about just about everything. God, what a witch! The mouth on her. Not that Chevy was any better. They would wake up yelling, spend all day yelling, and go to bed yelling." Chevy's college friend John Clements occasionally visited Chevy in California, and observed the turbulence of that marriage. "It was a wild relationship. They were always fighting."

Chevy faced verbal and physical abuse from his second wife, another reminder of his childhood, which he had been trying hard to forget. On one occasion, she threw a hot iron at him. Most fights, John said, ended "with Chevy hopping in his Porsche—Jackie scorned it as his 'silver penis'—and tearing through the hills at breakneck speeds. I joined him when I was fast enough to dive in as well."

The first time Chevy went back to host *SNL* after his departure was in 1978 and the cast's reaction was not a pretty picture. To Lorne, Chevy coming back was a great thing, but the cast had been dealt a difficult blow from the public and the press after his departure. Everybody in the cast had "taken it in," Lorne said, but it became tiresome hearing six months' worth of cracks (and worse) about "Saturday Night Dead." "They took it really hard." There had also been a shifting of power. John Belushi and Gilda Radner became bigger stars after Chevy left.

"But there was another side to it. They were angry." The perception was that Chevy had been the lead actor in a hit show, and the show was no good without the lead. There was a "winner to loser" perspective, Lorne explains.

A lot of feelings came bubbling to the surface when Chevy returned to host *Saturday Night Live*. By that point he was a rising star in Hollywood and he had not realized the extent of the jealousies that had existed among some of the cast members, most notably John Belushi. Before the first year of *SNL*, Bill Murray had auditioned but was not selected, and Chevy doesn't remember why. He was sitting next to Lorne in the Steinway Piano building in New York City when the auditions took place and decisions were made. The decision had been Lorne's, Chevy said.

Several of those auditioning for *SNL* in 1975 were already part of an ABC segment called *Saturday Night Live With Howard Cosell*, which began on air the same season. Bill Murray was part of Cosell's show. Chevy wanted to call their new show *Saturday Night Live Without Howard Cosell* but not surprisingly the title was vetoed by the powers that be at NBC. Cosell had called his cast members the "Prime Time Players" and Lorne called his *SNL* cast "The Not Ready for Prime Time Players."

The cast had shuffled its positions without Chevy. But Chevy, admittedly without thinking, stepped right back into the role he had played with Lorne, talking through the show and assuming that, because the audience would want to see one of his trademark falls and have him do Weekend Update, this would also be agreeable to the cast. Since his departure, Jane Curtin had taken over Weekend Update, and Chevy was unaware that the cast was very protective of Jane's new role.

Bill was already known for getting into fistfights while at Second City and was famous for his volatile and erratic temperament. Chevy had not realized that John Belushi had set the stage by badmouthing him during the intervening year, making up stories about his arrogance and ways in which he had supposedly behaved. The balance of power on the show had changed, and what had been a quiet jealousy on the part of some of the cast members the previous year had turned to anger when Chevy returned. The cast members were always in a power struggle of sorts, and Chevy remembers going back and being full of himself. "I always thought, I'll have plenty of perspective, I'm thirty-four, but this is all in retrospect now in my sixties!"

Between the dress rehearsal and airtime, there's about one hour, enough time for makeup and reviewing a few lines. Usually the host is left alone to look at his lines in a special dressing room. Chevy was familiar with the routine and didn't feel the need to separate himself. About fifteen minutes before going live on air, and shortly before Chevy's opening monologue, Chevy and Bill were seated next to each other in makeup. The dress rehearsal had been two hours long, and no personal problems had developed during the week of planning, writing, and rehearsing—except that Chevy had stepped right back into his former manner of communicating closely with Lorne, and others in the cast had noticed and resented it.

Bill began to make rude and provocative comments to Chevy—comments that included Jackie, Chevy's wife. And Bill was physically intimidating. Chevy, normally mild and unflappable, retorted with equally mean comments about Bill's pockmarked face. "I said, 'I'm gonna land Neil Armstrong on your face if you don't shut up.'" Bill, angered by Chevy's insults about his appearance, fired back at him, "Why don't you go fuck your wife?" and left the room.

When Chevy's makeup was finished, he went to look for Bill's dressing room. "There, I saw John on the couch, with Bill seated next to him. I saw a look in John's eyes that said, 'I've done something I wanted to do.' He was the instigator. There was no question, it was clear." Until that moment, Chevy had not been clear about John's issue. He never saw it coming. John—not Chevy and not Christopher Guest—had been the star of *Lemmings* a few years earlier. He wasn't prepared for the turnaround that took place during the first year of *SNL*. Chevy's rise to stardom had clearly made John upset and jealous.

Chevy was fuming. He shouted at Bill, "If you ever say anything about my wife again, I will . . ." At that instant, Bill jumped up and Chevy, still in the doorway, assumed the posture of a boxer, ready to fight. "I was angry and fully prepared to break his nose." There were only five minutes to airtime but Chevy didn't give a damn if the show started or not. He was upset about Bill's comments regarding his wife; it also hit a nerve because his new marriage was in trouble.

There he was in the doorway, ready for a punch. John Belushi jumped up, ready to be the hero, at which point, when the blows came, "neither Bill nor I landed a punch!" With John attempting to keep them apart, Chevy ended up punching John's forehead and Bill was punching at the back of John's head. Others in the cast heard the commotion and came in the room. "Bill had assumed I was a rich kid and he was from the other side of the tracks and he could just blow me away. I said to him at a party after the show, 'I'll eat you.' We never fought."

Had Lorne, who was not nearby, known what was going on he probably would have kicked Bill off the show. But it wasn't until moments before airtime that he heard what had happened.

"Bill is obviously disturbed," Chevy said. "But I have an underlying real affection for him, and I think he's a funny guy. He thinks I'm a funny guy. In retrospect, even with my body shaking from the adrenaline, I felt intimidated by him at the party. I never felt I'd lose a fight, and hadn't for many years of fistfights in my teens and twenties. I was bigger, stronger, and faster and would have lost a few teeth again, but I would have taken Bill!"

Doing the show wasn't a problem. "I simply compartmentalized and wiped it out of my head." He opened with one of his classic Gerald Ford parodies, spoofing the president attempting to answer his phone but spilling a glass of water on himself instead, a long scene culminating in one of his infamous falls. A few moments later, Chevy walked onstage for his monologue, relaxed and self-assured, and the audience cheered his return.

Jane Curtin started Weekend Update and the desk was shared by Dan Aykroyd. In a fake emergency phone call (from Chevy) telling Dan that there had been an accident involving his mother, Chevy got rid of Dan and took the seat himself, the audience cheering, an audible "All right!" coming from an audience member.

John Belushi joined the newscast, giving a bizarre monologue on boxing, finally boxing Jane onto the floor, and saying, "Okay, it's all yours, Chevy." In a scene making one wonder about the proverbial grain of truth, Curtin has a mock tirade about Chevy's departure and rise to Hollywood stardom.

"Don't tell me how to act," she says angrily. "This is *my* news show. You left. I took over and brought some integrity to it. None of your schoolboy cuteness. Go back to Hollywood and do it 'cause it won't work here. This is my show and I won't be pushed around by Belushi, or you, or her [Gilda, who is now on the set as well]."

At the end of the evening, senior *SNL* writer Herb Sargent, "the guru," came over to Chevy and said, "You haven't changed. *They've* changed." Coming from Herb, whom Chevy respected and admired and viewed as honest, "this sober remark meant a great deal to me. Until then, I couldn't be sure if I had done something out of character for me, and unethical, or if I had always lived in some sort of denial about my behavior during the first year. I was very confused and shaken."

Meanwhile, the now infamous backstage fight made its way around the country, and in short order all of Hollywood knew about it. The next time Chevy saw Bill was in Beverly Hills, at a party. Somebody warned Chevy that Bill was there, and the room was tense, wondering if the bad blood between the two would erupt into a fight. Chevy spotted Bill near the swimming pool, and in view of all the guests he walked slowly toward him with a look of great anger. He threw open the doors, walked over to where Bill was standing, and fell to his knees. "I began to unzip his pants, like I was going to give him a blow job, and Bill laughed. He laughed and I laughed. I didn't want to fight. But that doesn't mean I shouldn't be careful—on *Caddyshack*, I didn't turn my back." Chevy goes on to say he means that as a compliment. "The very thing that makes Bill so funny is the sense of danger in his work. One can never quite be sure what this comic genius is going to do at any given moment."

Although Chevy's first return as host of *SNL* had its trials, that did not stop Chevy from returning eight more times to host the show between 1980 and 1997. By that point, the casts had changed, and some of the cast members had been in high school during Chevy's time on the show. Martin Short joined Steve Martin and Chevy as the hosting trio on the December 6, 1986, show, the year the three scored a major success with their hilarious film *Three Amigos*. "Chevy is always happiest making people laugh," Martin Short says.

One of their *SNL* highlights that evening was their "Stumblebums Anonymous" skit, reprising Chevy's endless ribbing of Gerald Ford with a spoof on a clinic for klutzes. Martin Short almost didn't make it to the trio-hosting episode. He was filming *Inner Space* and the producers wouldn't let him off until Friday. "*Saturday Night Live* had promoted an appearance by the three of us, but by the end of the week, all the material was set." Somehow the show was pulled together, even with Short's late arrival.

6. SEX, DRUMS, AND ROCK 'N' ROLL

Chevy's fine musical ear was apparent early on. His mother was an excellent classical pianist, and the house was frequently filled with the music of Chopin and Debussy. (Chevy recalls sitting under the piano as a tiny boy, listening to the music with a milk bone in his mouth.) But Chevy did not learn to play the piano as a child. His mother didn't teach him. He had lessons in school for a few months, never practiced, and was dropped by the teacher.

Despite this, Chevy remembers loving music when he was a small boy. When he was about four, he began playing the harmonica and discovered he could play it well. He later picked up blues harmonica.

His interest in the piano surfaced in his teens. He has played several other instruments along the way: harmonica, twelve-string guitar, drums. He played in a jug band in high school. He wanted to play the saxophone, too, but never took it up. Chevy began drum lessons in high school with the head of the school's music department, who happened to be a fine jazz drummer. He showed Chevy some of the basics, which he learned quickly.

The unorthodox story of acquiring his first drum set still makes him chuckle. One evening, in his early twenties, he was with a young girl named Lucy, daughter of the writer William Saroyan. They were at a pool party at the home of a (nameless for the obvious reasons) married woman in her thirties and were engaged in swimming, tennis, and other sweaty activities. The woman of the house invited handsome Chevy to use her shower.

She was a wealthy and beautiful woman and Chevy had no second thoughts when he realized the shower invitation was indeed a seduction. "As push came to shove," Chevy aptly recalls, "the story came out that she was not sexually satisfied by her husband." Understandable, he thought, as the guy is so old—in his forties! "In some ways, it was delectable to me because she was a real woman, but I didn't learn anything much. Just did my job. At that age, I had learned nothing about the beauty and intricacy of the female body, and what gives her pleasure. It couldn't have been that great for her, but it sure sounded like it was."

Chevy spent the night with the woman, whose husband was out of town, and left early the next morning. She asked if she could call him in New York; he supplied his phone number and left. A few weeks later, Chevy received a phone call from the woman, inviting him to see her at her Park Avenue apartment in Manhattan. Once again, they slept together, this time during the late afternoon. Chevy had second thoughts. "Even at that tender age I knew what was wrong." He felt like a gigolo, and he told her so.

"I understand," she said, "but let me give you something." She insisted on giving Chevy money, further confirming his astute analysis of the situation. He kept turning down her offer of money.

"Well, isn't there *something* you want?" she asked.

Chevy said yes, there was a set of drums he'd seen, but they were expensive, $600. When he told her the price, she said, "That's egg money for me," an expression that became one of Chevy's favorites. She reached into her wallet and pulled out six crisp, hundred-dollar bills.

Chevy skipped all the way downtown to Manny's Music, whistling to himself, as happy to be out of the strange relationship as he was to obtain his own set of drums.

A short time later, he became a drummer with a rock 'n' roll group and his career started moving. For a while, he played with musicians Walter Becker and Donald Fagen, who later formed the group Steely Dan. But Chevy didn't think he was good enough and left the band, advising them to find a better drummer.

About a dozen years later, he saw the married woman after a *Saturday Night Live* performance. She was then in her late forties, and still beautiful. They spoke and he remembered her with some fondness, telling her she had given him his start. Chevy keeps drums in the music studio at his home. He had the "gigolo set" for a long time but he doesn't recall what happened to it.

"Music is my solace," Chevy says. He is at the piano in his living room. Chevy takes great pride in the fact that his own children are musically talented. He has provided music lessons for them. All three of his daughters sing and enjoy composing and playing instruments, including piano and guitar. They love listening to their dad play the piano and all three understand how important jazz is to his life.

Chevy has been practicing several hours a day so that he will be able to truly master the demands of "The Duke" by Dave Brubeck. He wrote to Brubeck to ask for his original version of the piece as he has been struggling with his own transcription of it for quite some time.

Chevy cannot bear to play a piano that is out of tune. "With perfect pitch, it's almost painful to hear a note on a piano that's not tuned. All the overtones can drive you nuts. It's an orchestra, the piano. The most beautiful thing in the world."

There are two pianos in the Chase household (both recently tuned): a Yamaha in the living room and a Steinway in a large studio that is set up next to the office, a building separate from the main house. He plays both instruments, and practices every day when he is at home. The studio contains his piano, drums, and a pool table, all of which get frequent use.

For four years after college, Chevy played with rock bands (drums, keyboards, and vocals), and he has several albums to his credit, including one with Chameleon Church, produced by Verve Records, which did quite well. Other albums include *Lemmings*, the *National Lampoon Radio Hour*, and a 1980 recording simply entitled *Chevy Chase*.

He was playing in groups and, at the same time, he was writing. He played for groups such as Chameleon Church, Orpheus, and Ultimate Spinach, ensembles that were part of the "Boston sound, which was known for its overuse of violins," Chevy says. "I was the drummer, drowned out by the violins. There were five of us, and we were told we sounded like the Association."

On occasions when Orpheus was overbooked, Chevy explains, "We toured *as* Orpheus." He recalls one tour where they were billed as Orpheus, playing at the University of Kentucky. "I remember being in that gym, which was filled with Orpheus fans. We knew all their songs. And someone in the audience yelled, 'You're not Orpheus,' and I shouted back, 'Yes, we are!'"

Boston sound was *the* sound. The members of Chameleon Church wore Nehru jackets on the cover of the album. "It was post-*Sgt. Pepper*, and every group was trying to be the Beatles. Had we been really attentive—that is to say, had the rest of my group not been heroin addicts, all of them dead today—we might have gone somewhere." Chevy was "a pothead" but did not follow the group in its heroin use. Chevy stopped touring with the rock groups when his work as a writer became more steady, and he did not have the time to do both.

Early in Chevy's career, he had a chance to combine his musical, acting, and writing talents. In his films, he often had suggestions for the music that would be used, and in fact he had considerable input at times. Directors came to trust his musical instincts and often asked his opinion.

Today, Chevy loves many styles of music although he plays primarily jazz. His favorite is the late Bill Evans, whom he knew and admired tremendously. He was also saddened to watch Evans's decline and death (in 1980) at the age of fifty-one from drug use and from a lifestyle that was common to many of the jazz musicians of his day.

Active with the Jazz Foundation, Chevy assists the foundation with helping elderly jazz musicians to pay their rent and get hospital treatment. Occasionally, he plays for their fund-raisers. "They are always surprised to see this white guy, with a style that's bluesy, among all these old African-American artists, such as Clark Terry or [until his death in 2004] Illinois Jacquet."

Chevy has played at the Apollo, as well as gathered in the basement dressing room crowded with "seventy- or eighty-year old jazz musicians I've adored all my life. I can feel all this love and all this music around me, without anything being played."

He prepared three pieces for the foundation's November 2006 fund-raiser: his rendition of "Alice in Wonderland," along with a Thelonious Monk and a Bill Evans piece.

Chevy is frustrated that he has to work so hard techni-cally to express the music he feels so passionately. "I still have to count the notes above the staff, and my biggest problem is with reading the rhythms. In college I would play the piano from midnight until two in the morning. I was awful, but kept getting better and better."

Family friend Natasha Garland says that Chevy's music has "blossomed" since the family moved back to New York. With Chevy at home more, "he really threw himself into that." When Chevy is away, he always manages to find some time to practice, even if it means playing a piano in a restaurant.

More than one of Chevy's costars over the years has enjoyed his musical talents. Beverly D'Angelo, the singer and actress, recalls, "I was thrilled to see the level of Chevy's musicianship. I think we did something together in a lounge at a hotel he was staying in, in Santa Monica, when he was in town. I think it stunned people too much for them to really listen. He plays the most beautiful version of 'Emily.' A good jazz player, for sure," she adds.

Dan Aykroyd is another costar quite familiar with Chevy's skills as a musician: "He's a master pianist. He understands music mathematically and artistically." Chevy's style reminds Dan of some of the great jazz legends, such as Oscar Peterson. Chevy identifies with Bill Evans more than anyone else. "I was just drawn to him, to his music," says Chevy. "The voicings, how they tug at your heart, and the fact that he never appeared to make a mistake, ever."

Evans's voicings (spacing of the melodic line in the harmonies) with closed chords are hard to copy, Chevy explains. "They are just different. His rhythm is what's remarkable about him. He played with both hands as if playing the drums, and the sense of rhythm and syncopations are remarkable."

Chevy demonstrates at the piano. Evans would start an idea "linearly, and you can see it work itself out—the rhythm, pacing, and intervals. All the stuff that makes a solo work. He completes a thought before going on to another thought. It's not a choppy solo, like Keith Jarrett's style, but this is more the Monet. You feel a sense of completeness and resolution in everything that he does." Chevy demonstrates another phrase. He has taken it right off the Evans recording, "but I'm missing a lot of the left-hand stuff."

Evans, who played flute and violin as a child, was a classically trained pianist who graduated with degrees in piano performance and teaching from Southeastern Louisiana College in 1950 and studied composition at the Mannes College of Music in New York. "He was about my size," Chevy recalls. "Evans became a junkie, like so many jazz musicians of his period. You can see the depression they were living in. They won Grammys but had no money, only for the heroin they needed after the gig.

"It's tragic—he died at fifty-one—an old man whose liver and kidneys failed from shooting up drugs. He was a sensitive, sweet man, and that comes out in his music. He was shy and distanced from people. It took a while to get to know him." Through going to jazz clubs frequently, Chevy also got to know Miles Davis, John Coltrane, Thelonious Monk, and Charlie Mingus. "All the greats. It's a time I don't think we'll ever come back to."

From listening to Evans, Chevy has learned "what moving block chords are" (a dense harmonic support of a melody). He demonstrates again, with the first chord of "Come Rain or Come Shine," as played by Evans. "It's not transcribed yet. I've found four books of transcriptions. Some are very good and some not close enough."

Chevy plays one of Evans's tapes from the sixties in his car, trying to absorb "Danny Boy" enough to do his own transcription, but he's his own worst critic. "I'm not anywhere near as good as the pianists who play in bars. I do have a feel and the feeling, and I'm proud of what I've taught myself over these years."

Harold Ramis remembers being struck by Chevy's musical ability when he saw *Lemmings*. They all played, he remembers, "like a lot of talented people, who tend to be multitalented. Music is an interesting pastime for him."

Chevy's LP recording entitled simply *Chevy Chase* was produced in 1980 by Arista and was an outgrowth of his musical work in *Lemmings*. The record has two sides—side one and side three—and includes Chevy as lead vocalist, musical director, and sound-effect artist, in such hits as "National Anthem," "Never Never Gonna Sing for You," "I Shot the Sheriff," "Let It Be," "Love to Have My Baby," "Sixteen Tons," "Wild Thing," and "Rappers' Plight."

The Randy Newman song "Short People" was also included on the album. Chevy appreciated the original, but was inspired to write parody lyrics, expressing some sentiments contrary to Newman's original. Newman's "Short People": "Got no reason to live . . . .Don't want no Short People 'round here." Chevy's "Short People," on the other hand: "Got more reason to live . . . I need more short people 'round here." Chevy insisted on including a long list of examples of short people, Belushi, Cagney, Chaplin, "many of the great comedians of our time." As an expansion of the joke he included Christopher Reeve, "six foot four and having already filmed *Superman*. Ultimately, the song parody is more in line with Randy's in its subtle insults," Chevy says.

Short People
(Randy Newman, with parody lyrics by Chevy Chase)
Short people got more reason to live,
They got quicker hands and quicker eyes,
They're built lower to the ground
Got better balance for their size
They eat much less food
They breathe much less air
They're much smarter with their money
Only pay half-fare
Well I just want more short people
Must have more short people
I need more short people 'round here.
Short people are so much better than you and I
(They're just the right size)
Some of my closest friends barely reach my thing
(It's such a small world)
Short people got more reason, etc . . .
They look further away than they really are
They don't crowd your space
You can get a dozen in a car
They'll give you all they got
If you give 'em half a chance
It takes them much less time

To press their pants
They look down at no one
They live longer lives, you know
They're just a bunch of crazy little guys
Well I just want more short people
I need more short people
I'd pay for short people
On me
Yes, I would
Chaplin, Napoleon, Olga Korbut
(Short people)
Pacino and Hoffman, Billy Barty
(Short people)
Carrie Fisher, Rod Stewart, Willie Shoemaker
Former mayor Abe Beame
(Short people)
Mickey Rooney, Alan Ladd, Belushi, Cagney, and
    Coozy
Toulouse-Lautrec
(Short people)
Judy Garland, Artie Johnson, Peter Lorre, Chris Reeve
(Short people)
Mason Reese, Rodney Allen Rippy
(Short people)
Truman Capote, Bella Abzug, Norman Mailer
Shirley Temple Black
(Short people)
Geraldo Rivera, Brenda Lee, Robert Blake, Paul
    Williams
(Short people)
Louisa May Alcott, Bobby Short, Tom Hayden (Short
    people)
Tom Thumb, Ricky Schroeder, Gummo
(Short people)
Groucho, Chico, Harpo, Zeppo
I need short people on me

CHEVY'S DESK I

The Weekend Updates on *Saturday Night Live* dealt with the news of the week, and no topic was exempt from merciless parody. During the first year, Spanish dictator Francisco Franco's health and ultimate (and ongoing) death were frequently visited. But Chevy's inspiration for the recurring Franco theme and updates on Franco's condition ("still dead") was the news following the demise of the renowned racehorse Ruffian in 1975. The race had been broadcast on TV worldwide, and the horse suffered a broken leg while running a close race, with Foolish Pleasure in second place.

"The news for a two-week period or so made the story of Ruffian's condition 'breaking news,' or headline fodder," Chevy said, "which *had* to be parodied.

"Franco's 'condition' was continually being updated by the wire services ad nauseam. Everyone was waiting for him to finally kick the bucket, but as he 'held on valiantly' to life, the headlines stayed with it. I saw the obvious pretense in all of this as a way for papers and TV news to sell their wares. Out of my cynical view of the press came my parodies, which in turn were the vehicles for more 'political' statements."

[All excerpts from NBC's *Saturday Night Live* are reprinted with gracious permission from *Saturday Night Live*.]

From a Weekend Update:

Well, after a long illness, Generalissimo Francisco Franco died Wednesday. Reactions from world leaders were varied. Held in contempt as the last of the fascist dictators in the West by some, he was also eulogized by others, among them Richard Nixon, who said, quote, "General Franco was a loyal friend and ally of the United States. He earned worldwide respect for Spain through firmness and fairness." Despite Franco's death and an expected burial tomorrow, doctors say the dictator's health has taken a turn for the worse.

Another popular sketch, performed not during the first season but when Chevy came back to host the show in 1978, involved a scene in which Chevy and Gilda are in bed, having just met at a party and had sex for the first time.

"After Love Discussion"

Man . . . Chevy Chase
Woman . . . Gilda Radner

[A couple begin a conversation after having sex.]
Man: You want a cigarette?
Woman: No, thanks, I don't smoke.
Man: Oh, good. Neither do I. [Pause] That was terrific. How was it for you?
Woman: Okay.
Man: Was it just "okay," or was it "really okay"?
Woman: Well, it was "really just okay."
Man: Did you, uh . . . did you . . . hmm? Did you have, uh . . . ?
Woman: Couldn't you tell?

Man: Well, I'm not very good at those things. I can't figure those things out too good. They confuse me.

Woman: Well, why did you ask?

Man: Well, you know, I figured we've just been very intimate, as intimate as you can be, you know? And, uh ... I'd feel sort of guilty if only one of us was satisfied, you know? I mean, it's not like I didn't try ...

Woman: Oh, I know.

Man: Well, did you?

Woman: Well, look, don't worry. Sometimes I do, and I don't even know it.

Man: Huh? I've never heard of that before. When it happens to me, I know it.

Woman: Well, girls are different, you know? I didn't even know I was *allowed* to have one till I went away to college.

Man: Do you *usually* have one, though?

Woman: Well, you see, it's like this. I never really feel them immediately. It's sorta like they, uh ... kind of store up, and then I feel them all at once. Usually, on the first day of Purim. A lot of girls are like that.

Man: Well, then ... you mean, you *did* have one?

Woman: Well ...

Man: You *might* have.

Woman: Yeah.

Man: Good. I feel better.

Woman: Could you hold me?

Man: What?

Woman: Well, I just wondered if you'd hold me. I mean, we've been so close and everything ... and I like that part, the holding part. I like that as much as the other part.

Man: Well, sure. I like that, too. [They adjust themselves.] Can I ask you something personal?

Woman: Sure.

Man: Um ... I don't want to pry ... but who's Phil?

Woman: How do you know about Phil?

Man: Well, in the middle of it, you said his name, you know?

Woman: Oh, gee. I'm sorry.

Man: It's okay. Who is he?

Woman: Well, Phil's my old boyfriend. We broke up a couple weeks ago. I'm sorry. I didn't mean to hurt your feelings, really ...

Man: Oh, no, no. That's okay, I understand. I was just wondering, that's all. It's okay.

Woman: You mind if I ask you a personal question?

Man: Of course. Shoot.

Woman: Who's Terry? Right in the middle of everything, you said, "Terry."

Man: *I'm* Terry. Terry Forrester?

Woman: Oh, I remember! You told me at the party! Right.

Man: That's just sort of a habit, from all those nights alone. I didn't mean to hurt your feelings.

Woman: Uh ... Terry?

Man: Yeah?

Woman: Can I ask you another question?

Man: Yeah, sure.

Woman: Who's Mommy?

Man: I said "Mommy"?

Woman: Yeah.

Man: "Mommy" is my middle name—Terry Mommy Forrester, I swear!

Woman: I believe you.

Man: I know that sounds funny. Well, it's getting pretty late. What time do you have to get up for work?

Woman: Well, my boss is out of town, I don't have to go in till the afternoon.

Man: Wow, you're lucky. I've got a nine-thirty class. It takes me forty-five minutes to get there.

Woman: Class?

Man: Yeah.

Woman: I thought you said you pitched for the Yankees?

Right: Ned and Chevy with Mom, c. 1950. (Courtesy of Chevy Chase)

Right: "Two Little Indians." Chevy, left, and Ned, 1946. (Courtesy of Chevy Chase)

Above: Smiling for the camera. Chevy, age 10. (Courtesy of Chevy Chase)

Below: "What are you all laughing at?" Summer camp, age 13 (far right). (Courtesy of Chevy Chase)

Left: "Did you say Champagne?" Ned and Chevy at their mother's wedding to John Cederquist, Feb. 14, 1951. (Courtesy of Chevy Chase)

Below: Chevy, Ned & Dad, c. 1974. (Courtesy of Chevy Chase)

Below: "Sorry, Dad. I like this shirt." c. 1989. (Photo © by Jayni Chase)

Left: "This is a good place to stop." Colorado, c. 1990. (Courtesy of Chevy Chase)

Below: "You can't have her—she's mine." Chevy with Cydney at 6 months. (Photo © by Jayni Chase)

Left: Passing on the talent—Chevy with Cydney, age 5. (Photo © by Jayni Chase)

Left: Chevy and Jayni, 1982.
(Courtesy of Chevy Chase)

Below: "Finally, our whole family has arrived." Chevy and Jayni, with Emily, Cydney, and Caley, 1988. (Courtesy of Chevy Chase)

Left: The whole family, with proud Grandpa Ned, 1992.
(Courtesy of Chevy Chase)

Above: "I'm so proud!" Chevy with (left to right) Caley, Cydney, Emily, and Jayni. (© Weston Luke)

Below: Ned and Chevy, c. 1980. (Courtesy of Chevy Chase)

Left: "No Martin, I'm not pregnant." Martin Short, Chevy, and Dave Thomas, 1990. (Courtesy of Chevy Chase)

Below: "My First Family" in DC for Press Corps Lunch at White House, December 1975. Dan Aykroyd, Jackie Carlin, Chevy, Lorne Michaels, John Belushi. (Courtesy of Chevy Chase)

Man: I did? Yeah . . . well.

Woman: You even promised you'd give me tickets for opening day.

Man: Look, I was lying. I just . . . I'll level with you. I just wanted you to go home with me. I wanted to take you home. I thought it would sound a little better if I told you I was pitching for the Yankees. I figured if I told you I'm teaching driver's ed for Rodell Junior High, you know . . .?

Woman: I understand. You must really like baseball.

Man: Never miss a game.

Woman: Yeah, me either. Especially the Yankees. I follow them closely, like I know the whole roster.

Man: Well, why did you let me lie to you like that?

Woman: Well, I didn't want to embarrass you, and I was afraid you wouldn't take me home. . . and I knew you'd tell me the truth, eventually.

Man: Well, that's real nice of you. That's real nice. I've gotta go. [Gets up.]

Woman: Well, where are you going?

Man: I told you, I've got an early class. I've gotta get ready.

Woman: Well, you can stay, if you want to.

Man: I can?

Woman: Sure. It's your apartment.

[The man turns the lamp off, as they both fall asleep.]
[Fade out.]

Chevy could not resist writing sketches that poked fun at television ads. From his earliest days of writing for Channel One, he'd look around to find things that were taken for granted in order to bring out their absurdity, or to show how a subtle twist of their reality could lead to the absurd. Parody was his vehicle, as it had been from the start, with Channel One, *Mad* magazine, and *National Lampoon*.

Chevy was intrigued by the ways in which products were advertised and sold, and he enjoyed poking fun at the marketing psychology employed by established corporations. Some of these early ad parodies were written by Chevy while working on *The Smothers Brothers Show* (often working in pairs or teams).

One of Chevy's favorite such parodies was his own innovative "Triple-Trak Commercial," written in 1974, and made slightly more amusing by the fact that the actual three-bladed razor did not come out until the 1990s.

The commercial was written for *The Smothers Brothers Show* but was not used. Chevy kept it and recycled it for *Saturday Night Live* and it was used on the first show, on October 11, 1975. The Trac II razor had just come out.

In 2004, the *Onion* published a satirical article announcing the five-bladed razor. Possibly it was on a hot tip, but the following year CNN/Money quite seriously announced that "Gillette has escalated the razor wars yet again, unveiling a new line of razors . . . with five blades and a lubricating strip on both the front and back."

In Chevy's prophetic script there are roles for "Cavemen" and "Announcer (voiceover)." Props were a rock, sharp rock, ax, straight razor, injector, double-edged, Trac II, and Triple-Trak.

[Open on Caveman outside his cave, alternately hitting and painfully rubbing his bruised and bearded face with a rock.]
Announcer (V/O): First, there was the rock . . .
[Cut to exterior of cave, another angle.]
[Caveman with reddened and badly scratched cheeks, scraping with a sharp rock at a scraggly beard. He is not as full-bearded as the first caveman]
. . . and soon after, still long before the Bronze Age, the sharp rock.
[Cut to exterior of cave.]
[Caveman swings axe toward face.]
Later came the most sophisticated beard-removing device of the Paleolithic period, the axe. Since then, man has

been ardently striving to design the perfect shaving instrument, from the rapier, to the machete, to the straight razor.

[Shows us straight razor. Puts down straight razor and shows us injector cartridge.]

But the truly close shave could not be had before the twentieth century, and the advent of the injector blade—smooth, comfortably close.

[Puts down injector cartridge, shows us double-edged razor.]

Then came the double-edged razor, with its incomparable stainless steel blade . . .

[Puts down double-edged, shows us the newer Trac II.]

. . . and, finally, the highly acclaimed twin-blade cartridge. Almost perfect . . . yet not quite the superlative groom.

[Cut to: product shot—Triple-Trak razor, looking just like the Trac II but with three blades, turning slowly in limbo and eventually passing the lens of the camera.]

(Music: *2001: A Space Odyssey* takeoff)

Introducing the Triple-Trak. Not just two blades in one system, but three stainless platinum Teflon-coated blades melded together to form one incredible shaving cartridge, easily fitted into your old twin-blade holder.

[Cut to: Cards with drawings of the following description.]

Here's how it works. We made the first two blades just dull enough to pull at your whiskers, not once but *twice*. The first blade grabs at the whisker, tugging it away from your face to *protect* your face from the second blade. Blade number two *catches* and *digs* into the stubble before it has the chance to snap back and injure you while pulling it farther out so that it is now ready for shearing. Triple-Trak's third blade, a finely honed, bonded platinum instrument, cuts cleanly through the whisker at its base, leaving your face as smooth as a newborn baby. The hair is severed at an angle so that there are no split ends to worry you. Your face will shine like a billiard ball.

[Cut to: Announcer holding the handle in one hand and the Triple-Trak cartridge in the other. He snaps the cartridge into place.]

The Triple-Trak. Because you'll believe anything.

Nothing is sacred in parody and satire. Chevy's sketches hit every subject, from Watergate to the Middle East to hot dogs. One of his sketches, the "Monday Night Domestic Argument," with announcers George Carlin and Tom Smothers, turned everyday activities into sporting events, using techniques from *Monday Night Football* broadcasts to illustrate. For example, in this short excerpt from a much longer sketch, as Selma Beckerman opens the oven instead of responding to her husband's greeting, the announcer, George Carlin, says, "Another look at that in slow motion."

George (commenting on the replay): Notice that she all but ignores her spouse, moving coyly to the oven. She's really working on the martyrdom angle here ... Back now to live action. [Part of Chevy's inspiration for this sketch was observing the relationship between his mother and stepfather.]

Selma (to her husband): I can't take it anymore! I just can't take it!

George (commenting): A surprise maneuver.

Part II

Hollywood and Fame

7. FOUL PLAY, IN MORE WAYS THAN ONE

During the period following Chevy's departure from *SNL* he was once again searching, although from quite a different vantage point than he had a decade earlier. He was a big star but still wondering why and how, and what to do about it. In an interview in the September 1978 issue of the magazine *Crawdaddy*, Chevy attempted to answer questions about the direction of his career.

Executive editor Mitchell Glazer wrote: "Chevy has this problem. He's intelligent and perceptive enough to rip apart those often-nameless desires which drive all performers. He understands it all—so he has to deal with it . . . He knows, and it's probably a raw knowledge, why he pushed for a prime-time special (top-rated for 1977 NBC specials) and why he took a role in a major Hollywood comedy."

Chevy is quoted as saying, "I have to think, 'What do I have to compromise? I don't want to lose my base. My base is, I make fun of bullshit.' But then I came to the realization that it's bullshit to think that wanting to be a star is bullshit. That's bullshit. Why shouldn't I want to be a star? Isn't the idea of any job upward mobility? In any job you name, people wanna be a star. And if they're honest they'll admit it.

"What's all this shit about compromising? When it comes down to it, I'm just a fuckin' American TV and movie personality. Sellout? Shit? We're not talking about Mao here, or the *Dialectics*."

Looking back on some of the comments he made at that time, Chevy now says, "I was just being cool."

Shortly after his marriage to Jackie, Chevy began to discover disturbing lies and important things Jackie had not told him about herself. For example, she was eleven years older than she had said, and she had been married before but had not mentioned it. In a casual conversation with a friend of Jackie's, Chevy was told that Jackie had previously been married and living in Florida. One day, the friend said, Jackie's ex-husband had come home from work and found all the furniture gone; Jackie was in Paris. Her ex was served with divorce papers. She was an actress and a model, Chevy says, "But I never saw her act in anything that I didn't put her in. Commercials on *SNL* and photos of her in magazines." Chevy's marriage to Jackie blew up after about a year, although it was five years until the divorce. He had asked her for a prenuptial agreement once but she had threatened not to marry him. When the relationship failed, he knew the financial part of the divorce would be challenging.

Struggling with his separation from Jackie was difficult. When the marriage was finally at an end, she did interviews with the press, including one for the *Star* where she blamed "hangers-on and meddling lawyers for breaking up the marriage." Jackie had reacted angrily when Chevy's lawyers asked her to sign a "postnuptial" agreement after they had separated and reconciled.

Once finalized in 1980, the divorce settlement gave Jackie $400,000, plus $4,000 a month in alimony. Chevy was very depressed about the breakup of his second marriage, and the negative publicity that surrounded it, although Jackie claimed publicly that she was the one who had been abused by the press. In the same 1980 interview, she had stated,

"All along I've been the one to be bad-mouthed. It was falsely stated that I was taking him for everything he was worth and I was getting everything."

During this period, Chevy continued trying to work with Michael O'Donoghue on a screenplay they first began in 1976. Somehow word got out that Chevy and Michael O'Donoghue had a long and stormy relationship. "I felt very close to Michael. He was a strange duck, one of the most brilliant satirists and writers of our time, but he had tremendous hate and anger in him, and it came out in his writing. It was hilarious stuff. There was some misguided belief on Buck Henry's part that Michael hated me. Well, he didn't hate me—he loved me."

Eventually, the film blew up. The screenplay, *Saturday Matinee*, was many pages too long, Chevy says, and a dispute arose over cutting it. "Normally a script would be about 90–100 pages, a page being a minute or so." Their script was 160 pages, and that was only for part of the movie. O'Donoghue wouldn't cut it. Chevy said he wouldn't cut Michael's work, and "Michael suggested some airhead girl. She didn't do it. It was his dark side speaking, saying go fuck yourself. I had my own life, my career. I moved on," Chevy says. This happened over a period of several years, during which Chevy became increasingly disillusioned. Other opportunities arose for Chevy, and he abandoned the screenplay.

"It was a sad thing we couldn't make that film. There was anger in Michael all the time over so many things, but we saw each other many times after that period." Michael's use of unique forms of insult was "the hallmark of his humor," Chevy explains, "the very language of which flowed like some never-heard-of blood type, always a hidden channel for his interminable anger."

The screenplay included called a song called "Let's Talk Dirty to the Animals." Some years later, Michael asked Chevy to release that portion so Gilda Radner could do it on Broadway. Chevy was fine with it, and it was a song Radner performed many times. Although the screenplay was never finished, Chevy said that he and Michael remained on very good terms until Michael's death in 1994, at the age of fifty-four from a stroke. Chevy was making movies "that were hardly up to Mike's standard" when Michael died at his Chelsea brownstone in New York. They had seen each other a few months before his death.

Chevy was offered a leading role in a film called *Foul Play* at the same time that he was being considered for *Animal House*. "When Doug Kenney's brother died, he transferred [his feelings as a brother] to Chevy," says Harold Ramis, who wrote the *Animal House* script with Doug Kenney and Chris Miller. Kenney had Chevy in mind for the role of "Otter," Tim Matheson's eventual role. "It was sideswiped by Chevy's *Saturday Night Live* rivalry with John Belushi," recalls Ramis. He also believed Chevy's management saw him as a leading man and "the next Cary Grant" and advised against "an ensemble youth comedy at that point."

In *Foul Play*, Goldie Hawn, as librarian Gloria Mundy, finds her peaceful existence shattered when a film cassette is by chance left with her by a dying agent. She unwittingly uncovers a plot to assassinate the pope. Chevy plays San Francisco detective Tony Carlson. In this wacky and complicated comedy spoof, Chevy and Goldie prevent the dreadful crime from taking place. Dudley Moore plays the role of Stanley Tibbets, a famous opera conductor, and he conducts *The Mikado*, a focal point of the pope's visit to San Francisco. Love blooms between Gloria and Tony.

This was Chevy's first Hollywood film and Dudley Moore's American film debut. Chevy recalled going to great lengths to get Dudley Moore for the role of Stanley Tibbets. Dudley had at first refused, and the role had to be recrafted. When music was brought into it, and Stanley was rewritten as a famous opera conductor, Dudley agreed to accept the role.

Foul Play had a bizarre and delightful plot and was a remarkable vehicle for the physical comedy styles of both

Chevy and Dudley, as well as Goldie's already well-known brand of comedy. It was also the start of a romance between Chevy and Goldie that developed ultimately into a very close friendship between the two.

Goldie recalled that she was asked to play the role of Gloria Mundy "at the last minute. It was supposed to be somebody else." And the first meeting with Chevy is clear in her mind nearly thirty years after the fact. "I knew I had to meet the guy. I had seen *Saturday Night Live* a bit and loved the show." But she hadn't been paying close attention to who did what on *SNL*. "I didn't know which guy Chevy was."

The first meeting was in the office of writer/director Colin Higgins. Chevy opened the door, "and he took my breath away," Goldie recalled. "He was so handsome, talented, funny, and he made me laugh. He had all of it." Goldie was carrying a purple crocheted purse that looked like a cow's udder. Chevy looked at it, looked her in the eye, and said "posh." Goldie was smitten. "I fell madly, truly, deeply in love." Goldie was drawn to Chevy because he was so different from everyone else she knew in Hollywood. "So talented, highly educated, well read. He was able to talk on any subject and was always questing for more knowledge. Nobody I've worked with has made me laugh harder than Chevy. He always gets the sense of the absurd. I feel that a sense of humor is a sign of intelligence."

Although their romance, which blossomed on the set of *Foul Play*, was short-lived, their deep friendship continued for many years. Goldie said they have maintained contact but regrets that they drifted apart after Chevy left Hollywood. "He's a great friend. He's very traditional, which I am as well. We've been together for those events that were passages, important times in our lives."

Goldie quickly got to know members of Chevy's family while they were filming *Foul Play*. Chevy had invited his brother Ned to come stay with him in San Francisco. It was 1978, and "Chevy's second marriage had failed, which was quite painful for him," Ned said. "I spent a lot of time hanging around the set while everybody took care of their job in completing *Foul Play*." To complete the foursome, Goldie invited her sister Patty to stay, and the two couples spent a fair amount of time socializing.

Goldie became part of the family, and Chevy introduced Goldie to his dad in New York. "When Goldie and I first met, I was in love with her, and she with me." Ned Senior had a devilish sense of humor and was often playing pranks.

The bathroom was right off the office where they had gathered to meet. "Excuse me," Dad said, closing the bathroom door, but not totally. A trick he played more than once, he would go in, having prepared a pitcher. "He had some anachronistic view of virility—peeing a long time. So he went in there, started [pouring the pitcher slowly into the toilet], went on and on and on, stopped, continued again, for about three minutes. Goldie's now in hysterics, and me because I know the joke." At that point in Chevy's career, he said, his dad "was a little jealous of me. I wasn't the son of Ned Chase, but he was the father of Chevy Chase."

Despite his success at that point, Chevy remembered thinking it was strange to have come from *Saturday Night Live* to *Foul Play*. "To go from current events, politics, affecting the vote in this country, to a B-level light romantic comedy to me felt like scud, and that's what kept me out of movies for a couple of years. One of the problems of making movies out there—what could I do that would have an impact on the audience, that would affect things *now*, not a year from now?"

He remembers feeling the same way about Dudley's role in the film. "The Monty Python boys looked up to him. Here he was relegated to being a guy who nobody knew had a clubfoot, asked to be in a bathrobe with no shoes on, and he didn't want to be seen that way. Portrayed as a guy who loved American rock 'n' roll, which he hated, and blow-up balloons of girls. There was more class to Dudley than playing that kind of a movie. He was too intelligent. He knew what Hollywood was."

8. "THE NEXT CARY GRANT"

Chevy's friendship with actor Cary Grant began in a way memorable even for Hollywood. Chevy recalls more with amusement than annoyance a disagreement that arose following a comment he made about Grant on a television talk show. The year was 1978. Chevy's career was on the rise and some critics had called him "the next Cary Grant," a description he found both flattering and irritating. On Snyder's late-night talk show, *Tomorrow*, Chevy was talking about being compared to Grant.

"Cary Grant is brilliant, elegant and athletic, can deliver lines with great humor—and he can also give you everything Jimmy Stewart and the great actors from that generation could deliver . . . and I understand that he is a homo."

There was a huge laugh from the audience. Tom Snyder suggested removing the comment from the tape, but Chevy thought that Cary Grant would find it funny. Within days, somebody had shown a tape of the show to Grant. Chevy learned the hard way that Cary Grant had a reputation as one of the most litigious actors in the business. Suing was top of the list among his hobbies. In his own defense, Chevy insisted that he had "no desire to defame this man. I couldn't care less if he was gay. I didn't take it seriously. I simply had a habit—with apparent arrogance—of using the term 'homo.' The word 'homo' was funny to me . . . an anachronism.''

It soon became clear to Chevy that the word "homo" wasn't funny to Cary Grant. He filed a $10 million lawsuit against Chevy (one of several suits he habitually filed every year). He would ask for millions and settle each suit for a few hundred thousand. "Maybe he made a living at suing," Chevy pondered.

Chevy didn't have $10 million and promptly wrote to Grant attempting to explain why the word "homo" is funny. There was no response. He wrote again, but the letters had no effect at all, and Grant remained determined to sue. When it came time for Grant's deposition, Chevy attended. Cary and his two elderly attorneys, and Chevy and his attorney all sat on plush sofas in a Los Angeles law office. Grant's attorneys, in a scene obviously replayed several times each year, were tired and bored. As the deposition progressed, they were sinking deeper and deeper into the sofa.

The case had been heavily reported in the press. Not reported in the press, however, were the details of the deposition. Halfway through the long list of questions, Chevy's attorney looked Cary Grant in the eye and asked, "Mr. Grant, how did you feel when you watched the tape and heard Mr. Chase say you were a 'homo'?" Grant sat up straight, looking thoughtful for a moment, and with perfect, theatrical, Cary Grant timing replied, "I felt I wanted to sue."

Chevy fell off the sofa, onto the rug, laughing. "The whole thing was worth that remark," he said. As it turned out, it was a $150,000 remark for Chevy. As part of the settlement, Grant asked Chevy to appear on the Johnny Carson show and apologize, but Chevy persuaded Cary that the last thing the case needed was more attention.

As soon as the dispute was settled, Grant's attitude changed. Much later, meeting by chance at the 1984 Olympics, Cary invited Chevy to dinner and Chevy, still in awe of the Hollywood legend, accepted without a moment's hesitation.

On more than one occasion, Chevy's acting style was compared to that of Cary Grant. He had the charm, the good looks, the smooth style of underplaying for laughs.

The change from live performance to film was a major adjustment for Chevy and in a way it was very strange for Chevy to see how audiences responded to his on-screen persona. Within a short period of time, he went from ensemble comedy and political satire to a leading man and romantic figure in comedy film—a natural transition but also a major distinction. As Chevy has observed, by the very nature of film, there's no commentary on the contemporary. By the time a film is released it may be a year or so later. He had left behind his ability to comment on the current political situation, and in interview after interview he spoke of having difficulty adjusting to his change in status.

But, with his good looks and smooth manner, he was very much into new territory as a leading man and film star. "Onstage I knew how to get laughs, if the writing was good," Chevy said. His new direction involved a major learning experience—dealing with directors, and taking the advice of others, when in the past he had depended primarily on his own instincts as to what worked and what didn't. He had been onstage with *Lemmings*, doing several shows a week: "Each time, it was a little different depending on how the audience is responding." And the energy and adrenaline of *Saturday Night Live* was a weekly performing high. "There's more feedback live than in film. The film crew is the only way to get feedback, and they can't laugh out loud while shooting, obviously, but they do give good feedback at the end of a shoot." On camera, Chevy made an effort to keep things spontaneous, adding little touches that were only his.

It is no secret that audiences love to stereotype actors and to typecast them. In fact, Chevy was showing too many talents to his audience. His transformations were confusing to his fans. First, he was the satirical political writer and slapstick comedian known for his famous falls and comical Weekend Update and then he was a romantic leading man in light comedy, an actor able to transform himself into many personalities. So in which category were they supposed to cast him? He had been a drummer, a jazz pianist, and was also an intellect who could seriously discuss many subjects and would later pal around with such luminaries as Bill Clinton before and during his presidency.

Chevy had the capacity to play a role in the manner of Cary Grant, and he had the good looks and charm to pull it off effectively, but there was no way that Chevy could stick with one style. He needed a broader challenge. Playing a romantic lead in a light comedy was easy for Chevy. He established that he could do it but he didn't want to be stuck in that stereotype.

9. *CADDYSHACK* ERA

An unusual prospect for becoming a cult movie, *Caddyshack*, released in 1980, deals with the bizarre and off-beat happenings at an exclusive golf club. It's a movie whose lines have become very familiar, often quoted by golfers, including Tiger Woods.

Considered a zany classic, the film concerns a loud, wisecracking land developer, played by Rodney Dangerfield, who wants to convert an exclusive country club to a condominium complex. Chevy stars as a well-oiled, smooth-talking golf pro, Ty Webb, whose caddy Danny, played by Michael O'Keefe, will do anything to raise college money. Ted Knight, head of the country club, plays the straight man, and Bill Murray plays a psychotic groundskeeper engaged in an all-out war against a gopher determined to ruin the grounds and drive him insane.

Confirming the film's "pop culture" status, Tiger Woods filmed an American Express ad spoofing *Caddyshack* in 2004, twenty-four years after the film was made. "Tigershack" looks at what happens when the world's most famous golfer meets the world's most famous gopher. The commercial uses some of the movie's script and original footage, and Woods has no luck getting rid of the gopher.

However, he has an American Express card, with which he is able to hire an exterminator to get rid of the gopher. The card is touted as "the official card of happy endings."

Caddyshack has many subplots, so many, in fact, that the reviews of it have a number of different takes on the film's plot. The movie grabbed the public's attention and held on to it. There are certain movies that inspire quoting, and *Caddyshack* is one of them.

Chevy's character, Ty Webb, is constantly giving advice to Danny, reminding him to keep his eye on the ball, to understand the force in the universe that makes things happen (good golfing, for example), to absorb the qualities of the ball—in fact, to *be* the ball. Ty is a character who tries to be sophisticated but finds himself tangled up in the demands of being slick.

The *Caddyshack* sequel was released in 1988, directed by Allan Arkush, but it did not hold a candle to the original. "Sequels screw things up," Chevy says. Like most actors, he wonders why film companies continue to take chances on sequels, when most of the time they are proven to fail. "I can't say that Rodney Dangerfield was the funniest guy who ever lived, but he was right for the part in the first one. Jackie Mason [who played the equivalent part in the sequel] didn't come up to par. Billy's character, to me, was what *Caddyshack* was. I only did the sequel as a favor."

The original *Caddyshack* was the first of the two Chevy films directed by Harold Ramis. Chevy raves about Harold as a director and as a person. The film was written by Ramis, Brian Doyle-Murray, and Douglas Kenney, and Ramis recalls that it was Doug who said that "Chevy embodied the character of Ty Webb." "*Of* that establishment, but not *in* it," he clarifies. For a director, there were interesting challenges: the four comedians had totally different approaches.

"They spoke different foreign languages. Chevy and Rodney were polar opposites. And Ted Knight had nothing in common with Chevy. Billy had 'issues,'" explains Ramis.

"I don't know if the four even liked each other," he continues. "And I liked them all, each in a different way. I worked with them each in their own way. Chevy would improvise. Rodney needed to prepare every syllable. Chevy used to do an impression of Rodney's hairsplitting precision. We would do our work the night before. Billy totally improvised, Second City style. I could identify with each of their characters.

"Some directors say the shooting period is the worst time. All sorts of pressures—psychological pressures, money pressures, performance pressures. I'm always a little scared but never show it.

"With Chevy there was always something funny happening. Jon Peters, the executive producer, said, 'We've gotta have a scene with Chevy and Billy together.' We had nothing."

Everyone was a little nervous, considering the history between Chevy and Bill. "I thought, I can be the peacemaker," remembers Harold. "I sat down in the morning and figured out where the scene could take place, fit in the movie. Started planning beat by beat, setting up for an improv. The actors went away and I turned to the set designer to create this room—a car seat covered with a blanket, fertilizer bags as a divider . . . We put it in the equipment garage, and the guys improvised. It was great. Filming *Caddyshack* was like a party in Florida for eleven weeks," he adds.

Caddyshack collected some excellent reviews and became a major box-office hit. While the *New York Times* described it as "an amiable mess," the *Arizona Daily Star* called it, "One of the all-time classic comedies. Lightning in a bottle, in a bunker." *Variety*, on the other hand, stated, "In *Caddyshack*'s unabashed bid for the mammoth audience which responded to the antiestablishment outrageousness of *Animal House*, this vaguely likable, too-tame comedy falls short of the mark. This time, the thinly plotted shenanigans unfold against the manicured lawns and posh backdrop of a restricted country club, generally pitting the free-living youthful caddies against the uptight gentry who employ them. Stock characters include Chevy Chase as resident golf-pro; club and jurist Ted Knight; and Rodney Dangerfield as the perfectly cast and very funny personification of antisocial, nouveau riche grossness. Beyond Chase, prime lure is Bill Murray as a foul-habited, semi-moronic groundskeeper, constantly aroused by the older femme golfers."

The critics had different opinions as to whether the film's primary character belonged to Chevy, Dangerfield, or Murray. Roger Ebert argued: "*Caddyshack* never finds a consistent comic note of its own, but it plays host to all sorts of approaches from its stars, who sometimes hardly seem to be occupying the same movie. There's Bill Murray's self-absorbed craziness, Chevy Chase's laid-back bemusement, and Ted Knight's apoplectic overplaying. And then there is Rodney Dangerfield, who wades into the movie and cleans up.

"To the degree that this is anybody's movie, it's Dangerfield's, and he mostly seems to be using his own material. He plays a loud, vulgar, twitching condo developer who is thinking of buying a country club and using the land for housing. The country club is one of those exclusive WASP enclaves, a haven for such types as the judge who founded it (Knight), the ne'er-do-well club champion (Chase), and the manic assistant groundskeeper (Murray)."

The year 1980 was a busy one for Chevy. He played not only humans but in one instance a dog. In *Oh Heavenly Dog* Chevy stars as a private investigator who gets killed while on a job and is sent back to earth to solve his own murder. The only available body is a dog, and Benji helps Chevy with this role. The quite intriguing group of costars in this film include Benji, Jane Seymour, Omar Sharif, and Robert Morley.

Seems Like Old Times, also released in 1980, wasn't one of Chevy's favorite movies, "although I suppose I could put it up there with some of the funny ones." He certainly appreciated the wonderful script by playwright Neil Simon, along with his renewed partnership with Goldie Hawn, enhanced by costar Charles Grodin. "People did want to see Goldie and me again." The film is a tightly knit comedy about what happens when writer Nick Gardenia (Chevy) is kidnapped from his California cliff house and forced to rob a bank. As a fugitive, he seeks help from his ex-wife Glenda (Goldie Hawn), who is a public defender remarried to a prosecutor (Charles Grodin). There's a double love story, according to Simon: "Goldie's character really loves her husband and her ex-husband, played by Chevy."

Neil Simon was on hand for some of the filming, and he rewrote some of the script for Goldie but not so much for Chevy. "Goldie really made the movie," Simon says. "Chevy's wonderful, funny. We worked a lot through the director [Jay Sandrich, who had directed many episodes of *The Mary Tyler Moore Show* and made his feature debut with the film]." Simon recalls not being intrusive in the rehearsals, with Sandrich being the one to request changes. Simon was there for the initial readings of the script. "I would come in, stay around, leave early," he said.

The script for the film was not drawn from one of Simon's plays, which made it quite a different type of experience for him. "Some movies I'm more involved in, if they're from my plays." If not, he says, "I'm a person watching a movie."

Janet Maslin, writing the December 19, 1980, review for the *New York Times*, gave Neil Simon credit for being "in very funny form." "Why can't the women in Mr. Simon's scenarios ever figure out to whom they ought to be married? Goldie Hawn here, like Jane Fonda in *California Suite*, is a high-powered professional with two men in her life, the current Mr. Right plus a very appealing ex."

Al Hirschfeld selected this movie as the basis for his characterization of all three stars—Chevy, Goldie, and Charles—and his drawing reflected one of the funniest scenes in the film, where Chevy is hiding under a bed.

Critic Roger Ebert was on hand again to provide his B-plus review of the film for the *Chicago Sun-Times*. "*Seems Like Old Times* is another one of those near-misses that leaves a movie critic in a quandary. It's a funny movie, and it made me laugh out loud a lot, but in the final analysis it just didn't quite edge over the mystical line into success.

"The movie's single best scene is probably a formal dinner party that Grodin and Hawn throw for the governor (George Grizzard). The butler gets drunk while Chevy Chase is hiding in the kitchen, so, while the statewide search for him continues, he puts on the butler's tuxedo and serves dinner. The scene develops into wonderful physical comedy."

John J. Puccio, writing more recently in *DVD Town*, was more in keeping with what most people seemed to feel about this movie. "*Seems Like Old Times* may not be the laugh riot of the century or even the most original story around, but it's got a gentle charisma that's hard to resist."

10. CHEVY AND JAYNI AND THE GIRLS

C hevy had to fight for Jayni. He had been through two failed marriages and was in the middle of his second divorce. It was early in the fall of 1980 and Chevy was filming *Under the Rainbow* on the *Queen Mary* in Torrence, California, when he had a chance meeting with a young woman who was working as a production coordinator.

Jayni Luke would not ordinarily have been on the set, but it was the first day of shooting and she had to give a message to the first assistant director. A little more than a year out of college, Jayni was a bright and independent young woman who had majored in communications at UCSB (University of California, Santa Barbara) and was very passionate about a range of social causes, including environmental issues and consumer rights. She had taken a job with NBC for a year after graduation and was working as a secretary in network programming. Her goal was to leave California, where she had spent her entire life up to that point, and travel in Europe, perhaps work for the BBC, and get to know more about what was going on in the world outside her own environment. The last thing on her mind was getting married and having a family.

Life was about to take a surprising turn. It was anything but love at first sight for Jayni, although the first time Chevy heard her voice, and then met her, he was determined to win her heart. She was twenty-two years old and wearing a pair of old overalls. "Not a day I was trying to look cute," she recalls. She had to wait on the set awhile before she got a chance to deliver her message. Chevy had just finished a take and immediately noticed her. He walked over and asked her to hold his hat. Jayni was not impressed. That's not my job, she thought, but she didn't say anything. Why is he asking me to do this? She took it from him and looked for a costumer, whose job it was to handle such things.

By this time Chevy was already well known as a film star. *Under the Rainbow* was his fifth film. Chevy's primary memories of the film were meeting Jayni, and dealing with a cast of hundreds—"more than a hundred little people." As Chevy recalls, it was a group not used to being in Hollywood films, and a lively group that partied continuously when not filming. The movie was made "during the height of cocaine and alcohol abuse, and there was an abundance of drugs. They were funny, happy, delightful people, and we were endlessly being goosed. We never knew who did it—all we could see was those little hats and costumes, and we heard the laughter."

Chevy had his eye on Jayni, who was barely aware of him. She had seen him on *Saturday Night Live* but had not followed his career at all afterward. Jayni was never the "fan type," and hadn't seen any of his films. But that day he was friendly, mildly flirting with her. Jayni handed over the hat to someone on the set, delivered her message to the assistant director, and left, not thinking anything more of her brief encounter with Chevy.

Flash ahead a few weeks to Lairds Studios, just before Chevy's thirty-seventh birthday. Jayni was working in the office, still in production for the same film. He dropped by to say hello and asked Jayni out to dinner. She had heard he was in the middle of a divorce, so she turned to him and said, "I don't go out with married men." Chevy was taken aback but he returned to the office a week later, informing Jayni that his divorce was final. He did not ask her out that day.

Not long after, they were filming at Union Station in Los Angeles. The production office was set up near a bank of pay phones in the train station. Jayni was working at one of the folding tables when she looked up and saw Chevy in costume, slightly winded. "Tonight is the premiere of my movie," he said. (*Seems Like Old Times* premiered while they were filming *Under the Rainbow*.) "Goldie [Hawn, his costar] is in Paris, and Jackie Bisset has the flu. I'm wondering if you would go with me." Jayni was quick to respond. "Well, not if I'm third choice." Chevy was crushed. "My heart jumped. I shouldn't have been so flip with him," says Jayni now. Chevy left, figuring he would go by himself.

Jayni thought better of it and phoned a short while later to ask if the offer still stood. On that first date, Jayni discovered that Chevy was "amazing, a sweetheart." She had been warned by others on the set; she had heard rumors that Chevy was "a druggy, a jazz guy, hanging out in clubs." She had heard stories that he wasn't a nice guy. "I expected him to be full of himself." Jayni never expected to be swept off her feet—it wasn't at all her style—but, according to her, that's exactly what happened. Their romance progressed quickly after that first date and soon they were living together.

Chevy's two previous marriages had been disastrous but now he felt older, more mature, and instinctively he knew that this relationship was going to work. In a way, he said, they were "perfect opposites." Jayni is athletic and practical, not easily rattled, and always able to handle problems in an upbeat way. Jayni doesn't stay down for long—she bounces back. Chevy is creative and prone to depression. Their early time together was spent learning how to communicate and to trust, which was a challenge for Chevy.

He had been hurt, betrayed by women, starting with his own mother from the earliest days of his life. Jayni was grounded, strong, and not trying to get ahead in Hollywood. She was levelheaded and practical and saw that world clearly in perspective. There was a lot of easy laughter between the two of them.

Chevy had an apartment on Kings Road in Hollywood, and after being together for a year Chevy and Jayni decided to buy a house in Pacific Palisades, "in an out-of-the-way gated community." Typical of inflated California prices, it cost about the same as the twelve-acre New York property they bought many years later, but it had only half an acre; it also had a tennis court and a swimming pool.

At the beginning of their time together, after *Under the Rainbow*, Jayni complied with his request that she not accept another job too quickly. He wanted time for them to be together, to get to know each other. Their plans were spelled out carefully. They would buy a house, live together for a year, get engaged, and start a family.

They spent a lot of time reading, talking, and playing. Chevy was a thirty-seven-year-old man and an eight-year-old boy combined. "One day I had been in the garage with a lighter killing black widow spiders," he recalls. Later, they were both sitting in the living room and reading, only Chevy's book was upside down and he wasn't feeling well. He was too embarrassed to tell Jayni that he had a fascination with spiders and that while he had been in the garage killing spiders like a kid, one of the black widows had bitten him and he was in pain.

"Chev, what's wrong with your hand?" Jayni asked. It was very swollen. He told her the whole story. "Good God," Jayni said. "I've heard that can be dangerous! Lethal!"

They went upstairs to their library and opened the *Encyclopedia Britannica*. They turned to "Poisons—black widow spider." The entry described what could happen: "First, the swelling begins, then there would be cramps in the body." Dangerous for a two-year-old, thought Chevy, but not for a 185-pound strapping guy, although lethal in four percent of the cases.

"And this word neither of us had ever seen—priapism . . . Painful priapism," he remembers. They found a dictionary and looked it up. "It's an erection, very big and painful." Both collapsed with laughter and Chevy decided not to seek medical attention. His hand became more and more swollen for a few days and then went back to normal, "although I have had a painful priapism ever since."

Another spider "incident" took place while visiting friends in Washington State. Chevy identified the dangerous brown recluse spider as the culprit. "It hurt like the devil, I shook it off, and it turned into a swelling and a bruise that changed every color of the rainbow. Then the skin began to come off. I'm terrified of them."

Chevy continues to communicate with spiders, but he is much more careful now. "That's why I have the 'Bug-zuka,'" he adds. The vacuum device allows him to move his spiders into an outdoor lantern, where he watches them spin webs. "I've always loved biology and anatomy, having once wanted to be a doctor and all that."

Chevy continued to have spider troubles and other minor incidents, but he could never have anticipated a serious electrocution accident that would affect his life for a very long time. Chevy was working on *Modern Problems*, a film written and directed by Ken Shapiro (Chevy's colleague from Channel One) and released in 1981 to an assortment of mediocre and negative reviews. It was a film that had all sorts of problems along the way—not just modern problems.

Bruce Bodner, who was in Los Angeles during part of the filming, recalled a meeting called by Sherry Lansing, head of the company producing the film. It was breakfast at the Bel Air, a very staid Hollywood hotel and a big industry hangout. She said she had heard rumors and was concerned that there was drug use on the film set.

In the middle of the meeting, Chevy excused himself, went to the men's room, found some Ajax under the sink, and sprinkled it on his dark shirt. He came back to the table as though nothing had happened.

"Now Sherry is bright, sophisticated, and pretty hip, not some old biddy, but her mouth dropped," Bruce says. So did his. "Then Chevy laughed and the joke was clear." During that whole period, Bruce says, "When Chevy walked into a room filled with celebrities, he had the charisma, the star power. It was very exciting to be around him, with him."

Drugs or not, the film was far from a hit. Vincent Canby's review in the *New York Times* claimed that 20th Century Fox intentionally launched the film on Christmas Day, with no advance screenings for the press, so that the public wouldn't be influenced, then went on to stereotype and insult the film's audience, "whose inner clocks are set by their television habits [and] don't worry much about consistency or point of view. And, having short attention spans, they immediately forget the long dull patches that separate the truly funny sequences."

Chevy plays an air traffic controller, the filming unfortunately coinciding with an air traffic controllers' strike. Chevy's character is accidentally exposed to radioactive soap suds and suddenly develops telekinetic powers. He makes use of his ability to move objects, sharing the screen with actors including Patti D'Arbanville, Dabney Coleman, Nell Carter, Mary Kay Place, Brian Doyle-Murray, and Mitch Kreindel.

For Chevy, the strongest memory of this film is the fact that he was the victim of electrocution. He was being prepared for a dream sequence in the film, in which he was landing a plane. Large lights were put on his arms for the scene, and the special effects and wardrobe people had arranged to attach the lights with plastic and rubber insulation over his shirt. Director Shapiro—Chevy was still angry with him for some issues dating back to their Channel One days together—thought the lights should be attached directly onto Chevy's skin. "The padding wasn't what I expected, but you trust the people who do these things.

"The way I understood it, it was not simply DC power, but AC power too—something to be wary of, enough so that I said, 'Look. I'm clammy, sweaty. I hate electricity, electric shocks. I think there's a danger.'" No one involved agreed with him. "It's perfectly safe," they said. "Don't worry. We can test it." Chevy agreed. They attached the lights and "turned the juice on. For ten seconds, I was screaming, as this electric current was going through my body. Screaming 'Turn it off, turn it off!'"

Known for being a prankster, everyone thought Chevy was kidding. They ignored him and continued the test. "They thought I was kidding, until I hit the floor. I woke up with a paramedic infiltrating my arm with a needle, trying to get an IV hooked up." The pain of the attempt woke Chevy up. "I remember opening my eyes and I was laid out on a blanket." He was taken to an emergency room.

The electric cuffs had left black burn marks on Chevy's arms, but, more seriously, they ended up burning the muscles in his arms and shoulders, and it took a couple of years to heal completely. He was weakened and depressed. He found himself crying uncontrollably while in the hospital. The doctor explained to him that the electrocution had been a near-death experience and that a strong emotional response was not unexpected. Chevy spent a few days in the hospital and went back to the set.

"For at least a year, I wouldn't turn a light on or off. I asked Jayni to do it," Chevy remembers.

In retrospect, he says, he probably should have filed a lawsuit, but it didn't occur to him at the time. He fought off the effects of his near-death experience by working, but he remained weak and depressed. A few months later, he was shocked to learn of the death of John Belushi. John's death (on March 5, 1982) from a mixture of heroin and cocaine was difficult for Chevy to handle. He couldn't figure out how to deal with it. He was angry, devastated, and yet couldn't seem to mourn Belushi's death. He didn't go to the funeral; the loss stayed with him for a long time, and it wasn't until several years later that he finally broke down and cried.

Chevy was eager for marriage and wanted to start a family. In fact, Jayni had become pregnant two months before their wedding date. They were married on June 19, 1982, in a small ceremony at their home in Pacific Palisades.

"Before Chevy got down on his knee and proposed, he called my father and asked for his permission to marry me," Jayni said.

"I knew she was young," Chevy said. "I told her father I was hoping for his approval. He said, 'Well, I reckon that's up to Jayni.'"

"I was never one to dream of a big wedding," Jayni said, "so we invited only those people we were in daily contact with," a small group of close friends and family. "We were married under a weeping willow tree that we had planted behind our home. I had two bridesmaids and Chevy had Ned as his best man. My father gave me away.

"We got married and then we all just hung out, ate, and played music. Chevy came to me about an hour after the ceremony and asked if it was okay if he played tennis with his father. I said, 'Of course!' So we have photos of me in my wedding dress and him in his tennis garb."

The press did not pick up the wedding at all. "We flew under the radar screen completely," Jayni said. A week after their wedding, Chevy started filming the first of the *Vacation* films. Jayni, ready to work and travel with Chevy, acted as production secretary.

The early years of their marriage were a whirlwind, with Chevy focusing on a quick succession of films as well as on Jayni and the girls. For many years, Chevy had wanted to be a father. He had always adored babies and small children and couldn't wait to have a family of his own and to put into practice his humanitarian philosophy of child-rearing.

He also needed to confirm to himself that he could be a good father despite his abusive childhood.

Cydney Cathalene was born on January 4, 1983, Caley Leigh two years later on January 19, 1985, and Emily Evelyn on September 29, 1988.

Jayni's family lived nearby and provided support when Chevy was away filming, but Jayni didn't mind his busy schedule. With their first child, Jayni said, she softened. Chevy had always been the romantic in their relationship, pursuing her, "writing notes that were wonderful and funny, of course." Jayni found that motherhood changed her. She had been competitive, career driven. "I changed. I softened, slowed down, the competitiveness melted. To this day I don't feel competitive," she says, "but I remember how that used to feel." She credits Chevy with helping to bring out the softness that came to her with motherhood.

There were other issues for Chevy, however. They had to work very hard to overcome some of the problems of his childhood as they began to affect their marriage. He was very particular in the way he thought Jayni should mother their children. "My own mother was not all over me. My generation had what we called Helicopter Moms, hovering over their kids all the time. Mine didn't hover. She was involved but not in my face," says Jayni, appreciatively. "I took my own mother for granted until I became a mother."

Chevy wanted Jayni to hover because his mother had neglected him so much. "There were triggers in him that I didn't understand. Subconsciously, he was expecting me to say horrible things to the children." One time, Jayni was watching Cydney on her baby blanket and picked up a magazine. The baby toppled over, not hurt at all. But Chevy was walking by and had seen it happen. "He was upset with me. He was expecting me to be the way his mother had been. It took some work in our marriage for him not to feel that way."

Chevy was aware that it is not uncommon for the abused to become abusers. In his case, he went to the opposite philosophy, never punishing his children in a physical way but giving them only kindness and affection. All three of Chevy's daughters have high praise for both their parents, saying they had truly put their child-rearing philosophy into practice.

Chevy's brother John remembers one summer afternoon in 1992 at Chevy's East Hampton place, discussing parenting with Chevy and Jayni. "Chevy told us his strong belief that talking to one's children was all that was ever necessary to work through any problems—any at all, be they behavioral or otherwise. He was convinced, he stated, that there was categorically no excuse whatsoever—none—to ever lay a hand on a child in anger, or to threaten to do so, ever, no matter what.

"Having never been treated with any hostility by their parents, his girls were trusting, felt safe, and knew for a fact that they were truly loved and cherished. This had been demonstrated by their parents. And so, they were well behaved by nature. Having followed this little speech to some degree, little Caley then piped up, 'And you know why? Because there's no hitting in this family.' She was all of six. I was floored, and there and then my own philosophy on the subject gelled for good and all. No hitting. No threatening. Never. Under any circumstance. Period."

Cydney, now twenty-four, says, "I think my dad had children because he loves children. He always wanted to be a dad. My dad emboldens me to make decisions. His confidence in me gives me confidence. He's really grounded, for what he's gone through."

Daughter Emily, at eighteen, sings her dad's praises. "He's a great father. We're buddies, a lot like good friends, and yet he still has that authority. Everything I've taken away from my dad is positive. He does have his insecurities as a parent. All three of us have taken the most positive things from him." Emily knows that Chevy worries about his parenting, and about how his career and celebrity have affected their lives. All three girls are aware of the abuse he suffered as a child. "He has never abused any of us. He's a big, powerful man, and the most gentle person. I think it's amazing how he overcame the abuse," Emily adds.

During the early years of their marriage, Jayni focused primarily on the children. She was very independent, very capable. She never sat at home complaining. "We always did what was best for the girls." When it was possible, Jayni packed up the girls and took them to wherever Chevy was filming. They would "watch him work, see what he does, then go home and let him do his job." One thing Jayni was very thankful for was that she totally trusted him. "He's a really attractive man. You see a lot of actors, even in the same town, and there are actresses in their trailer [on the set]. I knew Chevy wasn't doing that. Neither of us has ever had that tug."

The family spent most of their time in California through 1985, when they began spending summers in East Hampton, New York. Eventually the contrast in lifestyle, and many other factors, led them back to New York to stay, and the whole family moved east in 1995.

11. NATIONAL LAMPOON'S VACATION

The public and the media had been following Chevy pretty closely since his arrival in Hollywood. It seemed every move he made, and every movie, would be analyzed under a microscope and measured against his career and his life. An Associated Press story in January of 1983 referred to Chevy's arrival in LA in 1977 "with the promise of becoming a bright new film star. Five years and six movies later, the Chevy Chase promise still seems to be on hold. Historically, that's not unusual. Cary Grant was a slick-haired leading man before finding his niche. Burt Reynolds was a star of a failed television series. But today's movie industry deals in instant success or instant failure. Chase lands somewhere in between," the article stated.

Chevy said, at the time, "I didn't come out here with any direction in mind. Being a movie actor was never a major desire of mine, but I find I enjoy it. Like everyone else, I like the affection and the attention, as well as the feeling of accomplishment. The main thing I've learned is how to separate the fantasy part from actuality."

Filming of the *National Lampoon's Vacation* movie, the first of four, was completed in 1982. It was followed by *European Vacation* (1985), *Christmas Vacation* (1989), and

Vegas Vacation (1997). The constants in the cast were Chevy, his screen wife, Beverly D'Angelo, and Cousin Eddie, played by Randy Quaid.

Chevy believes the first *Vacation* film is the funniest of the four. He loved working with director Harold Ramis: "A very funny person with a good head on his shoulders." It was a good time in Chevy's life. He and Jayni were still newlyweds, and she was able to work on the film as a production secretary. She was also pregnant with their first child, Cydney.

The film was shot all over the country. "Harold had it all set up, with the ugliest car he could find. The interior and shell were mounted on a trailer, on which a camera dolly was set up." While filming some long stretches in the desert, they had huge air conditioners blowing into the car. "It was brilliant directing on the road," he adds. Ramis was a comic actor, with his roots in Second City, so he understood comic directing well. "He said to play it over the top, so I did, and I found Clark Griswold.

"I knew my career was going completely downhill in comparison to the effect I had in New York City with *Saturday Night Live*. The election, Carter, satirical writing. To the critical world I had gone to the lowest form of family comedies." Nevertheless, and despite all of Chevy's concerns, the *Vacation* films became major hits, one after the other. Certainly the partnership between Chevy and Beverly D'Angelo had a lot to do with this success. A friendship quickly developed. "Beverly is a very funny person, a very talented singer and actress," Chevy says.

Beverly recalls, "I first met Chevy in an office at Warner Brothers Studio. I think I may have done some sort of reading from the script. The truth is I was twenty-eight, and I was to play the mother of a fifteen-year-old, but my husband laughed out loud at the script, and I idolized Chevy, so I went in for the audition. The rule of the day was: 'Don't play a mother, don't do a comedy, don't act with animals.' Thank God Chevy was an animal."

The Griswold children were different in each of the four films (for many reasons, including the number of years between the films), with no apology or explanation made for this, although by the last film, *Vegas Vacation*, Chevy ad-libbed a wisecrack: "You guys are growing up so fast, I hardly recognize you any more!"

Vacation was a great success, for its zany, exaggerated spoof of a comedy film, for the extreme mishaps that occur in it and others in the series, and for the extraordinary and hilarious occurrences as this strange but "typical" American family makes its way across the country. Clark Griswold's character (the family name is not spelled consistently through the four films) has been quoted liberally.

The screenplay was written by John Hughes. Harold Ramis and Chevy rewrote a lot of the script: "Chevy and I both saw the strengths of the script and the problems." Because of Writers Guild rules relating to the writer's credit, it is possible for a director to change most of the dialogue and not get a writer's credit.

Harold immediately identified with the story. He and his wife had bought a nine-passenger station wagon and traveled with their children—in fact, Harold and Chevy rewrote the journey to conform to Harold's trip. Chevy did not have children yet so, Harold remembers, "I was trying to explain my conception of the story from a father's point of view. You always know a little more than your kids— that's all you have to know." Harold's own five-year-old daughter, Violet, was cast as the mute daughter (Daisy Mabel) of Randy Quaid's character, Cousin Eddie. On the most basic level, Harold explained to Chevy, it's simply, "Look, kids, wheat!" Chevy said, "I've got it. I know exactly what you are talking about." Clark Griswold, Harold added, is the guilty father: "He does what he can to avoid parenting fifty weeks of the year. For two weeks, he had to be Superdad."

Beverly D'Angelo said that Chevy was so effective in the character of Clark Griswold because "he seemed to be tapping into someone he knew, definitely a character he had a handle on that everyone instinctively knew but had never seen before. He spawned a genre, by the way. I can't begin to tell you how many people have come up to me and said either 'I am Clark Griswold' or 'My husband is just like Clark.'"

There were two principal changes in the script, as rewritten by Harold and Chevy. Says Ramis, "John Hughes was always fascinated with adolescent sex—puberty and awakening desire. Rusty [the Griswolds' teenage son] keeps running into a thirteen-year-old girl. As a husband and father, I was far less interested in a thirteen-year-old than the frustrations of a grown-up in a decent marriage, suffering the frustrations that come with marriage. So the thirteen-year-old girl grew up into Christie Brinkley. A fairly adult theme. That was a principal change in it. Not just a 'sometime father' and now the challenge of staying interested."

Another major change was the ending. "The original ending was shot and tested, from the point at which Clark buys a fake gun." In the original ending, Clark stopped and found Wally's house (the old *Dynasty* house in San Marino). "He bursts into the house, where Roy Wally and the Disney directors were having a meeting, and he takes them hostage, saying 'I want my dime's worth of entertainment.'

"We tried it and it didn't play at all. The audience was with us for seventy-five minutes, embracing the film, and then dead silent—not another chuckle. I analyzed the problem. They've waited an hour and fifteen minutes to get to Wally World and now they can't go." Harold realized they would have to hijack the park. "Everyone's fantasy, to be alone in an amusement park. We got John Hughes to rewrite, and got John Candy for the guard. I thought John and Chevy would be great together."

Traveling across country filming *Vacation* was a major challenge. A lot of it was in hot weather and Harold recalls the cast and crew arriving at Wally World (they were using the parking lot of the Santa Anita Racetrack). "It was a hundred and fifteen degrees on the pavement and the air temperature was a hundred." Chevy had to run in and out of a hot garage, take after take, to load the station wagon, and he kept blowing the takes. Usually easygoing, Chevy was starting to lose his cool.

Chevy was holding a duffel bag, Harold recalled. "I thought, 'He's gonna throw that bag.' He was frustrated." In the split second between realizing what was going to happen and what did actually occur, Harold thought, "He can't throw it at the lights, the camera, or the sound. He's gonna throw it at me. The bag came whipping at me. I lifted my foot a bit, knocked it down, and thought maybe we ought to take a break! I was glad he trusted me enough to throw it at me."

"Chevy worked in a way unlike any other actor I had ever worked with," said Beverly D'Angelo. "He kept himself alive by keeping in the moment, whether he knew it or not. He played poker nonstop. Then when it was time to work, he'd walk straight to the set and shoot. When they'd call 'Cut' he'd say 'Deal 'em' and go back to his ferocious winning streak.

"He'd had a hand in [writing] every scene, and he *was* the character, so what he was actually doing was just staying completely relaxed. No one ever gives Chevy credit for having anything to do with acting. He knew what he was doing with the character of Clark Griswold. It was a character and it is embedded in the hearts and minds of several generations. That's acting.

"Chevy was the star, and he led the way in terms of where the whole thing should go. It was R-rated. I don't think anyone imagined it would become a family picture. There was nudity—mine—lots of political incorrectness. It was satire. The public saw itself in these characters instead of seeing a satire, 'identified with' instead of 'laughing at.' That's my theory, anyway.

"It was an official box-office hit—number one at the box office for a while. A family picture, even with the R-rating."

The next film to come out was *Deal of the Century*, also in 1983. In the film, Chevy plays an American arms dealer (Eddie Muntz) trying to sell a high-tech military vehicle to a South American dictator. The plot involves Chevy's character trying to persuade his girlfriend Catherine (played by Sigourney Weaver) to seal an arms deal by sleeping with the dictator. The cast features Chevy with Weaver and Gregory Hines, directed by William Friedkin.

Chevy liked Friedkin personally but had difficulties with him as a director. The entire cast and others knew about a fight that took place during filming. "Bill had a temper like I've never seen, and a propensity to strike out," says Chevy. Chevy was angry that Friedkin had fired a perfectly good director of photography for what he considered little cause. Friedkin tended to intimidate Sigourney Weaver. Chevy recalls, "I felt she couldn't do her best in the film. It affected the way she read her lines. Greg wasn't affected. I wasn't affected." Chevy took Friedkin aside and asked him to treat people better on the set. "Bill laughed it off, saying I'm a 'scorpio.'" They had an argument while filming in a converted church whose upper balcony area served as a kitchenette and living area. All the weapons for the film were kept in the church. There was a scene between Chevy and Sigourney in the raised balcony area. Overnight, Freidkin changed the blocking for the next day without telling anyone. He directed from a tall ladder, twenty feet high, so he could be eye level with the cast.

"As time went on," Chevy explains, "it became clear that the rehearsal the night before was obsolete—because he had totally changed the blocking." Chevy called him on it, and "Bill went batshit in front of a hundred people. He said 'Clear the room' and a hundred people filed out the front door." Chevy pointed out to him that it would have been easier for the two of them to step outside. "But he stayed on the ladder—yap, yap, yap across the void—notably as he pointed out later, he didn't want me to be able to be get to him. I couldn't take it seriously, and let him have his temper tantrum." Chevy didn't hold a grudge. "He's a complicated, intelligent man, and one of the most brilliant directors I've ever worked with," Chevy adds.

After Chevy's near-electrocution during the filming of *Modern Problems*, he was extremely cautious when Friedkin wanted him to fire a bazooka, which he planned to rig with a flame thrower so that the flames would shoot out the back. He presented the idea to Chevy at the end of one day's filming. Chevy refused, saying he would "burn my face off with the bazooka against my head." Eventually he told Bill he would do it if Bill would. The next morning, as Chevy was getting ready, he noticed that Bill kept his right side away from him. Finally, Chevy got into position to see a large bandage on Bill's ear. He had tried the bazooka shot, and burned his ear.

12. FEAR OF FAME

"First I was an observer. Then I was the observed." For Chevy, as for so many stars, fame was an uncomfortable burden, and quite frightening. Everyone recognizes you. Life is no longer private. People think they know who you are. Really, Chevy feels, the public should have a little more pity for celebrities. Not for him, he says, but for celebrities in general. "Fame leads some people to self-medicate. They're at the Betty Ford Center, trying to get off one drug or another, trying to get off alcohol or pills or ecstasy. I was there, I know what they are talking about."

Celebrities are medicating their depression: their guilt for being so highly paid, the feeling that they don't deserve it. "The sort of guilt you have when others die in a plane crash, but you've made it. This is the guilt of 'Why me?'" Chevy says. And it's compounded by the rest of the world believing celebrities are sitting on top of the world, when they are dealing with the same struggles as everyone else, only in full view of their public.

Chevy has spent a lot of time looking around and wondering why he rose quickly to the top when others he respects greatly have not had the same success, and an equal amount of time persuading himself that he is deserving of the acclaim—talented, better, funnier than others. Inside his head is a battle of strong and scary forces. Chevy is thinking to himself, " 'The funniest guy in the room is Martin Short, but where is he? He's not a movie star.' How many actors go through that struggle? Probably all of them," Chevy insists.

Chevy's career began as an observer, a writer. His appearances on camera changed everything, transforming him into "the observed." Walking down the street and hearing "Ch . . . Ch" and knowing his name was being whispered. Putting on sun glasses, so you don't have to make eye contact, so others can't see if you are sad. The fear of being "discovered, caught, found out one day—that you're not worth this at all, not worth anything, in fact."

In the early years of his career, Chevy smoked pot, but once his career took off his drug use progressed to a combination of cocaine and painkillers.

When Jayni and Chevy met on the set of *Under the Rainbow*, Jayni recalls, "Almost everybody on the film was doing, taking. People didn't even realize how addictive it was, cocaine. People were taking quaaludes and doing cocaine. I didn't see this, it was kind of done quietly, and people were smoking pot. I'm sure it affected them. The film kept going on and on because people were on drugs." Indeed, the film took much longer to finish than the time originally allotted.

"It was rampant then, but Chevy wasn't the worst by far. He always had a head on his shoulders. He was never stumbling around, or acting jerky. It was the beginning of his anesthetizing pain from his childhood. His back was killing him. It crept up on him and on me." Chevy did not realize until years later that part of his drug problem had to do with his abusive childhood, and trying to ease the pain he continued to suffer.

In the 1980s, Chevy began to realize that he had been depressed all his life, but he continued to cover it up. He described himself as a "cokehead" for about eight years, until 1986, when he went into rehab. "I was self-medicating. Not only did I take coke but I ruined my sinuses doing it, caused tremendous pain, and therefore got painkillers to kill the pain in my sinuses. I was addicted in both ways." The cocaine, he said, was easy to give up. He recalls the day, October 1, 1986. But the use of painkillers went on for a few more years. "I had to get them in a gray-black market, or by going to different doctors."

It had taken Chevy a while to realize he needed to do something. He had been deeply affected by John Belushi's death, but it still took time to internalize the fact that he could break the cocaine habit.

During the 1960s, when everyone was experimenting with drugs in college, Chevy never touched them. He was a soccer player and a runner. His physical health was very important to him and he was never even tempted to try acid, all the rage at that time.

As he began working professionally as a writer, the temptations to use were strong. Chevy has no recollection of his first encounter with drugs but figures it must have been at a late-night party. Then began the years of pot smoking: "We laughed a great deal, we were well received for the writing we did on pot. Basically our audiences were potheads all through the sixties and seventies. Being a pothead just meant being a person at that point."

The heavier use of cocaine, however, began during the late nights of working on *Saturday Night Live*, and having enough money to be able to afford it. Friday night was a heavy drug night at *SNL*, staying up late and working on the scripts for Weekend Update. "It was everywhere. I remember receiving my Emmy for acting in *Saturday Night Live* [presented by Redd Foxx]. I gave my speech, came offstage out of view of the camera, and Redd Foxx shoved a spoonful of cocaine up my nose in a congratulatory way. It was a common way of expressing joy or feeling it, part and parcel of the way we lived at that time."

During the mid-eighties, Jayni was becoming increasingly concerned about the effects of Chevy's cocaine use. "I was going to the ENT [Ear, Nose, and Throat] specialist so much, hurting my septum, hurting inside my nose, yet I couldn't seem to stop. [Jayni] suggested the Betty Ford Center." The Rancho Mirage Center had opened in 1982, founded after Betty Ford admitted to being an alcoholic.

For a long time, Jayni was not aware that Chevy's cocaine use continued on a regular basis. She hadn't asked; he hadn't disclosed. She was aware of the painkillers, and she knew there were mood swings, but "not a Dr. Jekyll and Mr. Hyde" type of thing. Even after she received a phone call from Chevy's doctor, asking her to come in to discuss a problem, she believed Percoset was the problem. One of Chevy's other doctors had been prescribing painkillers on a regular basis. Jayni and the two doctors did an "intervention," although she had to threaten one of the doctors with a malpractice lawsuit before he agreed to it.

Faced with such a strong trio, and recognizing that Jayni was concerned for his health and their family life, Chevy quickly agreed to get help and said he would go to the Betty Ford Center. His reaction, Jayni recalls, was, "Oh, thank God. I knew I shouldn't but I didn't know how to get out of this."

In the preliminary phone calls to the clinic, Chevy learned that he could sign in under any name. He was promised that his privacy would be protected, that nobody would know he was there, and that he could be treated as long as necessary (generally three to six weeks) without his identity being disclosed. Chevy checked in under his doctor's name.

Jayni drove the two and a half hours to the center, Chevy finishing up the last of his cocaine in the car, realizing this was going to be the end of an era. Arriving at the center, Chevy checked in and was escorted to his first-floor room. It was dark, and the first thing he saw while unpacking was a flash from outside his window. The next day, the story was big news, the press announcing Chevy's stay in a "drug clinic." Chevy never learned who told the press about his stay. He did find out that somebody pretending to be Tim

Hutton called Jayni at home, saying he wanted to wish Chevy a happy birthday (Chevy's birthday is October 8). Jayni was unaware that Chevy barely knew Tim Hutton and that he would not have called their home. She gave the caller the number and a reporter evidently called the center and learned that Chevy was there.

Chevy's stay at the Betty Ford Center was all over the news. The *New York Times* published a small piece on Sunday, October 12, 1986, reporting, "The comedian Chevy Chase, known for his slapstick humor and pratfalls, is addicted to painkillers and has checked into the Betty Ford drug rehabilitation center, his public relations agent says. Mr. Chase, 43 years old, who gained fame on the television satire series *Saturday Night Live*, voluntarily entered the drug program several days ago, the agent Pat Kingsley said on Friday. She said the treatment was for 'dependency on prescription drugs relating to chronic and long-term back problems' resulting from years of pratfalls and stunts dating to his days on *Saturday Night Live*."

Despite his feeling of betrayal, Chevy remained at the center and participated in the program for just under three weeks. He did not complete the treatment program but left over an incident regarding the interpretation of "leisure time." It was early evening, and Chevy was reading a novel. The head of the "dorm" ripped it from his hands, saying he should have been reading his twelve-step book. Chevy was incensed. While benefiting greatly from the program as a whole, he had difficulty dealing with the authoritarian rules. "I didn't like either the God-squadding or the twelve steps. Or having to put my arms around people or hold hands and say the serenity prayer. I already had my problems with that sort of stuff." The high rate of recidivism was also an issue for Chevy. People were coming back to the center "based on what they were told—it wasn't their fault, it was a genetic problem, which in some ways it was."

The combination of addiction being a "genetic problem" and the "higher power thinking" accounts for people relapsing, Chevy believes. "It was the result of the excuse being given to you by saying it's a problem of genetics, when in fact it's a behavioral issue that you controlled or you didn't control!

"I'm not a hard ass, but I saw in my case I quit the second I went in. One reason I never took it [cocaine] again was because I never wanted to be back in a place like that."

Once Chevy's book was snatched, it was all over. His anger over the promise of confidentiality surfaced. He left the center that day. Despite the many Hollywood situations where he was tempted to use cocaine, Chevy never touched the drug again.

On October 22, 1986, a press notice circulated widely stating: "Comedian Chevy Chase has been released from a hospital with 'his system cleaned of drugs' and will continue private therapy for back problems that led to a dependency on painkillers."

Chevy had many negative things to say about the experience. The *San Francisco Chronicle* stated: "Comedian Chevy Chase has dared to criticize Hollywood's Holy Land: the Betty Ford Center. 'They get you to believe that you're at death's door, that your family is at death's door, that you've ruined it for everybody, that you're nothing . . . They used the phrase "Thank you for sharing with us" so much it made me nuts.'"

Once Chevy got control of his cocaine use, he became increasingly concerned about the life-threatening drug use of some of his friends and colleagues.

He was also worried about his brother John. In 2006, John was able to say, "I just celebrated twenty years clean, thanks in great part to my elder brother Cornelius, who called me in out of the cold while he was languishing at the Betty Ford clinic, paid my way through drug addiction treatment, and helped me to get back on my feet out on the other side.

"A very loving and generous man, Chevy. He compensates for the abuse and neglect of his own childhood by being a stellar father, uncle, brother, and son. He's a truly decent man."

The loss of his closest friend, Doug Kenney, several years earlier was extremely difficult for Chevy. Their relationship was both personal and professional. Kenney had been founder of the *Harvard Lampoon* and cofounder of the *National Lampoon Magazine* and *National Lampoon Radio Hour*. He and Chevy had used cocaine together, but drugs were not considered to be the cause of his death, which remained a mystery. The first time Chevy spoke openly about Doug's death was in a 1988 *Playboy* interview, in which Chevy spoke at length about his friendship with Doug and the tragedy of his mysterious death.

Chevy said: "*Caddyshack* was a big thing for Doug. It stood out apart from *Lemmings* and [*National Lampoon*] *Radio Hour*. Now we were in the grown-up world of movies, Warner Brothers. Doug had been loaded throughout filming. Somebody said, 'Take him away,' so I took him to a tennis camp 80 miles south of LA. We did nothing but tennis, eight hours a day for two weeks. The idea was to dry Doug out and dry me out. At that point I was coked up, drinking, living the high life from being so popular. Doug was way over the top. I was in control, never out of control."

Chevy and Doug went to Hawaii after the tennis camp. They did reasonably well in their attempt to dry out, but it wasn't complete.

"Doug needed it more. I was bigger, older, more aware and remained in charge—not overtaken by it. You would never find me with my head flat down on the table, dead drunk."

Theirs was a friendship filled with humor, companionship, and love, Chevy acting much like a big brother to Doug. "I loved having a friend of Doug's caliber, taking care of him. Doug genuinely thought of himself as the most handsome man in comedy, except for me." Doug was bowled over by the work in Hollywood, "looking at a world of big bucks. I was looking askance, having been there a couple of years."

In Maui, Hawaii, they stayed at one of the major hotels, on the fifteenth floor, with a pool that was "an acre, a beautiful seashore, all the time in the world, and money."

After a couple of weeks Chevy had to leave Hawaii and get back to work. Doug stayed on, and his girlfriend Kathryn Walker came to visit him. "They fought all the time. She was very strong-willed and they were intellectually connected; also by the heart. But they fought." When she arrived, she stayed only a couple of days, leaving after another fight, Doug told Chevy. "I got a call from him a couple of days later and he sounded sad and depressed. I don't know why. I said I would come back."

Chevy performed one of his now well-known pranks during his time in Hawaii with Doug, Chevy had grown tired of Doug's obsession "over the numbers on *Caddyshack*. I said, 'I can't take it anymore.'" Their rooms were directly across the hall from each other, and the doors were open. "I'd been on the balcony and I had my cowboy boots on. He was in the other room and I just went 'Ahhhhhh' like I was falling and he rushed out to the balcony. I was hidden behind the curtains and all he saw were my boots. It looked like I had jumped out of my boots."

A few days later, Chevy got a call from Alan Greisman, a producer who had joined them in Hawaii. "Chevy, nobody can find Doug. He's not in the hotel." It took another couple of days before Doug was found at the bottom of a ravine on the island of Kauai, "a small version of the Grand Canyon." Chevy flew there immediately and stood at the edge of the ravine, in shock, with other colleagues and friends. "We stood there looking at the spot where they had taken his body, bloated from laying in the sun for days, fifty feet down on the rocks."

Doug's shoes, and his glasses, had been found at the top of the cliff. "The last thing you'd have expected Doug to do was to take his own life," says Chevy, although for years he believed that was a possibility because of the shoes. The official cause of death was an accidental fall that occurred when the cliff on which he was standing collapsed under him. He was standing overlooking the Hanapepe Valley on the island of Kauai, Hawaii. "If you stepped too far out on that cliff, the dirt would give way. And that was the explanation the police had given us.

"Naturally I wondered if Doug had pulled some incredibly strange suicide joke," says Chevy, "but as I said, I can't believe that he was ever *that* unhappy."

Two decades later Chevy had an experience he found hard to discount. Jayni was going to see a "translator," who could speak to the dead, she claimed. At that time, Chevy was the world's biggest skeptic. When Jayni invited him to join her, he laughed. "I thought it hideously funny and idiotic," he recalls, but out of curiosity he did join her.

"A lovely lady, with a bit of a Spanish accent. Living in a small house, a crucifix around her neck. There was nothing odd or séance-like. Marie didn't know who I was. She explained what she does and immediately locked on to me. Standing next to me are my grandparents. It was so incredible. She got her name, Mabel, and my grandfather, 'who is choosing to show himself in his thirties. They are proud of you,' Marie said. 'You have made many people happy.'

"Now I'm starting to freak out. She was changing my whole view of life. I'm a skeptic, not religious. And the things there were phenomenal. Maybe there is something after death."

Marie asked if there was anything else Chevy wanted to know. He said he had often wondered about a friend who had died, and how he died. His name was Doug, he said. "Don't tell me any more, he's here." Her eyes closed. "He's very funny, isn't he, a good-looking man. He says it's taken him twenty-two years to get you here." Her feet began kicking out and she had to grab the table to hold on. "He doesn't want to show the end," Marie said, "but says it was the silliest way he could have died. He fell off and left you a present—his glasses." She explained that his glasses, flimsy rimless glasses, landed near where he had taken off his shoes.

Chevy believes he took off his shoes to walk around, and says, "I would rather take her word it was a mistake and he fell than think it was suicide." The experience with Marie, he added, "really changed my view of life."

Chevy was fond of quoting Lorne Michaels' statement that "cocaine was God's way of telling you that you had too much money." People around Chevy in New York and California "were taking cocaine and then painkillers to balance out the high. John Belushi never explained it to me that way. He just overdid it. Nobody bothered to stay on John's ass. They all feel that, I'm sure. I don't want to engender guilt. But Chris [Farley] was a clear example of going the way of John. We all had the opportunity. With Chris, I gave him lecture after lecture. He was just trying to level out. I told him, 'You won't be seen as another thirty-five-year-old Belushi. You'll be seen as a fat comic who wanted to seem like Belushi. Drinking a quart of Scotch in order to get back to the level of being calm enough because you just had two grams of coke.'

"I had learned that many, many years ago. You want to be high because you're depressed and frightened of pain or whatever it is, want to be out of that world of fear and in the world of fantasy, and at the same time fighting to get straight so you can have a real perspective. But you are killing yourself.

"The last talk I had with Chris was literally two weeks before he died [on December 18, 1997]. And he died exactly the way I said: 'You'll just be found.' The people who knew him better worked with him and probably tried very hard. I'm sure Lorne tried too. I would say, 'You're heading down the road to killing yourself.' Very overweight, an alcoholic, taking coke."

After moving back to New York in 1995, Chevy began going regularly to a therapist and "getting to the root of it," and learning why his television show, which should have been a big success, did so poorly. "I was in a situation where I couldn't tell the world this is what's wrong, because I didn't even know what was wrong." For the next decade Chevy went to therapy every week.

Chevy feels strongly that the public doesn't understand the burdens as well as the advantages of celebrity. Fans may say, "Oh, poor baby, if only I had your troubles, your money, your influence, your fame," but Chevy wants them to understand that for every positive aspect about stardom there's an equally destructive negative aspect.

The celebrity may live in a whirlwind of fame and glory, "half-blind from the popping of the flashbulbs, endless parties, huge amounts of money," but there is always something there to remind you that fame is a dream world, "insidiously taking away layer after layer of skin until you are raw. You have fame and fortune and here you are in a depression and seeing a shrink."

Carl Reiner said, "It was most amazing, funny, when Chevy started making it as a movie star. He was guilty about his success, but also [in] a kind of competition [with his colleagues]: 'Wait a minute, what am I doing here?' He was amazed he was a major star."

During the mid-1980s and early '90s, Chevy was part of an exclusive group, the Hollywood Gourmet Poker Club, with fellow card players Steve Martin, Johnny Carson, Carl Reiner, Barry Diller, and Neil Simon.

Carl remembers Chevy as a "fun player, a smart man, a smart poker player, and he was a graceful loser. We were all graceful losers. We took it seriously but there were a lot of laughs. He's a hard one to figure personally. [During our games] Chevy was two people, really—one was sentimental and the other a comedian. He talked about his wife and kids. He was a real person with his family. The other side of him was a wonderful invention, like his *Saturday Night Live* character."

But neither Carl nor Neil Simon felt they got to know Chevy very well. According to Simon, "The poker games were great. I like him, but there's so little I know about him. The group had a lot going. The worst were Carson and me. I went for the fun and would lose, generally."

They played for money, but not big money. "Steve was the best," states Simon. "Chevy hid everything behind the humor. He's a strange, terrific person. I'm not a big talker. I didn't get to know him well."

Chevy's three children, against all the odds (of children of celebrities), are well balanced, polite, and grounded. Chevy credits his wife Jayni for this, although his endless hours of in-depth discussions with the girls, as well as the conscious decision to leave Hollywood during their most formative years, has clearly helped the situation. Still, there are issues that are troublesome—dealing with gossip, or with the childhood friends who are there only because Daddy is famous. "When one of my children is hurting, I explode inside. Parts of me are crying so deeply, and there's nothing to do to fix it."

He worries when his children read things in the press that aren't true. "A perpetuation of these kinds of writings can change the perception of who you are . . . until they can get to know you." Chevy finds himself explaining things frequently, helping his daughters through it, telling them that no matter what hurts them he loves them deeply. "The act, the fact, of being famous is frightening and it's oppressing. And it's mostly frightening to by and large emotionally immature people who are in need of a quick fix of hugs, of nurturing."

"It's a funny, disparate thing going on. Whereas the world sees you in magazine photos and articles, and *Extra*s and *Entertainment Tonight*s, you are—I speak now for my cohorts who are famous—you probably come from a place that's very private and very introverted, frightened," he says.

"The idea of being emotionally healthy and secure is one of the most difficult things in this business. It's so much about *you*, and that's a dangerous perspective," says Goldie Hawn. "This business is now more about celebrity than acting—it has gotten out of hand, a feeding fest that chews kids up and spits them out. Celebrity was in 'those days' a little more respectful. People weren't wanting to know what color your poop was."

13. *FLETCHES* AND A FLURRY OF FILMS

Fletch, released in 1985, was a good film for Chevy. Directed by Michael Ritchie, it was an Andrew Bergman adaptation of a novel by Gregory McDonald.

Irwin "Fletch" Fletcher is a Los Angeles journalist whose profession is his life. As Jane Doe, he publishes articles that have caused heads to roll in the past. Now, Fletch is in disguise as a vagrant living at the beach, where he is actually doing research for a story on drug dealing.

Fletch is approached by wealthy Alan Stanwyk (played by Tim Matheson) who asks Fletch to kill him for $50,000. Stanwyk says he has cancer and wants Fletch to shoot him so that his wife will get the insurance money. The investigative reporter in Fletch discovers that Stanwyk is healthy, but the story is complicated by drug dealing, the police, and a piece of land in Utah.

The film provides an opportunity for Chevy to show his talent for assuming many identities, including a government investigator, an insurance salesman, a doctor who passes out during an autopsy, and a black basketball player in a dream sequence, a scene that includes Kareem Abdul-Jabbar. This is one of Chevy's top films and one that continues to be popular.

In his extensive *Playboy* interview in 1988, Chevy spoke of being comfortable in the role of Fletch. "Fletch feels very much like me, so he's easy to play," Chevy said. "There's a certain tongue-in-cheek, cynical attitude about Fletch that is me in many ways. The way in which he handles people, the way in which he talks, the way in which he performs, are not unlike the way I am with people."

Speaking now, Chevy says, "In real life, I'm not so insistently arrogant and rude. After all, it *is* a performance, larger than life. But the fact that Michael Ritchie allowed me to 'wing it' whenever I wanted to lends credence to what *Playboy* published."

Over the years, Chevy says, he has done many "favors" for Warner Brothers, including a number of sequel films. "It was always, 'Do us a favor and we'll return the favor.' One after another, lousy pictures that I didn't want any part of. They were always a favor, and I never got the favor returned."

Fletch 2, or *Fletch Returns*, was a Universal film and not one of the "favors" for Warner Brothers, but nevertheless Chevy was not happy with the sequel. The original *Fletch* received many favorable reviews. "Universal assumed that me in different costumes made *Fletch* work. In this one, the sequel, they put me in ridiculous-looking costumes."

The sequel was already handicapped by a writers' strike that began shortly after they started shooting. The director, Ritchie once again, began writing the script himself. "When the strike kicked in," Chevy said, they were on a tight schedule and "we still couldn't stop shooting. The sequel was based on the fact that *Fletch* had done so well. I was not happy with it. I think it stank."

The critics concurred. Vincent Canby, who reviewed both films, four years apart, in the *New York Times*, noted the contrasts between the two. Writing on May 31, 1985, about the first *Fletch* film, Canby had stated, "In the syntax once favored in advertising for John Wayne movies, Chevy Chase *is* 'Fletch.' The 'Fletch' ads don't say so, but Mr. Chase's screen personality—subversive in an entirely benign way, a slightly mussed-up example of the neat, buttoned-down class that bred him—defines the easy charm of this comic mystery film about a Los Angeles investigative reporter, dope-dealing cops and a wealthy business executive who takes out a contract for his own murder. Mr. Chase as Fletch, the hard-nosed reporter who writes under the name Jane Doe ... is very much like Mr. Chase the television personality ('Saturday Night Live'). He manages simultaneously to act the material with a good deal of nonchalance and to float above it, as if he wanted us to know that he knows that the whole enterprise is somewhat less than transcendental."

Canby went on to call the film "a lightweight, breezy experience that, by never pretending to be anything more than what it is, disarms criticism."

By contrast, his review on March 17, 1989, was another matter entirely. "Michael Ritchie's 'Fletch Lives' is the overly optimistic title of the follow-up to the far more entertaining 1985 Ritchie comedy 'Fletch,' about a wise-cracking investigative reporter played by Chevy Chase. 'Fletch Lives' looks less like 'Fletch 2,' which it is, numerically speaking, than 'Fletch 7,' the bitter end of a worn-out series."

Between *Fletch* and *Funny Farm*, Chevy had occasion to host the Academy Awards twice in Los Angeles; he has also presented awards several times in subsequent years. In 1986, at the Dorothy Chandler Pavilion, he cohosted with Goldie Hawn and Paul Hogan, and in 1987, at the Shrine Civic Auditorium, he hosted the Academy Awards on his own.

Funny Farm, a film released in 1988, the same year as *Caddyshack II* and just a few months before *Fletch Lives*, is just about Chevy's favorite film: "The best movie I made, with a great director [George Roy Hill] who knew what he was doing."

Bruce Bodner was executive producer of *Funny Farm*, one of three of Chevy's films he produced (*Fletch Lives* and *Memoirs of an Invisible Man* were the other two). "Chevy asked me to get involved," Bruce explained, adding that he often looked for material and there were several potential projects he looked into developing with Chevy that never actually became films.

The story of *Funny Farm* is an appealing one. When Andy (Chevy) and Elizabeth Farmer (Madolyn Smith) buy a farm in Vermont, they are in for a series of surprises. Andy has quit his job as a sports journalist and is intending to write the Great American Novel. From the moment of the move, everything starts to go wrong—the movers get lost with their furniture, there's a body buried in the garden of their new country home, an insane mailman harasses them, and townspeople set to drive them to distraction. Andy's novel is a disaster, and their marriage is threatened by Elizabeth's success when she writes a children's book. It's a delightful story and a film with many quite good reviews.

"One of my favorite moments in *Funny Farm*," says Chevy's sister Pamela, "was a shot of the fireplace, and the dog sleeping, with his tail in the fire. Chev's hand comes in with the tongs to get the dog's tail out. There was a very specific way he was doing it—one hundred percent Chev— just hysterical."

Bruce was concerned that Chevy "got caught in a little bit of a trap, and I saw it in *Funny Farm*. George [Roy Hill] had a certain style, approach, a nice kind of story, and he would try to play it relatively real. There's a scene in the film with some schtick with Dutch doors. About ten to fifteen minutes into the film, he [Chevy's character] gets hit in the groin. He's rushing, and Madolyn Smith, who plays his wife, is rushing. They each grab one part of the door and he gets hit in the groin. It was a big slapstick Chevy Chase moment, and the audience laughed, out of relief: 'Okay, so it will be a Chevy Chase/*Vacation* slapstick type of film.'"

Bruce remembers thinking the audience wasn't prepared for Chevy to do films that were "more conceptual. It was a trap. The audiences wanted physical broad comedy out of him. He is capable of smarter, subtler, more original work but they wanted that stuff."

Bruce, like Chevy, said that working with George Roy Hill was one of the highlights of *Funny Farm*. He was "a man of real substance. The film was a wonderful experience for Chevy—that professionalism. He [Hill] was just getting ill and this was his last movie," Bruce adds.

Speaking in a New York *Newsday* interview a few months after the film's release, Chevy said, "I was low-key, staid, reserved, contained—contained by George Roy Hill. It was a point of contention between us, but a wonderful point of contention. He felt the comedy would work better that way.

"I felt that if I didn't give my audience the broader stuff, they might feel I was disloyal to them. Then people were misled by the ad campaign, which gave the idea that it was a wacky summer comedy, when actually it was a comedy of more sensibility and sensitivity. So the director was right in concept and the studio was right that the audience wanted more Chevy Chase mugging, goofing and falling down. I blame the low box office on the way it was sold."

In a print interview with Gene Siskel, Chevy discussed some of these issues, including the fact that his films, while often attacked by the press, nevertheless did well with fans and at the box office. Chevy never pretended to love his films when he had complaints. Speaking of the discrepancy between the reviews and the ticket sales, specifically referring to *European Vacation*, he said in an interview, "It's rather astonishing and kind of sad, isn't it? I thought it was pretty lame, but it grossed nearly $100 million worldwide."

Concerning *Funny Farm*, Chevy said, "George is a strong director . . . He wouldn't allow me to fall back on my old bag of mannerisms. I couldn't raise an eyebrow. Sometimes I would plead with him, saying, 'George, if you'll just let me do this one little thing, I know it will get laughs.' And he'd say, 'I don't care. If it's not real, you're not doing it. Stay away from mannerisms. Play it for real and the humor will be funnier.'

"We had a running joke during the production where if I began doing my old tricks, George would say, 'Down, boy.' He said it a lot. And so I did more acting and less mugging ... I really owe a lot to him."

"Film is a director's medium," says Bruce from his vantage point as executive producer. "When you read about old Hollywood, it was a producer's medium, and the producer would take it over when the director finished and make the film. A large degree was subject to the director's vision and what they ultimately do."

Roger Ebert, who wrote negative reviews of some of Chevy's films, adored this one and gave it a good dose of praise and three and a half stars out of four. "*Funny Farm* is one of those small miracles that starts out like a lot of other movies and then somehow finds its own way, step after step, to an original comic vision. It's funny, all right, but it's more than funny, it's likeable. It enlists our sympathies with the characters even while cheerfully exploiting their faults. And at the end, I had a goofy grin on my face because the movie had won me over so completely I was even willing to accept the final gag about the two ducks.

"None of this, I imagine, sounds as good as it plays. *Funny Farm* has a good screenplay by Jeffrey Boam, and yet in other hands it might have yielded only a routine movie. George Roy Hill, the director, makes it better than that because he finds the right tone and sticks to it—a sort of bemused wonder at the insanity of it all in a movie that doesn't underline its gags or force its punchlines but just lets everything develop naturally. Notice, for example, the timing in the sequence where the sheriff first comes to chat about the corpse in the garden.

"Chase is not exactly playing a fresh kind of role here—his hero is a variation of the harassed husband he has been playing for years—but he has never been better in a movie. He has everything just right this time, and he plays the character without his usual repertory of witty asides and laconic one-liners. It's a performance, not an appearance."

Despite Chevy's feeling about sequels, his *Vacation* costar Beverly D'Angelo said, "*Christmas Vacation* was one I know Chevy loved and a lot of people think it was the best one. It is outstanding in general, beautifully shot. The director [Jeremiah Chechik] kept telling everyone he was going to elevate the franchise, like the *Vacation* movies were dog turds that he, the great artist, was going to polish into pure gold.

"As usual Chevy was consistently Clark," Beverly says, "and everyone fell into place around him. I had some problems with the director. I felt like he kept trying to talk to me like I was an idiot about filmmaking and it bothered me. I was very childish then. One day, my stand-in told me she overheard the director blaming me for a delay on the set, when it actually had nothing to do with me, so I called a friend to pick me up and just left.

"John Hughes, who wrote the script, called me into his office late that night and said, 'Is it Chevy? Is he too hard to work with?' And I had this sudden insight. I realized that everyone who idolized Chevy was afraid of him, was envious of him at the same time. I said it wasn't him. It was always the same. Directors were afraid to direct Chevy, so they would try to direct him through other means, misdirecting all the actors around him, instead of giving him guidance if he needed it. Chevy ends up getting punished for that, just because directors get intimidated by his intelligence and persona." Chevy had a hand in the script for *Christmas Vacation* and planted his seed for the story about a huge family Christmas. "Jeremiah and I rewrote it," Chevy says, an uncredited role he actively accepted in several of his films.

Chevy's musical instinct also came into play when the film was being edited. Although film directors didn't always take advantage of his musical ear, there was one scene in *Christmas Vacation* where his special touch worked wonders. There was a forty-piece orchestra for the film score. When Clark struggles to get the lights on the roof to work, and finally succeeds, Chevy says, "Clark is alone outside, it's a very sentimental time." Chevy asked for a harmonica. "The guitarist played harmonica and gave it its distinctively American flavor. He winged it, and it had a very nice kind of feel, not blues, but a sense of 'on the prairie.' It completely fucked up his score, but it was *right*."

Christmas Vacation deals with the Griswold family's preparations for the annual family celebration and the series of hilarious and unpredictable mishaps and disasters that involves. It's a houseful this time, with Clark's parents, Ellen's parents, Aunt Bethany, and Uncle Lewis. And of course the inevitable visit from Cousin Eddie and his family. Clark places 25,000 light-bulbs on the outside of the house and awaits his Christmas bonus to install the swimming pool he has already ordered. There are many classic moments in this film, including one electrocuted cat and a squirrel in the Christmas tree.

It's another of Chevy's films from which fans quote liberally from one Christmas holiday to the next. Classic lines include:

Bethany: Is your house on fire, Clark?
Clark: No, Aunt Bethany, those are the Christmas lights.

Clark: Where do you think you're going? Nobody's leaving. Nobody's walking out on this fun, old-fashioned family Christmas. No, no. We're all in this together. This is a full-blown, four-alarm holiday emergency here. We're gonna press on, and we're gonna have the hap, hap, happiest Christmas since Bing Crosby tap-danced with Danny fucking Kaye. And when Santa squeezes his fat white ass down that chimney tonight, he's gonna find the jolliest bunch of assholes this side of the nuthouse.

Clark: Hey. If any of you are looking for any last-minute gift ideas for me, I have one. I'd like Frank Shirley, my boss, right here tonight. I want him brought from his happy holiday slumber over there on Melody Lane with all the other rich people and I want him brought right here, with a big ribbon on his head, and I want to look him straight in the eye and I want to tell him what a cheap, lying, no-good, rotten, four-flushing, low-life, snake-licking, dirt-eating, inbred, overstuffed, ignorant, blood-sucking, dog-kissing, brainless, dickless, hopeless, heartless, fat-ass, bug-eyed, stiff-legged, spotty-lipped, worm-headed sack of monkey shit he is. Hallelujah. Holy shit. Where's the Tylenol?

Ellen: What are you looking at?

Clark: Oh, the silent majesty of a winter's morn . . . The clean, cool chill of the holiday air . . . An asshole in his bathrobe, emptying a chemical toilet into my sewer . . .

[Eddie, in the driveway, is draining the RV's toilet.]

Eddie: Shitter was full.

Clark: Ah, yeah. You checked our shitters, honey?

Ellen: Clark, please. He doesn't know any better.

Clark: He oughta know it's illegal. That's a storm sewer. If it fills with gas, I pity the person who lights a match within ten yards of it.

14. A FEW GOOD AMIGOS

Chevy had truly become part of the Hollywood "in-crowd." He had joined the elite celebrity group. He was respected and admired by actors who had been his idols, many of whom had complimentary things to say about Chevy's willingness to speak out.

On one occasion, Chevy was a guest on the Johnny Carson show, and Carson did an impersonation of Sylvester Stallone. "I was fed up with the endless impersonations of him," Chevy said, and he spoke up. After the broadcast, Stallone wrote to him, saying: "Dear Chevy, The world is littered with very small and often cruel inhabitants. Every now and then a man will defend an unpopular position. Some call it audacity. I prefer to call it class. Sincerely, Sylvester."

On another occasion, Paul Newman wrote to him: "Dear Chevy, You are some special kick in the butt. You've had oral encomium enough but thought I'd put it in writing in case you wanted something to burn. You add luster and dimension to the word 'class.' Best, Paul."

Chevy received the letter around the time he had offered to help Paul Newman with his summer camp for children. Newman also admired Chevy's willingness to speak his mind on important subjects. Interestingly, both Newman and Stallone independently used the word 'class' to describe Chevy's way of dealing with people and situations.

It was a big deal when Chevy and his *Saturday Night Live* colleague Dan Aykroyd made the film *Spies Like Us* in 1985 and an international group of reporters was brought to LA to help promote the film. The pair were committed to the project, which involved a screenplay written by Aykroyd and comedian Dave Thomas five years before the film became a reality. At that point, Dan's successes had been *Ghostbusters* and *Trading Places*, and both Dan and Chevy were hoping *Spies Like Us* would be a hit.

Chevy's strongest memories of *Spies Like Us* involve the process of filming and the striking contrasts of their locations. "The fjords of Norway, in eight-foot-deep snow, and the beauty of the Sahara Desert, when it could as easily have been done in Death Valley and Canada," Chevy says, still a little amused by the choices that were made at the time. "But, hot as I was, the studio was gonna spend the money. It was either twenty below zero or a hundred and thirty degrees," he added. The film script was written by Dan Aykroyd, Lowell Ganz, and Babaloo Mandel. John Landis directed.

"I imposed upon him to do *Spies Like Us*," Dan Aykroyd said. And it was a whirlwind of a film. Chevy's friendship with Dan was a major factor in agreeing to do the film. The actress Donna Dixon, Dan's wife, was also in the cast, along with Bruce Davison, Steve Forrest, William Prince, and Vanessa Angel. Chevy was extremely fond of both Dan and Donna.

Some of the filming was also done at the Twickenham Studios in London, where Christopher Reeve and John Gielgud also happened to be working on separate projects. "Chris went into the lunchroom in full Superman garb," Chevy says. "And there was John Gielgud eating lunch. Chris was taken aback seeing Gielgud, whom he idolized as one of the greatest Shakespearean actors of all time.

"He went up to Gielgud and said, 'Mr. Gielgud, I'm sorry to interrupt, but I'm a great fan. I'm here from the US shooting *Superman.*'

"'Oh, really?' Gielgud replied. 'And what part do you play?'"

In *Spies Like Us*, Chevy plays the role of Emmett Fitz-Hume, who wants to be a government information officer. Dan Aykroyd plays the role of Austin Millbarge, a Pentagon decoder. Both are bumbling and socially inept, and so good targets for a diversionary espionage mission.

The plot unfolds as the two incompetent applicants, Fitz-Hume and Millbarge, are chosen from a CIA recruitment program. They are parachuted into Pakistan and end up in Afghanistan. They are chased by Russians and finally learn the truth, that they are being used as decoys to draw out the Soviet defenses while two real spies are sent in. Their mission is to hijack and launch a soviet missile launcher and test the new US orbital defense laser. The missile is fired. As it is heading for an American city, the laser system manages to miss its target. The contingency plan would be World War III but Fitz-Hume and Millbarge save the day.

The film features several directors and celebrities doing cameo spots and one-liners, including Michael Apted, Martin Brest, Costa-Gavras, Joel Coen, and Bob Swaim, as well as Bob Hope, Frank Oz, and B. B. King, who is on hand to ask, "Won't you gentlemen have a Pepsi?"

Dan recalls an incident that took place while they were filming in Morocco, "way out in the desert. Chevy and I drove to work together in a jeep. One day after work, we were coming back around four in the afternoon. We passed a dump truck, filled with mud-strewn soldiers and heavy weapons. I took a picture and they chased us. Chevy drove right through the markets in Ouarzazate and avoided the Moroccan police patrol."

It was an "elite unit of paratroopers," according to Chevy, "and Dan knew he shouldn't have taken the photo."

Eventually, after a high-speed chase through the town, Chevy pulled over into the parking lot of his hotel, abandoned their car, and hid in a VW bus (a taxicab that had curtains). They were not caught, but as they left the parking area, very nonchalantly, they noticed the soldiers from the truck standing in a line, machine guns in position, guarding the entrance and exit. "Close call!" Chevy says. They learned that because the soldiers were from an elite group in battle on the Algerian front, having a photo taken of them was a high-security risk for the unit.

The next day, Dan arrived early for his call, told director John Landis what had happened; Landis went along with Dan's plan to let Chevy think Dan had been arrested and taken to Casablanca. Chevy was incredibly upset by Dan's "arrest" and became terrified, thinking he would be next. "I was thinking about my wife and kids. After about half an hour, there was a knock at the door, someone with a heavy accent. I was sweating, crying to myself, looking at pictures of my wife and children." He opened the door and it was Dan and John.

In fact, Chevy was both furious and relieved when he learned the truth. But, Dan said, "Chevy took it in good stride—he was a great sport. How could I resist?"

European Vacation was made in 1985. "Lots of people love this film but I didn't like it and I didn't like doing it. I had problems with the director, Amy Heckerling—a very lovely person, but I didn't think her direction smacked of energy and humor." Chevy felt that nobody could hold a candle to Harold Ramis, "who gave me the character of Clark Griswold. My expectations were higher. I didn't think *European Vacation* was funny enough." However, the film has become a classic from which lines are often quoted.

Filming *European Vacation* was a big production, involving a lot a touring around Europe. For some reason nobody has been able to explain, this is the only one of the four

Vacation films in which the Griswold family name is spelled "Griswald"!

Because of the success of the first (R-rated) *Vacation* film, Beverly D'Angelo says, "Very quickly a sequel was written, and it was G-rated, and no one really knew what the formula was. It went downhill from there, I think. I was living in Europe with my husband the duke [Duke Lorenzo Salviati], so I was glad the second one was in Europe, but I know Chevy really missed being home.

"Jayni was pregnant, it was cold, etc., etc., the script wasn't that funny. At one point my husband had a birthday party for me and Keith Richards was there, got everyone singing all night, and Eric Idle ended up so hoarse he had to loop most of the scenes in the movie."

Of the complexities of the production, Chevy says, "I didn't understand Hollywood enough yet—didn't understand big money and sequels," he adds. It was seven years into his Hollywood career but he was still not the expert on how it all operated.

The Griswald family—Clark, Ellen, Rusty, and Audrey—win a trip to Europe in a game show called *Pig in a Poke* and begin the "trip of a lifetime," encountering in one trip every mishap that the average tourist might encounter over many years. Yet all the mishaps are close to the reality of the traveler's nightmare.

The movie contains scenes that have been echoed over and over and recited by fans: having their camera stolen (in it, an erotic videotape of Ellen that Clark had filmed and forgotten to erase); innumerable car accidents caused by driving on the "wrong" side of the road; getting stuck driving for hours around one of the infamous London "roundabouts" (what American driving in London *hasn't* done that?). The latter gave rise to the famous and often-quoted line: "Look, kids, there's Big Ben ... and Parliament ... Look, kids, there's Big Ben ... and Parliament." The sun begins to set while they continue to drive around and around.

More than twenty years after making the film, and despite its comically shallow national stereotypes, Chevy still finds that his fans quote lines from the film and laugh about scenes in each of the countries visited. "People ask me a lot about the turn: 'Look, Big Ben!'" Chevy laughs. "It's unbelievable. You just can't get out of it."

And what could equal the tragic irony of Eric Idle's repeated accidents and injuries (all somehow caused by Clark Griswald), and the exaggerated British stereotypes of downplaying catastrophes? During Chevy's 2006 visit to London, he said, "I was reminded of Eric Idle's character," the *Monty Python*-isms still creeping into conversation. Chevy couldn't help laughing as he thought of Idle's injuries throughout *European Vacation*. "We hit him on his bike, and he is bleeding—gushing from an artery, in fact. And he says, 'It's only a flesh wound, a minor problem.' I did actually meet some people like that on our trip," Chevy says.

The critics had a field day with the film, and the fans of the first movie were a little disappointed in the sequel. Janet Maslin's *New York Times* review claimed the sequel was less effective than the original, which was "a funnier film that established their provincialism with a less heavy hand. [*European Vacation*] has a jokey, loose-jointed comic style. While it's very much a retread, it succeeds in following up the first film's humor with more in a similar vein . . . The gags tend to be broader and the director, Amy Heckerling, has a way of repeating them."

Three Amigos, released in 1986, is a movie filled with fond memories. Chevy's warm friendships with Steve Martin and Martin Short developed on the set. "We had a great time, maybe more fun than I've had on any movie," Chevy said.

When silent film stars Lucky Day (Steve Martin), Dusty Bottoms (Chevy), and Ned Nederlander (Martin Short) get fired, they accept an unusual job proposition from Mexico—doing a job with El Guapo, whom they presume to be the most famous actor there. Traveling in the hopes of being paid good money, they arrive in Mexico only to learn that El Guapo is not an actor but a deadly Mexican gang leader. He abducts the mayor's beautiful daughter Carmen (to be his wife) in revenge for the people's cry for help. The trio of comic actors is now responsible for saving Carmen and the village.

The film was written by Steve Martin, Randy Newman, and Lorne Michaels and directed by John Landis, recommended by Chevy, who had worked with him on *Spies Like Us*. Chevy was, he said, "guilty for having told Steve and Lorne to hire John. He was okay on *Spies*, but uncaring about his stunts," Chevy said. The actor Vic Morrow and two small boys had been killed in a tragic helicopter accident while filming *Twilight Zone: The Movie* in 1983. Landis had directed that film and was later acquitted (with four others) in a 1986 trial relating to the deaths.

"I was able to get the scope on *Spies* but had not seen his postproduction work." After he was hired, and seeing the final cut of *Spies*, Chevy says he realized Landis's editing and postproduction were filled with bad choices. "He was more of a bully to people on the set than I cared for."

The enjoyment all three stars seemed to have had on the set, and the long friendship that developed among them and their spouses (who for years would meet frequently for dinners and vacations and still refer to themselves as the "Amigos and Amigoettes"), contrasted with the press's reaction to the film, although not with the delighted response from the public.

Martin Short recalls "a million dinners with the Amigos and Amigoettes" and many drives with Chevy from home to the set. "We both lived in Pacific Palisades and spent a month shooting in Simi Valley. Chevy would drive me—he loved to drive. We talked about everything."

While driving to and from filming one day, Chevy and Martin were talking and Chevy stopped. Martin glanced to the left to see Chevy with his head on the steering wheel, apparently asleep, but still driving. Martin panicked. "I believed him. But he had his left eye looking out onto the road."

Whenever there was a formal "showbiz evening," Chevy always had the comedic perspective, remembers Short. "Vintage Chevy. He was like a kid in boarding school making other kids laugh. Sinatra forgot the lyrics at one performance. Chevy turned to me and said, 'Should we call 911?'"

At another event, Chevy and Martin were sitting in the audience and (Hollywood "superagent") "Swifty" Lazar was in front of them. Chevy put a pair of glasses on the back of Lazar's head, causing an explosion of laughter when Lazar didn't notice at all.

"What I remember about the film is the fun we had on the set," Short says. "Memories not so much of what Roger Ebert thought, but what the *experience* was. I like to work in a room of looseness and likeness. It was all the fun of working with Chevy and Steve."

Roger Ebert gave the film one star, writing, "The ideas to make *Three Amigos* into a good comedy are here, but the madness is missing. All great farces need a certain insane focus, an intensity that declares how important they are to themselves. This movie is too confident, too relaxed, too clever to be really funny. And yet, when the cowboys sit around their campfire singing a sad lament and then their horses join in, you see where the movie could have gone. My guess is they made it with too much confidence and not enough desperation."

For Chevy, the social part of the experience stands out. He remembers one occasion, long after filming, being at a steak restaurant in Aspen, Colorado, with the Amigos and their spouses, having one of many riotous restaurant dinners. On this particular occasion, the six were having dinner when Steve Martin was shocked to discover a tooth in his salad.

"There was a molar in his salad. Nobody could believe it.

Steve couldn't believe it. He called the waiter over. Not a 'fly in my soup' but a 'tooth in my salad.'"

"I'm so terribly sorry, Mr. Martin," the waiter said, quickly removing his plate.

After a few minutes, Chevy said to Steve, "Steve, has it occurred to you that it might be your tooth?"

He felt around with his tongue and said, "Don't be silly ... Hey, it *is* my tooth!"

The plates had been scraped. "They were going through the garbage and we were all in hysterics. Probably a crown, but it was still funny as hell, and he did manage to get it back!"

Chevy was a big poker player, and everyone seemed to know about the Hollywood Poker Club, founded by Johnny Carson. They met at homes once a month to play poker, eat, and exchange stories, first at Dan Melnick's house, then Steve Martin's.

Chevy was part of the group for years, until he moved back to New York in 1995. Although Neil Simon has stated that he didn't get to know Chevy very well, Chevy was extremely touched by one example of Neil reaching out to him. Shortly after Chevy's birthday in 1992, Chevy received a letter from Neil, which he has framed and hanging on the wall of his home.

Dear Chevy,
You didn't think I forgot you, did you? It was just a question of finding the right gift. [Simon had sent him a $10 gift certificate to Robinson's, which is framed along with the letter.] Just as an aside, regarding the conversation you had with all the guys. ["I would talk about the most personal stuff with these guys," Chevy says. "They were my friends—they were not about to tell some newspaper. I was probably talking about a personal problem."] I always thought you were one of the most open, honest and forthright people I ever met. You were so open and honest about your feelings that

night, which consequently leaves you very vulnerable. But I find that a very endearing and accessible trait. Just thought I'd mention it. Happy belated, Neil.

"This letter was very touching to get," says Chevy. "I know what he was saying. I am very private. It makes me think—was he right? Everybody in that room was a comedian. Everyone needs a cover, their own foxhole."

15. NOTHING BUT TROUBLE

T alk about a bad choice for a title . . . The film's working title was actually *Valkenvania*, which might have been more intriguing. This film, indeed, caused nothing but trouble for Chevy. Before the script was finished, Chevy knew it was going to be the worst film he would ever make. He got himself into a jam by agreeing to star in it before Dan Aykroyd had written enough of it to confirm Chevy's worst fears. Chevy always liked and admired Dan, who was excited about the project, and he wanted to do whatever he could to help him. He had made a promise, and Chevy is a man of his word, though at certain times in his life he clearly wished he hadn't been.

The story concerns a wealthy stock investor and businessman, Chris Thorne, played by Chevy, and an investment lawyer, Diane Lightson, played by Demi Moore. On a trip to an Atlantic City conference, they take the wrong New Jersey Turnpike exit and encounter a local cop (John Candy) who stops them for speeding in a bizarre town. The rest of the film deals with the strange and unusual punishments heaped on them by a 106-yearold judge, Alvin Valkenheiser (Dan Aykroyd).

Even Dan Aykroyd, who had put a great deal of work into the production, had to admit it was a flop. In a letter to the other cast members, Dan graciously took full responsibility for the film's failure at the box office and with the critics, and he didn't want anyone else to feel their work hadn't been sufficient.

The film collected several Razzie Awards, including worst picture of 1991. Dan Aykroyd felt the film wasn't helped by an ill-timed release, with several major films competing for attention the same weekend. From Dan's perspective, there were also stresses between the two stars. "Demi was very demanding. Chevy was resistant to her demands." Their acting styles clashed, and they didn't get along. Later Chevy said he thought he had gone a bit too far in his criticism of Demi. In any case, Dan said, "That film ended my directing career." It was in fact his directing debut as well.

Hal Hinson, writing in the *Washington Post*, stated that, "*Nothing But Trouble*, which distinguished itself by being Dan Aykroyd's directorial debut and in no other way, certainly lives up to its name. But you could go far beyond that—it's nothing but trouble and agony and pain and suffering and obnoxious, toxically unfunny bad taste. It's nothing but miserable."

Fan sites have often disagreed with the critics. From one anonymous fan: "I am surprised so many people don't like this movie. *Nothing But Trouble* starts off as an urbane comedy, but soon spirals into macabre madness. You never know what's going to happen next. It turns into a William Castle-style horror film with extra gimmicks. Very much like an old *Twilight Zone* episode, with references to Poe and Lovecraft. There is no blood and I'd say this is safe for anyone over twelve; but it is a bit creepy. The music scene alone is worth the price of admission. The cast is excellent, but they are highly upstaged by the art direction, makeup, and costume. I think the script is very good too, and the ending is great. Maybe you have to be a little weird to like this. I think it's pretty good."

Chevy didn't take the negative reviews well—they hurt—although he managed to joke about them. Chevy has worked hard to develop a thick skin about criticism from the press, but it still nags at him, and he continues to feel that most critics have it in for him. In one interview in the early 1990s, he spoke about the reviews. "Some people are relatively review-proof," he said. "I'm one of those guys who, if the audience likes it, they couldn't care less about what the reviews are. And I don't believe I've had a good review since I was born," he said.

The explanation? "I've thought about it. When I first came into this business, on *Saturday Night Live*, I felt very full of myself. I thought I was good at what I did. And I projected an arrogance, which was part and parcel of my character and the character of the show."

In 1988, Chevy had very publicly stated, "I don't particularly care for critics. There's an ad running now on one of the local LA stations promoting a movie critic—Steve Kmetko—and it shows him sitting back and saying, 'I can't write, I can't act, I can't sing, I can't dance, so I'm a critic.' And it's supposed to be funny and charming. But basically, that's the way I see it. These are guys who can't do it, so instead, they beat down a guy who spends two years of his life making a picture—in two minutes, on television!"

Chevy once ran into Rex Reed when he was with Jayni, Steve Martin, and his wife Victoria. Reed had smashed a recent film and Chevy's instinct was to hit him. But what he actually said to Reed was, "'Rex, I think you're going to like my next movie a lot better.' He batted his eyes, and with that unctuous tone, replied, 'Oh, I hope so, Chevy.'"

It wouldn't be until 2002, however, when Chevy finally got tired of negative reviews and "myths and lies" being written about him in the press. He finally said, in yet another newspaper interview, "Don't believe anything you have read about me in the press."

He has always understood how much of the problem stemmed from his success on *Saturday Night Live*. If he had sprung fully formed into *Vacation* or *Fletch*, his relationship with the press might have been very different.

"*Saturday Night Live* is a very different kind of art form than making movies. For a long time, people expected me to be the same satirical guy that I was on *SNL*, and they expected movies with *that* guy. The only one I did was *Fletch*, where I gave that a little bit more of who I am."

During the early 1990s, Chevy maintained many friendships in Los Angeles and had a lively social life with invitations to all the in-groups' parties. It was in 1990 that Chevy had his first Friars Roast at the New York City-based Friars Club. As Beverly D'Angelo explains, "A roast is where you toast a great comedian over the coals and lift him out before he burns to death, by reminding everyone of what brought him to be honored in the first place." It is an event at which old friends make jokes about the person being roasted. The 1990 event was a traditional roast for which many of his close friends turned out. Typical of a roast, and contrasting with his more biting 2002 roast, Chevy thinks of the first event as "a real roast, respectful and funny." Dan Aykroyd was roastmaster for the 1990 event, and among those doing the honors were Rita Rudner, Dana Carvey, Phil Hartman, Gilbert Gottfried, Robert Klein, Paul Reiser, Richard Belzer, Freddie Roman, and Kevin Nealon.

Chevy also did a number of guest appearances around this time. In the summer of 1990 comedian and writer Dave Thomas got his own comedy/variety show on CBS—a sketch-based, half-hour show that was on the air for five weeks. Thomas, of Second City fame, was well known to Chevy from projects including the film *Spies Like Us*, for which he was one of the writers. The show debuted on May 28, 1990, and the summer series featured many of Dave's good friends and Second City colleagues, including John Candy, Dan Aykroyd, Catherine O'Hara, Valerie Bromfield, and Rick Overton.

Dave asked Chevy and Martin Short to do a sketch with him that involved some funny wigs. "We pushed something in our pockets and the wigs would go up in the air from fright." The sketch was set on a plane. "All of us had a fear of flying, and anything that happened, or was said, our wigs would go up in the air, just like that. Cut to a few months later at Dave's house to watch the show. There was a shot of Dave. The first sketch was ours. As he begins his monologue, there's a close-up of his face introducing himself. And superimposed subtitles—a flight has crashed, killing everyone on board."

In reality, a commercial plane and a small plane had collided. "We couldn't believe what was happening to Dave, not just the impact of the story but the fact that we were obviously missing everything Dave said. They continued with the show and totally ruined it. The next sketch was 'Fear of Flying.'

"It was an actor's nightmare, so funny and sad at the same time. Hideously terrible and hilarious. In a Woody Allen movie, it would be just funny as hell," Chevy said. But not for Dave Thomas. "The reactions of the people gathered around, looking at Dave—he had the complexion of a toad's inner thigh. It was unbelievable. He looked completely dead. It was clear that nobody would watch the show the next time it was on. They would immediately connect him with bad taste. We loved Dave. He truly deserved his own show, but that was the end of his career in television at the time."

16. VISIONS OF A VISIBLE MAN

Chevy was feeling good about the direction of his career in 1992, with a collection of hit films and a strong fan base devoted to him, willing to ignore negative reviews and turn out for all of his new films. He had more or less adjusted to the meaning of fame and had put it into perspective, finally recognizing that all Hollywood careers have big ups and downs and that, no matter what happened in his career, his family would be there for him and would always come first. With three small children of his own, whom he adored, he was beginning to think more and more about his own childhood.

Chevy was constantly searching for new projects that would hold his interest. Two movies released in 1992—*Memoirs of an Invisible Man* and *Hero*—seemed to indicate that Chevy was beginning to take on slightly more serious types of roles, although he himself thinks of both films primarily as comedies. *Memoirs of an Invisible Man* and *Hero* showed different sides of Chevy as an actor, dealing with themes that had not been dealt with in any of his other films.

Memoirs of an Invisible Man, a film that Chevy believed signaled the end of his relationship with Warner Brothers, was adapted from a book by H. F. Saint and was a film long in the creation. Chevy produced it with Bruce Bodner, his attorney and friend. "The book was a marvelous one. I wanted to replicate the book as best I could," Chevy said. The film was directed by John Carpenter, and the creative process ended up backfiring when Chevy and Carpenter clashed on many issues. "We didn't have the same taste, and it didn't come off the way I wanted it to. There was a lot of comedy, but also mistakes made by Carpenter. It didn't work; it was too dramatic and difficult to get the comedy out of it." Chevy disagreed with some of Carpenter's ideas for the film—"a dream sequence with sexual innuendos. He thought it was funny, but it was salacious and not funny."

Memoirs is the story of a San Francisco stock analyst who becomes invisible when a nuclear fusion experiment goes awry. The film stars Chevy as Nick Halloway, who becomes invisible in a freak lab accident just as he is about to date a beautiful lawyer (played by Daryl Hannah). Sam Neill plays a government agent. Chevy was fascinated by the theme of invisibility, and it seemed like a story that could effectively combine romance, adventure, and comedy. "It felt like it was right for what I had done in the past, and right for a move in the future—a little more dramatic and a little more of a challenge."

There were contrasting opinions as to whether it was more a comedy or a serious film, and differing theories about whether or not the film dealt with isolation and detachment. For Chevy as an actor, it was a film that showed he had made a lot of progress in learning the craft. He had spent quite a few years in Hollywood, and he was finally feeling thoroughly at home as an actor, "of really knowing your lines until you understood and found the character."

The film took five years to make in all. "It was a mistake that we didn't go with the easy humor of the first production team," Chevy said, referring to a team potentially headed by Ivan Reitman as director and William

Goldman as writer. Reitman quit when he realized it was not going to be a typical Chevy Chase comedy.

The special effects in the film were many and generally impressive, although there were problems with invisibility in the initial round of shooting. Chevy's role is seen from two perspectives: sometimes the audience will see his character and the characters in the film will see "invisibility or me when I was wet or glistening." There was a lot of makeup for the special effects. On one occasion, Chevy had to wear a body suit "that went over my entire head so that I'd look like Spider-Man, with a blue material that I could just see through."

Around the time of these two films, Chevy still had a tendency not just to go to the official screenings but to sneak into the film and see how the audience was responding. The industry screenings were hard to attend, "but going, just sneaking into a theater where it's playing, I've done it frequently. It's fun and it's nerve-wracking." Chevy would occasionally turn to the audience member next to him and ask for an opinion. "They'd freak out a little. You don't want to read the critics," he added, although he does generally check the reviews himself.

The reviews of *Memoirs* emphasized the intriguing theme of the film. "Chevy Chase manages to tone down the pratfalls and mugging in *Memoirs of an Invisible Man*, which is neither strictly a comedy nor strictly a rehash of science-fiction 'invisibility' conventions. In fact, this is arguably Chase's most restrained and effective performance and could attract an audience beyond his established, indiscriminate following," wrote the *Desert News* movie critic, getting in a jab at Chevy's loyal following.

In 1992 Chevy said yes to a last-minute request to play a small part in the movie *Hero*. With Chevy's input, the part grew and his role, although not one of the leads, was nevertheless notable. Chevy didn't play the part with his characteristic look and acting style.

"I was told to talk like Walter Winchell. I suppose you could call it a dramatic role, but it was more of an impression of sorts." Chevy decided that "I didn't want to look like Chevy Chase. I had my hair slicked back with grease. The director liked it. It was different from anything else I'd done." This was not because the role was un-credited, he said, but because he wanted to try a different acting style.

At the time he shot *Hero*, Chevy rarely made guest appearances and he asked not to have his name in the credits. He would regret his decision later, particularly when he heard he might have been considered for an Oscar nomination as a supporting actor. An actor cannot be nominated without having his name in the credits.

The film is a reverse Cinderella story involving a beautiful television reporter, a criminal who remains a mystery hero, and a Vietnam vet heroic in his own way. Geena Davis plays reporter Gale Gayley, who falls into a major news story when she is a passenger on a plane that crashes into a Chicago bridge. She is saved by a foul-mouthed crook, played by Dustin Hoffman. He cannot take credit or disclose his identity, and Andy Garcia's character ends up taking credit and claiming the reward, donating it to the city's homeless people. Chevy's role as Gayley's editor adds color to the unusual story.

"My part was a man who had about as much compassion and depth as this bag [a large plastic bag sitting on the coffee table]. It wasn't a great movie. On the other hand it had a lot of good stuff. And of course Dustin and Andy Garcia. A great story, but something was lacking. Maybe marketing when it was released."

The first weekend of its release, as Chevy had done previously, Chevy and Dustin went to a movie theater in Santa Monica. It was three-quarters full. "This is common—to sit in the back or next to somebody who recognizes you and have them jump," he says with a smile.

* * *

In February 1993 Chevy was honored at the Harvard University Club as Hasty Pudding's Man of the Year. He was greeted by male students in drag, who presented him with a green and white brassiere with the letter "C" embroidered in red on each cup. One of his more memorable honors, he accepted it wearing the oversized bra over a Lakers basketball jersey on top of a tuxedo.

The forty students in the group hung on to every word uttered by Chevy and liberally quoted from his many movies, obscure lines of dialogue that even Chevy didn't recall. It was proof that the magic was still there, that Chevy was revered by a new generation.

He received the Hasty Pudding's traditional brass pot. "I really am proud to get this," he said. Chase was in distinguished company. He was awarded the pot and roasted prior to the Hasty Pudding performance of *Romancing the Throne*, the 145th production of a club whose members have included Oliver Wendell Holmes and William Randolph Hearst. The theatrical group was founded in 1795 and is the country's oldest undergraduate theatrical club. Chevy was its twenty-seventh Man of the Year, following the likes of Bob Hope, Bill Cosby, Robin Williams, and Michael Douglas. The event took place shortly before Chevy began filming *Cops and Robbersons* and a few months before his Fox television talk show.

A Harvard senior who was one of the producers of the show asked if Chevy would do one of his traditional falls. Chevy refused. "No, I might hurt someone," he said. "But I'd be happy to be on the band," he said to an outburst of laughter.

17. *THE CHEVY CHASE SHOW*

When the Fox Television network approached Chevy with the idea for a late-night talk show in 1993, he was interested but not enthusiastic. Chevy had carried an underlying depression for many years, probably since his turbulent childhood, and he was just beginning to get the feeling that something was wrong. While he had been at the top of his career, the excitement of starring in major comedies, coupled with the public acclaim, had kept him going, and he was so busy that he didn't stop and think about what was going on inside of him. He didn't recognize that emotions were brewing that one day would come bubbling to the surface.

He was very happy with Jayni, and thrilled to have a family and a stable home life. Several years earlier he had addressed the issue of his addiction to drugs and painkillers, but he had only scratched the surface and begun to deal with the underlying causes of his addiction. He had done only half the job. The rest was difficult and painful, an uphill battle.

Chevy had been off cocaine since 1986 and continued to struggle off and on with painkillers even as late as 2005, when he had a hip replacement. It was partly physical pain he was medicating, and justifiably so, as he had done some damage from his very athletic years and from film stunts, *SNL* falls, and the beginning of arthritis. But it was also the pain of his childhood, the pain of the abuse that he had not yet fully addressed.

At the time he was contacted about the talk show, film work was slowing down and not going as well as Chevy had hoped. The wildly successful *National Lampoon Vacation* series had not yet seen the last of its four installments, but there were a lot of films getting negative reviews. *Nothing But Trouble* "was pretty bad," Chevy said, and there were others. The fact that *Memoirs of an Invisible Man* hadn't done well at the box office was another blow. Chevy hadn't followed his instincts well enough. This was perhaps another result of his childhood: he wanted to please people, and help his friends, even while knowing that the best decision would be to say no and to stand up for what he believed in.

Chevy was also feeling betrayed by factions in the Hollywood establishment. In the early nineties, Chevy had a run-in with Terry Semel, head of Warner Brothers at the time. Chevy and Jayni were attending the annual Christmas party that Michael Eisner and Michael Ovitz held at a lodge in Aspen, Colorado. About a hundred people attended, and the room was set up with tables seating eight or ten people.

"We had gone to choose a table in the back, and I was with Dustin Hoffman and Barry Levinson." Chevy sat down with his friends and saved a seat for Jayni.

Semel's wife Jane came over to the table and sat down where Jayni would have been sitting. (Jayni was still talking with people and not yet at the table.) Jane was talking, holding a coat on her lap. "She was there long enough for me to say, 'Jane, are you planning on sitting there, because I'll save this other seat for Jayni.'" Before Chevy could finish, she got up and left in a huff. A few moments later, Semel came over to Chevy and in front of the other guests said to him, "You have insulted my wife and I owe you big time."

"That sounds like the mob to me. It was outrageous and disgusting, and I wondered what she had told him to elicit such a response." Chevy went over to speak privately with both of them, to apologize profusely, to say he never would have intentionally been rude to her, but his words had no effect. They were in the cloakroom dressing to leave. Ovitz came over and tried to save the day, asking Terry and Jane to stay. "It was a mess. Ultimately they left," Chevy said. "What a hell of a thing to say to an actor when you are the head of Warner Brothers. It's been fifteen years since that happened, and it should have been cleared up easily."

Apart from the talk show, there was little Hollywood work for Chevy after that incident. Although he has no proof, he believes that Semel's influence was a factor.

Chevy accepted Fox's offer to do the talk show, *The Chevy Chase Show*, but he was not in a good frame of mind and in retrospect realized he went on the air depressed. Before the show launched, however, there was a positive feeling and some good publicity.

On September 6, 1993, the day before the show first aired, a *New York Times* headline read: "Is there any late-night audience left over for Chevy Chase?" "Apparently so," the story began. "The expectations for Mr. Chase's premiere tomorrow night as a late-night comedy-talk host on the Fox network are rather high." The story concluded that the flood of Letterman publicity would help Chevy's show. "There's been so much interest in the late-night period I'm sure Chevy is going to get something from all that heat," said Jon Nesvig, the senior vice president of sales for Fox.

Chevy's show was a topic of conversation all around, with CBS executive David F. Poltrack commenting, "I'm sure Chevy will open well." Contrary to what Chevy thought of the time slot, the *New York Times* saw it as an advantage to start at eleven p.m., thirty-five minutes earlier than Letterman, Jay Leno, or Ted Koppel on ABC's *Nightline*.

Even the advertising rates were different for the two time slots. Nesvig explained that Fox was selling the show as Chevy Chase One and Chevy Chase Two, with a higher price for the first half hour: $30,000 for each thirty-second commercial and $20,000 for the time slots in the second half hour. Fox also set high-ratings guarantees for the first half hour of the show. Advertisers for Chevy's show included Nike, Levi's jeans, and film companies.

Chevy started working on the show with as much enthusiasm as he could muster. "There was tremendous pressure on me to outdo Letterman and Leno." But Chevy was very unhappy with Fox's plan to air the show at eleven p.m. instead of the typical post-news eleven-thirty-five time that has remained popular. He argued the point with Fox but lost. He was told it would give his show an edge on the market, a plan that in fact backfired, producing a smaller audience.

Chevy never wanted a talk show to compete with the others. He wanted more of a comedy/variety show, with parodies. Chevy's original idea was to open the first show in an "expressionistic, surreal" way, on a gray floor. "Two gentlemen wearing gray full-body uniforms, carrying a burlap sack." They would release a rattlesnake, with Chevy lip-synching an operatic aria sung by Caruso. The real rattlesnake would be replaced with a fake (animatronic) snake, which would bite Chevy . . ." Blood coming out of my leg, emergency medical services. Dissolve to credits, me on a stretcher, an ambulance, an empty stage." Chevy wanted "comedy, danger, and music." Fox wanted a huge glittery set and a traditional talk show. "I knew going in I didn't have a chance," he said. "I wanted something far out. I wanted the kind of television that you couldn't get." Nevertheless, against his better judgment, he proceeded.

Chevy had as much input as he possibly could, working hard to provide unusual and imaginative openings to the show, sketches drawn from his previous writings, wacky skits, and news spots reminiscent of Weekend Update on

SNL. He had a star-studded lineup of guests, including many of his Hollywood friends and former costars. The opening shows included Goldie Hawn and Whoopi Goldberg, Beverly D'Angelo and Martin Short, all in the first week. Others to follow included Burt Reynolds and Queen Latifah.

Chevy's flair for the bizarre was put to good use. Contrary to the formulaic openings of other talk shows on the air at the time, each show opened with an unpredictable scene or skit, as well as Chevy shooting nightly basketballs into a hoop, a gimmick at first endearing but later criticized as Chevy's attempt to be "hip." He opened one show in the theater parking lot playing tennis against Billie Jean King and Chris Evert. Less charming, but amusing to the audience, was one juvenile skit that featured throwing water balloons at an unsuspecting driver in the studio parking lot.

Another, quite hilarious episode was taped in a wax museum, with Chevy pretending to be a wax figure of himself, then talking or moving to frighten the tourists. Chevy was seated on a chair in the middle of one of the exhibits, looking very much like a wax figure but real enough for tourists to stop and look twice. Chevy would choose that moment to come to life, scaring the hell out of the unsuspecting museum guests, whose varied reactions were hysterical. One young girl was terrified of touching Chevy's hand when he put it forward to shake hers. This skit was very popular and the tape of it was repeated on a show just a couple of days later.

Chevy insisted on certain elements in the show. While the monologue was written by "the writers," with Chevy having little control over the content and tone, he did have considerable creative input with regard to much of the show. But the monologue was somewhat doomed from the start. "I'm not a stand-up comic," Chevy says, although he tried to infuse life, and his personal brand of comedy, into it.

Chevy seized the opportunity to reinstate his famous news feature so familiar to *Saturday Night Live* audiences, writing every word and gesture of the sketches. Many times, after his opening line, "I'm Chevy Chase" (pause), the audience filled in the missing "And you're not," which Chevy had deliberately decided not to include in the 1993 version. This was early in the Clinton administration, and Chevy took some jabs at his friend Bill Clinton, but nothing too harsh.

It was also the era of the first Michael Jackson trial and Chevy's writers had a series of slightly off-color jokes relating to the Jackson news of the day. When it wasn't featured in the monologue, Chevy put something into his mock newscasts. Unlike any of the competing talk-show hosts, Chevy's musical talent was apparent every night, as he joined the band for musical interludes. His "Goofy-vision" camera showed a close up of his face and his hands on the keyboard. Like the amusement arcade mirrors of the "fun house," Chevy's features were distorted. Moments later he would return to his desk, back to his usual self. Fox wasn't happy with it, Chevy recalled, wanting him to appear strictly as handsome Chevy.

He also had a repeated segment with three faces singing—all the faces were Chevy's—a feat of rhythm and coordination. He had done this feature many years earlier and was happy to bring back a new version for the talk show. One high point around this time was his receiving a star on the Hollywood Walk of Fame. The presentation took place on the first show. Chevy opened by attempting to put his handprints in cement—three feet deep—and falling in completely.

Underneath, however, things were not right. "I was locked in, depressed, and I didn't know it." He had just started seeing a psychiatrist who prescribed Zoloft, the wrong medication for him. He had never felt so confused in his life, and he wondered what was happening to him. Of the show, he said, "I was acting and not enjoying it. I was frightened and bored at the same time, onstage in front of millions of people. I'm much more edgy as a person. Dave

[Letterman] gets away with it." Again, in retrospect, Chevy realizes he should have told Fox they weren't honoring his wishes and told the writers they weren't funny. But everybody assumed it was Chevy who wasn't doing the job.

Chevy's friend Andy Aaron worked as a writer on the talk show, and has some strong opinions as to what happened. "I think the choice of the executive producer was the genesis of everything that went wrong. Steve Binder was in the wrong universe. A nice guy, but he didn't begin to understand Chevy. He was old Hollywood TV. He was clueless about modern ironic comedy, he was into 60s laugh track television. We were about to go up against Letterman at the top of his game in his new home at CBS, and he didn't think of Letterman as competition." But the writers knew that the competition would be huge, he says.

"We had brilliant, amazingly funny writers. Binder was the filter. He was changing what was being written." The show began the day after Labor Day, Andy says, explaining that they all expected to practically sleep there over that three-day weekend. However, Binder had said " 'Take the weekend off.' When we returned on Tuesday morning, he had rewritten and thrown out all the good stuff. Everyone in the room [eight or ten writers] knew it was the end. There were hilarious taped pieces that were shot in July, and they were sitting on a shelf.

"There wasn't a person there that would say Chevy wasn't nice to work with. Never blaming, nothing mean, not throwing things. He said, 'I'm sorry I'm letting you guys down.' Binder would come into the writer's room from time to time with 'helpful ideas.' " On one occasion, Andy recalls, Binder came in with a suggestion from his old producing days. He said, " 'If you're ever stuck for a segment on the show, just get a bimbo—put her out there in a short skirt and a low-cut top. Put a sash around her, something written on it like 'Miss Forest Products' or 'Miss Pork Bellies.' And have her spend the day cramming, just fill her head full of facts about whatever it is she's representing.

And put her out there. The audience loves it.'" The writers were discouraged.

"I think with the right producer," Andy says, "the show could have been done well, could have at least had a respectable year run. It wasn't the perfect idea for a show, but it could have been executed well, and it would have been funny."

The reviews of the show were terrible and the chat rooms and online postings were filled with nasty comments, calling it dull, corny, and lacking in humor. Chevy was both devastated and relieved when it ended, but the circumstances were disastrous, and the show triggered a low point in Chevy's life and career.

The talk show lasted only five weeks and was canceled without notice. The harsh manner in which this took place was not forgotten by Chevy. Chevy's fiftieth birthday was October 8, 1993. Jayni had put together a huge birthday bash/charity fund-raiser show for about six hundred people at the Beverly Hilton. Just as that night's celebration was about to begin, Michael Ovitz (at that time head of CAA, the agency that represented Chevy) came over and whispered to Chevy that the talk show had been canceled and asked if he would prefer to stop immediately or continue for one more week, to which Chevy replied that he would prefer to end it that day. He tried in vain not to let this news ruin the evening Jayni had worked so hard to prepare. The birthday show had been planned as a major tribute to Chevy's life and career but, ironically, was one of the most disappointing days of his life.

It was hard for Jayni to watch what was happening to her husband. "When his career slowed down that was bad for him. When the show was canceled, it was the worst. My stomach churned. He wasn't emotionally set up for that— all those years of pulling himself up by his bootstraps."

Suddenly, it seemed to Chevy that his childhood was all coming back: not just bubbling up but "bubbling over." The ways in which he had no control over the content and direction of the show; the manner in which all of his best efforts seemed to backfire; forces larger than he not listening to his wishes; ultimately the callous way in which he was fired and the public embarrassment of it all—all these elements felt a lot like abuse and Chevy felt very much the victim.

Chevy took a long time to recover from the failure of the show. He realized later that he shouldn't have been surprised that things hadn't gone well. At the time, he didn't understand what was happening to him, to his career. He'd had his share of bad reviews but this time the nastiness seemed to go to an extreme he hadn't seen before.

A *Boston Globe* headline on October 18, 1993, was "Fox Chases Chevy Chase Off the Air." An AP story written by James Anderson, dateline LA, began, "Chevy Chase has reported the news many times: Generalissimo Francisco Franco is still dead. Now 'The Chevy Chase Show' is too. Chase became the first casualty of the late-night television wars yesterday as Fox Broadcasting Company announced it was canceling his show, effective immediately. He began Sept. 7 and battled David Letterman, Jay Leno, Arsenio Hall and Ted Koppel for viewers. But his show was savagely mauled by critics, and it performed a ratings pratfall much as Chase himself had done in his famous sendups of ex-President Ford."

The story went on to quote Fox executives, who claimed they had brought in an emergency team of writers and consultants when things seemed to be going wrong, and quoted actor Dennis Hopper, who said after a guest appearance on the show that Chevy had been very nervous and was feeling a lot of pressure.

"Had I been honest instead of sweet, I would have taken charge, railed at Murdoch and his people at Fox. Instead I blithely went along with things, and at the same time was in the midst of severe depression and didn't know what it was," Chevy says now.

Chevy did not try to hide his disappointment about the show and attempted to put it into perspective; he did not refuse interviews and spoke about the subject many times over the next year, and later.

In a May 1994 Associated Press interview at the time *Cops and Robbersons* was released, Chevy said, "I think you have to understand the cyclical nature of life. I think you need to have a side of you that has that perspective and knows what trivial is. Trivial is moping about because you lost the talk-show wars. Not trivial is moping about because your children have chicken pox, as mine do—they're really suffering.

"There are things in life that are more important than other things. You need that perspective. It's very difficult in this business to have what is considered and written about as a failure and make it back in a business sense. You have to consider that business we're talking about was never really part of the artist's life. The artist must continue to do his or her art. If you don't like that, then you're not an artist."

In an interview the following year with Larry King, Chevy was asked why he took on the talk show. "Good question," Chevy replied. "The fact is I felt I wanted to get back on TV and do what I had done before . . . You know the feeling that you have many people working for you, around you, and you like all of them. They work hard, they're good people, but they don't quite find your voice, as they put it in the vernacular? And I had a sense that we weren't going to be doing what I wanted to do. I mean, the very first show I wanted to open up with a rattlesnake biting me while I'm singing opera. In the grand scheme of things, kind of trivial that I've lost the 'talk show awards,' in quotes. I mean, life is . . . You go up and down. You miss, you hit. And I just wanted to put it behind me."

Not so far behind, however. He was willing to make fun of himself in a Dorito commercial—a very highly rated Super Bowl commercial, in fact. In it, Chevy arrived on the set, "and they were cutting me from the commercial. In the end I say 'tough year.'" It was an expensive commercial; the reference point was the talk show.

Heidi Schaeffer, his publicist at PMK/HBH, recalls how difficult a time that was for Chevy. She had worked with him since the 1981 film *Under the Rainbow* and was surprised that Fox stopped the show after only five weeks. "They gave it no time to develop." She acknowledged that the format wasn't the best for Chevy. "Chevy wasn't really in love with the interviewing process," she said.

"Transitions are very important in guiding a career," said Goldie Hawn, who was among the first guests to appear on Chevy's talk show. "Chevy wasn't comfortable in that venue. It was devastating for him."

18. HOLLYWOOD AND THE WHITE HOUSE

C hevy has always been very outspoken. Whether he is discussing his career, his relationship with the press, or the political climate in the United States, Chevy refuses to be gagged. He doesn't stop to measure his words and determine if what he is saying is "politically correct" (the term implied broadly) or not.

Sometimes his words have been misunderstood, but in the case of one widely publicized political incident they were not misunderstood at all.

Late in 2004, Chevy was invited to be the master of ceremonies for an awards dinner in Washington, D.C. Because of Chevy's known and outspoken liberal politics, he was the choice of the organization "People For the American Way" to present awards to actors Alec Baldwin and Susan Sarandon. Among the other speakers were Bobby Kennedy Jr. and Senator Tom Daschle.

People For the American Way was founded in 1980 by acclaimed television and movie producer Norman Lear as his response to the disturbing public and political influence of the religious right. Chevy agreed to speak but somehow found the evening increasingly disturbing. On this occasion, his public persona and his private views were in conflict, and his private views won the battle.

As host of the evening, Chevy started well, and kept it light, with quotes like, "This just in—resignations in the upper echelon of the Bush administration. The Bush sisters have resigned and are being replaced by Paris and Nicky Hilton. Back for more news later." After Baldwin and Sarandon accepted their "Defender of Democracy" awards, Chevy took the microphone one final time and, seemingly, snapped. Kennedy's use of the term "Hollywood collateral" had made him furious. His immediate next job was to introduce Tom Daschle but Chevy couldn't resist answering Kennedy, saying he was embarrassed to be there, embarrassed to be called "Hollywood collateral," and embarrassed at the lightness of the evening, especially "after that dumb fuck [Bush] was reelected."

Chevy ranted on, feeling the light evening was too much of a contrast with what he considered a dangerous administration in the country. Using the filthiest language, he ranted on about Bush: "This guy in office is an uneducated, real lying schmuck . . . and we still couldn't beat him with a bore like Kerry." At the end of it all, he remembered he still had to introduce Tom Daschle, who, essentially, needed no introduction. Daschle, the former minority leader, was a little rattled, saying, "I've had to follow a lot of speakers, but . . ."

Chevy's comments, in the midst of a liberal audience, earned him some cheers, but there were also a lot of people, even the most liberal, who were shocked and offended. The incident earned Chevy some bad press and a letter from Lear saying the comments had been inappropriate, to which Chevy replied: "When's the last time a comedian was appropriate?"

"I was so frustrated last year. Bush's reelection was despicable. My mood was sour, really angry, and I had never done anything like that in my life."

Many people were up in arms over the incident. The *Washington Post* wrote about it. The five hundred people at the event were supportive, with the exception of a few who

Left: A *Vacation* break, during filming in 1982. (Photo © by Jayni Chase)

Below: "Now everybody try to look happy." *Christmas Vacation* (1989) with the Griswolds. Chevy with Beverly D'Angelo, Juliette Lewis, and Johnny Galecki. (Photo © by Steve Schapiro)

Left: "Practicing for the big shot." Chevy and Kareem Abdul-Jabbar. *Fletch* (1985) (Photo © by Steve Schapiro)

Left: "Some tips on catching the bad guys." *Cops and Robbersons* (1994). Jack Palance and Chevy. (Photo © by Steve Schapiro)

Above: "Now Rusty, it might *seem* like we're stranded in the desert..." *Vacation* (1983). Chevy and Anthony Michael Hall. (Photo © by Steve Schapiro)

Above: "Helpppp..." Chevy between takes while filming *Caddyshack* in Florida (1980). (Photo © by Steve Schapiro)

Right: Goldie and Chevy, *Foul Play* (1978). Chevy's first Hollywood film. (Photo © by Steve Schapiro)

Above: "Olé!" Chevy, Steve Martin, and Martin Short in *Three Amigos* (1986). (Photo © by Steve Schapiro)

Below: "Unbelievable!" Rodney Dangerfield, Michael O'Keefe, and Chevy, *Caddyshack* (1980). (Photo © by Steve Schapiro)

Left: "Before DNA testing, so how can I solve this crime?" Chevy in *Oh Heavenly Dog*, 1980. (Courtesy of Chevy Chase)

Right: "Clark, what's that on the road?" Beverly D'Angelo and Chevy, *Vacation* (1983). (Photo © by Steve Schapiro)

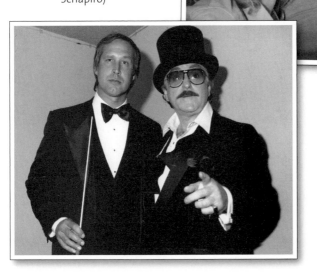

Left: "Where do you want this baton?" Chevy with Marty Feldman, LA fund-raising event, 1989. (Courtesy of Chevy Chase)

Left: "Two Fords." Ford and Chase at the opening of the Gerald Ford Library, 1981. (Courtesy of Chevy Chase)

Below: "I'm not a great golfer, Mr. President." Chevy with Pres. Bill Clinton during Camp David Easter Visit. (© The White House)

Left: "Christmas at the White House," Jayni and Chevy with Bill and Hillary Clinton. (© The White House)

Left: Raising funds for Chris Evert's Pro-Celebrity charity event. Chevy on the court in 1997. (Courtesy of Chevy Chase)

Below: "Please go easy on me!" Sam Waterston as the tough prosecutor McCoy and Chevy as Mitch Carroll on the set of *Law and Order*, October 2006. (Photo © by Rena Fruchter)

Right: Black bow tie event—Jayni and Chevy at a charity dinner in 2000. (Courtesy of Chevy Chase)

Below: "Who stole my oxygen tank?" Chevy on vacation with the family in East Hampton, 1993. (Photo © by Caley Chase)

walked out. Chevy said he only felt sorry that he hadn't given Tom Daschle a better introduction. "At the time, I regretted the fact that I used the language. I used it in a place where people could be shocked, but I know in my heart of hearts that nobody was shocked. I said what we all felt.

"I also knew all along that this was language everybody in that theater used at home. It wasn't new to them, just 'out of place.' More importantly, I wanted the People For the American Way to see the absurd juxtaposition of having a light awards—'Let's pat each other on the back'—evening so close to an election that surely spelled doom for millions of Iraqis, an outcome that would give another mandate to an administration which had lied to America. And People For the American Way felt this was a time to party and congratulate themselves? This goes against every ethic and principle I believe in. Why not express feelings in an honest way and share them with the very group that has the same view? I figured, 'I'll take the hit.' After all, when is a satirist and comedian most effective? When he's inappropriate. That's his job."

Chevy is often willing to assist at charitable events, but he objects to being called upon "in the guise of the bumbling Griswoldian character, when in fact I'm an intellectual and I have very strong feelings about politics. At least I was able to clear my own kidneys onstage."

The whole group, People For the American Way, is "totally liberal and democratic, but they were up there giving awards, nobody saying anything negative. They ought to be in Washington, beating the crap out of this guy. And I was only saying 'Let's do it.'"

Jayni, every bit as liberal as Chevy, said the incident was hard on both of them. "The fact that Bush got reelected was hard. What were people thinking?" Chevy couldn't get up the enthusiasm for the event and, she says, "something just snapped. He blurted it all out there and left. I was thinking, 'I can't believe he's done this.' It's not okay in public. He knows that. He apologized, a few letters of apology, in fact, and he will never do that again. There are better ways."

Chevy, like many Hollywood celebrities, understands well the connection between Hollywood and the White House: two worlds connected in a somewhat bizarre way by their mutual understanding of their situations. Film stars, larger than life and viewed as unreal—loved, hated and envied by the public that put them there; presidents, on a pedestal and seemingly untouchable—loved, hated, and envied by the public that put them there.

Linked to the White House through three presidencies—Ford's, Carter's, and Clinton's—Chevy Chase had become accustomed to the rarefied atmosphere, being invited to state dinners, readily able to share his political views with the country's leadership, and being called upon informally for his opinion or advice.

His relationship with Ford was mixed: a cordial personal friendship somewhat compromised by Chevy's endless and riotous *Saturday Night Live* portrayals of him. Chevy's satire put him high on the political radar, and Carter was already a fan who had very likely appreciated Chevy's depiction of his bumbling predecessor.

Chevy felt sad and nostalgic when he learned of Gerald Ford's death in December of 2006 and was surprised that so many articles published around that time spoke of the connection between Ford and Chevy. Chevy, after all, had parodied Ford mercilessly, and felt a little guilty about it. Ford had a great sense of humor and never held a grudge. Chevy remembered Ford as an extremely nice and kind person. "I valued our friendship and the gentle and kind qualities both the President and Mrs. Ford had. And Jayni and I will always know how lucky we are to have known 'Jerry and Betty.'"

Chevy was skiing in Colorado and was on top of a snow-packed mountain when his daughter Emily's cell phone rang. It was, surprisingly, a call for Chevy from a Reuters journalist based in San Francisco. President Ford's death that morning had prompted several calls to Chevy's publicist inviting Chevy to be interviewed—on ABC, CBS, and in print. He felt it would have been inappropriate to comment "during the Ford family's private time of grief." But the press and the public clearly had not for a moment forgotten Chevy's ridiculing Ford's "stumble-bumbling," although Chevy was quick to add that Ford was "perhaps the best athlete to have been the president."

Chevy credited Ford's presidency, and the *Saturday Night Live* parodies of Ford, as a factor in his own fame. He also credits Betty Ford, and the Betty Ford Center in Rancho Mirage, California, with giving him the help he needed in 1986 at a critical time in his life.

One of Chevy's favorite visits with the Fords, in fact, took place while Chevy was in treatment at the center, a decade after his departure from *SNL*. President and Mrs. Ford invited Chevy and Jayni to their Palm Springs home for lunch. A network television program about Betty Ford was being planned, and Gerald Ford suggested the four watch a videotape of several actors under consideration for the role of President Ford in the film.

President Ford and Chevy sat at the dining room table talking before lunch, while Jayni and Betty attempted to conquer the intricacies of the complicated tape player. The two women ended up "literally on their hands and knees in front of the confusing tape machine," wires leading in every direction, Chevy said.

Chevy suggested helping them out and began to stand up. At that moment, President Ford took Chevy's arm gently, encouraging him to sit down again. "No, no, Chevy," he said. "Don't even think about it. I'll probably get electrocuted and you'll be picked up and arrested for murder."

At first, Chevy was surprised by the strength of the Hollywood/White House connection. He was invited to Carter's inauguration in 1977, along with a hefty contingent of other stars, and he was stunned by the arrogance of the group. Thirty top film stars, flown first class to Washington, D.C., were put up at a luxury hotel. The night before the inauguration, there was to be a performance at the Kennedy Center. There was a major dress rehearsal all day, and the performers were kept in subfloor dressing rooms. In many of the rooms, Chevy recalled, people were getting drunk or stoned. "John Wayne was on a chair in a small room. Six-foot-seven, two hundred and eighty pounds, cowboy boots, a bottle of tequila." Paul Newman and Chevy were sharing beers, "into which Wayne would pour tequila as he leaned forward from the wall in his chair." Chevy shared a dressing room with Wayne, Newman, Dan Aykroyd, and James Dickey. "Dickey was completely loaded, lying on the makeup counter—a hilarious day. And there was the Leonard Bernstein follow-up."

A couple of years earlier, during his *SNL* season, Chevy had been commissioned by Lorne to get Bernstein to host the show, "so we could do our version of *West Side Story*," Chevy explained. "In the hopes of having John and Danny, these two lummoxes, jump up on stage and dance to 'Boy, Boy, Crazy Boy.'" So Chevy sat with Bernstein at Kurt Vonnegut's fiftieth birthday party. It was a year when Chevy was the toast of New York and was invited to every important event. Bernstein said he would think about the invitation, although it seemed to depend in part on how Chevy might respond to the maestro's attentions. When Lenny and Chevy ended up alone in a room later, and Bernstein planted a kiss firmly on Chevy's lips, Chevy simply wagged his index finger at him admonishingly. Lenny took the not-so-subtle hint; he never hosted *SNL*.

For the Kennedy Center performance the night before the inauguration, Bernstein was brought in to conduct the National Symphony behind James Dickey (the author of *Deliverance)* reading his poem. "He was the Robert Frost for Jimmy Carter," Chevy said.

The performance was to be shot live, with some things cut—one of Paul Simon's songs and part of James Dickey's poem. "It was like performing an Elizabethan sonnet and taking a couplet out—so senseless. But Dickey was too drunk to complete his poem. Cutting it short saved him from embarrassment."

As the group was called upstairs to begin rehearsing, Dickey, who had already begun drinking, invited Chevy to go swordfish fishing in Florida. ("I had never fished in my life," says Chevy.) Dickey then approached Chevy and said, "Chevy, maybe you can tell me how to lighten up my portion."

"It was in the days when I was somewhat full of myself," recalls Chevy. "I said, 'Play the laughs and I think the music can be more up-tempo.'"

Chevy knew perfectly well there was no room for levity in the solemn work about to be performed. He was backstage in the wings while Bernstein was conducting the orchestra in one full run-through. There was a pause, and Dickey walked up to Bernstein. By now, Chevy had told Jack Nicholson and Paul Simon what he'd said and they were all watching while Dickey asked Bernstein to play the music "a little more up-tempo." Chevy was sure Dickey wouldn't have mentioned his name to Bernstein, but Bernstein would have smelled the Scotch. He looked in the wings and caught the culprit's eye. "He knew. Who else would play a practical joke like that?"

For the inauguration ceremony the next day, the group was assigned seats directly in front of where Carter would be speaking. It was freezing cold that mid-January day (about 10 degrees Fahrenheit), Chevy recalled, and the group had been on a "major binge" the night before. The group included Jack Nicholson, Warren Beatty, Linda Ronstadt, Dan Aykroyd, John Lennon, Yoko Ono, and Chevy, and they all sat around in a producer's room indoors.

The stars sat in a circle staring at a TV that showed the inauguration preparations. There was a large table filled with food. Joints and other substances popular at the time were being passed around. Chevy sat down on the sofa next to Nicholson. One member of the group got bored watching the endless preparations for the inauguration and switched the channel to a talk show featuring a taped interview with British actor Peter Finch, who had died just a few days earlier, and two other guests. The program was closing with an ill-timed discussion of their upcoming appearances.

Warren Beatty was at the buffet table. "So there he was, carefully, fastidiously preparing his bagel . . . a layer of cream cheese, the smoked salmon, next the capers and a little egg yolk. Now carefully placing a slice of tomato, a slice of onion, and closing up the toasted bagel. It looked beautiful."

Warren was wearing a pastel-colored sweater, looking the picture of perfection. He was about to take the first bite when the host of the television talk show, wrapping it up in the final moments of the show, said to the first guest, "Now, you'll be appearing at the Desert Inn in Las Vegas next week," and to the second, "Your new album is out, and Peter . . ."

Chevy cut in dryly. ". . . and Peter, you'll be dying?" Jack Nicholson laughed. John Lennon laughed.

"Warren had just taken the first bite and did a spit-take I've never seen the likes of. All over the beautifully set table. Hit the wall, into the coffee cups, on his pastel sweater.

"It was such an obvious line—my persona and arrogance, and way of saying things. But Jesus Christ, it was so damn funny."

By this time, someone in the room realized it was too late to join the audience for the inauguration. The group, flown in at great expense purely for its celebrity value, watched the event on TV, and their empty seats were filled with families of senators and others brought in at the last minute to avoid an obvious block of vacant seats directly in front of President Carter during his speech.

There was no backlash after the incident. No one outside the group ever mentioned what went on in the room, and

Chevy's friendship with Jimmy Carter continued through-out his administration. Chevy, still new to the Hollywood/White House connection, would sometimes call the Oval Office on speaker phone, just to shock his friends when Carter would answer, "Hello, Chevy."

By the time of the Clinton administration, the White House was no longer a novelty to Chevy. Chevy had a closer connection, his political opinions were welcomed in confidential discussions, and he and Jayni were frequent guests at the White House, Chevy and Bill retiring to private quarters to discuss Bosnia or other pressing issues of the day.

Chevy first met Bill Clinton when Clinton was a young governor of Arkansas, in 1988, when Clinton made a speech at the Democratic National Convention. Chevy recalls that Clinton was "coming off as a young, arrogant, brash kid, and George Bush looked like the president, with the respect of the CIA." Chevy liked Bill Clinton from the start—his intelligence, outgoing manner, and sense of humor—and a friendship developed quickly. Chevy liked Clinton's approach to politics but was concerned about Clinton's approach to an audience. He talked to Clinton after observing him in action and had some theatrical suggestions for him. "You should take a minute before you answer questions," Chevy advised. "Make it *look* as if you are thinking about it."

"He's so fucking smart he can just extemporaneously pull the answers out of the air from this incredible memory of everything that he's learned since third grade, at Oxford, and since." Chevy was impressed and flattered to observe that Clinton took his advice. When he was running for president, he changed his presentation. Every so often, while on a long bus trip during the campaign, Chevy would get a phone call from Clinton after a televised appearance, asking, "How'd I do?" "It just *looked* like the wheels were turning—he was probably thinking of something else."

Once Clinton was elected, Chevy and Jayni had many invitations to the White House, including one overnight visit and an Easter weekend trip to Camp David. Chevy's daughter Emily recalls the Camp David Easter visit well. It was quite an extraordinary experience for a girl who was only eleven at the time. "Dad has a great relationship with Clinton, a lot of respect, sharing music and humor, playing golf and telling jokes," Emily said.

At the time of the Camp David trip, Emily was very worried about school shootings and asked the president about it. She sat with him and had "a half-hour conversation about the issue, and generally about social issues with kids in the country."

In his autobiography, Bill Clinton wrote about receiving praise from Chevy for his long speech in Atlanta. Clinton had been criticized for it by others so hearing words of praise from Chevy had lifted his spirits. "I had always liked his movies," he wrote. "Now he had a fan for life." At another point, during his 1992 presidential campaign, Clinton was in Los Angeles and having a difficult time. "Just as he had done on Long Island four years earlier," he wrote, "he showed up at a low moment to lift my spirits."

Clinton seemed to enjoy the Hollywood connection as much as Chevy enjoyed the invitations to the White House, Camp David, and political functions. Clinton invited Chevy to play golf, Chevy protesting that his role in *Caddyshack* hardly qualified him as a golfer. Nevertheless there were many golf outings, Chevy attempting to hold his own and engaging in an exchange of increasingly dirty jokes on the golf course. Chevy says his own jokes were dirtier.

"I kept saying to him, 'Mr. President, I don't play golf. I stink.' I had a pro with me every time I was filmed who would show me the shot. How to do the stroke. And that's why I looked good. That's why I got lucky."

On the golf course Chevy called Clinton "Bill," although at other times "Mr. President." When Clinton called from the White House, he would say, "Bill Clinton . . . Oh, sorry, Mr. President," and chuckle. "He told me some joke about a threesome—maybe a Jew, an Arab, and a black guy, or some such group. I told him a cowboy joke but I'm not really a joke teller.

"A cowboy rides into town, gets off his horse, straps it to the hitching post in front of the saloon. There were two old guys on rockers. After the horse was strapped, the rider goes and picks up the horse's tail, kisses the rear of the horse, and puts the tail back down.

"One of the two old guys asks, 'What did he do that for?'

" 'I don't know . . . Chapped lips?' replied the other.

" 'Well, how's that gonna help?'

"After a pause, 'Keeps him from licking them,' replied the first."

Clinton loved the joke.

The first time Chevy and Jayni visited the White House, it was following a fund-raising dinner in Washington, D.C., for Senator Ted Kennedy. The Clintons showed up unexpectedly and took the lectern. There were a thousand people, and the Secret Service approached the Chases, issuing a Clinton invitation to stay at the White House.

The trip to the White House for the first time was exhilarating, surprising, even for a celebrity accustomed to special treatment. Chevy remembered the door of the presidential limousine: "It must have weighed six hundred pounds, and the glass is two or three inches thick. It's a great trip, from somewhere in Virginia. The sirens go off, and the motorcycles. Everything stops, traffic everywhere, and suddenly you are at the White House."

Chevy and Jayni were escorted upstairs to the private quarters, where they were shown to the Queen's Bedroom. Then they went to sit out on the Truman Terrace and talk. The terrace looks out across the water and the Mall. Chevy recalled a mark, a chip out of the wall, where Truman had broken something in a fit of anger. "We closed our bedroom door and saw the original handwritten words to the national anthem. Every tchotchke is a genuine, real thing. It's just amazing."

Chevy wanted to discuss Bosnia and Clinton was ready to settle in for a conversation. He went right into the kitchenette, Chevy recalls, and the refrigerator door was opened.

"Bet you're hungry, huh?" he called from the other room.

"No thanks, Mr. President. We just had that huge dinner."

"Okay, I'm just gonna have a little dessert," Chevy heard from the other room.

Chevy recalls, "He comes out with a huge ice-cream cake, chopped up. He had obviously been eating away at this thing for the past week. He had to watch his weight, and the next morning, as I peered down the hallway, I waved 'good-bye and thanks' to the president as he was being dragged away by Secret Service to go exercise."

Chevy doesn't know whether he influenced the president on Bosnia or not, but Clinton "had a good response in terms of national interest as to why the US had not yet joined the process." He indicated to Chevy he was going to get involved in Bosnia but was cautious about going into every trouble spot. His decision would depend on the press buildup, the editorials, and what was best in terms of national interest. "He wanted to remind the European community, and NATO and others, who we were and what we stood for." Chevy brought up the discussion because he was "just curious" as to why the United States hadn't at that point stepped in.

Though Chevy and Jayni attended many functions and parties at the White House, they were only once invited to a state dinner, "which is an entirely different affair," Chevy said, a black tie dinner and a very formal situation, unlike the more casual visits to the White House and the Oval Office. There were about fifty tables in the room, eight or ten to a table, and a dais at the front of the room for the guests of honor, including the president and the first lady. The president, in white tie and tails, walked in that particular evening with the prime minister of India, whose gait was unusually stiff "and who looked like the most dour and boring guy in the world." Chevy and Jayni were seated at a table with other dinner guests, not far from the president.

President Clinton winked a greeting in the direction of Chevy's table just as the dinner was starting. A White House employee came by and Chevy, not at all sure how to act at an event where everything seemed so serious, said to the woman, "I don't know the protocol at these things, but the president has been indicating, and is it all right if I go up and say hello?"

"Absolutely," the woman replied. Chevy got up from the table, started slowly across to the dais, and, while Chevy was still a few feet away, Clinton put out his hand to say hello and caught a foot-high goblet of red wine with his hand.

"It exploded all over the prime minister of India, whose expression did not change at all!" The Secret Service, the president, and various waiters wiped him down, and still his expression did not change. In fact, the only one to react at all was Clinton, who was embarrassed and apologetic. Upon witnessing this, Chevy, without a smile, did an immediate about-face and returned to his seat. "He knew I had gotten away without showing any expression toward him. Our table had seen it but everyone had kept a straight face. Inside, I was laughing so hard—without showing it—I was sweating. I darn near wet my pants."

Chevy continued his relationship with the president through to the end of the Clinton presidency. Afterward, Clinton called upon Chevy to accompany him on a week-long World Economic Forum trip, as well as to political meetings, including one with Israeli and Palestinian ambassadors attending an event for "Seeds of Peace."

Chevy was seated next to Clinton, just recently out of power and still trying to work for Mideast peace. Seeds of Peace is an organization that works to secure lasting peace in the Middle East by bringing together Israeli and Arab teenagers, nurturing friendships through various projects at a camp for two weeks, allowing them to interact in a way that helps to erase prejudices against each other as the enemy.

The cause was important to Clinton and to Al Gore during their time in office, and they continued with it afterward. Chevy was called upon to help raise funds through a concert in New York in 2003. At the meeting that day, six leaders were assembled around a table. "Clinton knew every street corner in Israel, and I'm sure Bush thought the Middle East was near Canada," Chevy said. During the meeting, he found it surprising that Clinton was very deferential regarding his successor, who was not at the meeting, speaking of him as a good leader and telling the assembled group not to worry. When the ambassadors were talking among themselves, Clinton turned to Chevy and whispered a brief, unprintable, derogatory comment about Bush. Chevy was reassured.

Chevy's political involvement has not diminished, even though his White House visits have stopped. He was very active in Kerry's presidential run, donating $65,000 to his campaign. He had known Kerry for a number of years and was one of those advising him to select John Edwards as his running mate. Chevy remains in contact with the Clintons, socializing occasionally.

CHEVY'S DESK II

In Chevy's writing, he poked holes in conventional thinking. He deflated institutions that attempted to control people's actions and thoughts. Religion was certainly not exempt from Chevy's sketches. Taking a satirical look at the idea of confession in a Catholic church, Chevy wrote the following sketch with Pat Proft, his writing partner on *The Smothers Brothers Show*. It was one of a series of confessional sketches (and a "running gag") performed on the show.

[Open on Don Novello as a priest in a confession booth.]

Voice: Forgive me, Father, for I have sinned. It has been three weeks since my last confession.

Don: Yes, my son.

Voice: I took the Lord's name in vain at the office seven times. In fact, Father, business pressures being what they are these days, I must confess that I swore many times last week.

Don: Go on.

Voice: I lied to my mother over the phone. And I ate meat last Friday evening at the office. I was working late.

Let's see ... I had a sandwich ... It was a tongue, corned beef, and pastrami on rye bread [Chevy selected this sandwich because it was a favorite of his.]

Don: Go on.

Voice: ... with coleslaw and Russian dressing.

Don: Russian dressing?

Voice: Yes, Father.

Don: Ecch. Please continue.

Voice: Yes, Father. I committed a terrible sin this weekend, which is difficult for me to speak of.

[Pause.]

Don: Do not be afraid. We are alone with our maker.

Voice: Well ... I have committed adultery. It was at a motel with a girl from the office, Sherril Phat.

Don: Sherril?

Voice: Phat.

Don: Could you spell that?

Voice [somewhat confused]: Why ... yes, Father, if you wish. P-H-A-T.

Don: P-H-A-T?

Voice: Yes, "T."

Don: Funny name. Go on, my son.

Voice: I robbed the office vault of twelve thousand dollars in securities and—

Don: One moment. We'll get to that later. What about the adultery? Please, continue.

Voice: Oh, Father, it was nothing. Just a short afternoon in a motel room. I felt very bad after, but somehow relieved.

Don: What do you mean, "relieved"?

Voice: Well, I knew right after that I really loved my wife and family very deeply. I guess I needed an experience as traumatic as this one to prove it to me.

Don: "Right after"? Right after what, my son? You must get the details off your chest and into my ear.

Voice: Right after we ... we ... did it.

Don: Tell me something more about the trauma.

Voice: I don't understand, Father.

Don: My son, what I am trying to say to you . . . What I am hoping for your sake you may be able to lessen your burden with, what I am essentially looking for in you is an answer to a question of this adultery about which you speak which must sooner or later be faced by all who sin before the eyes of the Lord.

Voice: Yes, Father?

Don: How was it?

Voice: Oh! I guess . . . about a "B" minus.

Don: "B" minus? Hmmm. Phat, Sherril. Phat, eh? All right, my son. [Looks at his watch.] For your penance, I want you to say five "Hail Marys," twelve "Our Fathers," and six "slick slimy snakes slid slowly southward."

Voice [confused, he tries but he can't say it]: Six slick slappy slimes slow . . .

Don: Try, "Peter Piper picked a peck of pickled peppers." [Fade out on voice trying it.]

Watergate was a serious scandal but in the manner of all scandals it provided wonderful material for comedians and satirists. Chevy looked back on Watergate and found the turn of events surprising. Writing from the perspective of a prophetic judge, the following excerpts from a longer Watergate sketch look at what might happen.

Judge: Robert Haldeman, you are found guilty of four-teen counts of obstructing justice. You are sentenced to two and a half to eight years. You will not serve immediately because of your pending appeal. You will accept $25,000 from CBS for an interview describing your part in these crimes. [Gavel and echo.]
John Erlichman, you are found guilty of making false statements to the grand jury and fourteen counts of conspiracy to obstruct justice. You are sentenced to two and a half to eight years. You are to be free

pending appeal, which will give you time to negotiate with the Mutual Broadcasting System to be a commentator.

Richard Nixon, you have been found guilty of nothing, never having been given the chance. You have been pardoned for it. Having resigned the presidency just in time, you are hereby sentenced by this court to remain in seclusion at your beautiful "adobe"-style ranch on the beach, with a nice pension and a staff. You will be too ill to testify at any hearings and will only be allowed to attend parties in your honor.

Chevy wrote many *Saturday Night Live* sketches in late-night sessions with Lorne Michaels, and frequently there was input from other writers. Chevy is careful to note that he does not take a hundred percent ownership and that the process of editing went on until the very last minute before showtime. There were often more than a dozen writers for any one *SNL* episode, and teamwork was an important part of the concept. Many people have made the observation that Weekend Update spawned later satirical/political news shows, such as *The Daily Show with Jon Stewart*.

These sketches are reprinted with gracious permission from *Saturday Night Live*.

The following, another Ford parody, is the opening scene of the sixth *SNL* show, November 22, 1975.

[Up on the presidential seal.]

(V/O): Ladies and gentlemen, the president of the United States.

[Dissolve to Chevy at desk. Shaving cuts with tissue covering them are on his face. On the desk is a pitcher of water with two glasses. Also a red phone and a black phone. A desk set and various accessories are on the desk. Camera left, behind him, is the American flag. Camera right is the presidential flag. Right is an easel with a chart showing an increase in presidential popularity.]

Gerald Ford: Toy boat, toy boat, toy boat . . . My fellow Americans, I have called upon the networks tonight to make two pressing issues clear to the American public.

[Super: impersonation slides.]

Number one: the possible default of New York City, and number one: my stand on the Ronald Reagan announcement.

[SFX: telephone ring. It will continue to ring until the phone is picked up later.]

Ford (cont.): Excuse me.

[Picks up full glass of water and puts to ear, spilling it.]

Hello . . . Nessen? I can't hear you. Well, I guess the other phone's ringing. You get it, will you? Firstly: the default of New York City. Let me be clear on my feelings here. As president, I will change my mind whenever I want. Okay, so I did say I might favor limited loan guarantee legislation put before me by Congress.

[Picks up phone.]

[SFX: phone ringing stops.]

Hello. Hotline. Anwar, just a second . . .

[Picks up another phone.]

Henry? Talk to Sadat, will you?

[Puts phones together.]

The point is do I really care? Do I really know what the issue is? "Relevant," "Irrelevant," "Fault," "Default." These are just hard words.

[SFX: buzzer.]

Yes, Henry. All right. I'll talk to Anwar. Okay. The bail-out bill now before the House of Representatives does not address the current situation, and I would veto it . . . the current situation being that the longer I hold out, the better chances I have with those conservative Republicans who might otherwise support Ronald Reagan. Pretty smart, eh? Which brings me to the first point. Let's take a look at the recent popularity polls, shall we?

[The chart is upside down, showing his popularity rising when it is actually declining.]

[He gets up and moves to the easel.]

Clearly, my popularity is on the up and up. While Reagan's ...

[He drops card. Leans down to pick it up, falls through easel and across desk to camera left. He looks into camera.]

LIVE FROM NEW YORK, IT'S SATURDAY NIGHT!

The following Weekend Update shows the range and balance of topics typically covered. Chevy says that he often wrote in "roving reporter" parts in the Updates for *SNL* cast members when he felt they were underused in the rest of that night's show.

The following excerpts are taken from *SNL* 8, December 20, 1975. Candice Bergen hosted the show.

Chevy: Good evening ... I'm Chevy Chase, and you're not. Our top story tonight. A Harris Poll has revealed that Humphrey is ahead of both Ford and Reagan. Harris said that if the election were held tomorrow, Hubert Humphrey would be the president. Humphrey could not be reached for a comment today. He's running around the country trying to get the polls open. Humphrey, delighted by the news, held a press conference, in which he struck six classic poses for photographers.

[Hand appears with paper.]

This bulletin just in ... from Madrid, Spain, comes the word that Generalissimo Francisco Franco is still dead. Doctors say his condition is unchanged.

The character of Emily Litella was a recurrent one on Weekend Update—an elderly woman, somewhat hard of hearing, whose editorials are always based on hearing the news reports slightly incorrectly.

Chevy: Recognizing our obligation to present responsible opposing viewpoints to our opinions, Weekend Update invites Emily Litella to reply to an editorial.

Gilda: What is all this I hear about firing the handicapped? It's a filthy, dirty idea. Firing the handicapped . . . especially at Christmastime . . . where there's so much more opportunity for the handicapped to find employment . . . like licking envelopes and stamps, making lightbulbs, putting the outfits on Barbie dolls and recording the little voices in Chatty Cathies, posing for Christmas Seal photos, and playing Santa Claus sitting down in large department stores. The holiday season is the time when the handicapped need money to buy Christmas dinner for their families. Why, they'll have to buy cheap, unplucked, frozen turkeys and they'll hurt themselves trying to pull the feathers out and they'll freeze their laps off. Why, they'll end up having to eat toast. Whoever heard of Christmas toast?

[Chevy interrupts her.]

Chevy: Miss Litella, the editorial was about "*hiring*" the handicapped!

Gilda: Oh . . . Well, that's lovely . . . Never mind.

Chevy ended every Weekend Update with "Good night, and have a pleasant tomorrow," a phrase that remained with the show long after his departure from *SNL*.

Chevy: And now, as a public service, to those of our viewers who have difficulty with their hearing, I will repeat the top story of the day aided by the headmaster of the New York School for the Hard-of-Hearing.

[His story repeated by Garrett Morris shouting Chevy's words]: Our top story tonight. A Harris Poll has revealed that Hubert Humphrey is ahead of both Ford and Reagan. Good night, and have a pleasant tomorrow.

Part III

Over the Rainbow

19. NEW YORK HERE WE COME

There were several final straws that led to Chevy's move back to New York. Those close to him knew that no matter what he did in California, he was a New Yorker at heart.

After the talk show came the films *Cops and Robbersons* and *Man of the House* and another appearance hosting *Saturday Night Live*, but there wasn't enough work to keep him busy, and not enough to justify him staying in California. *Cops and Robbersons* got a lot of press, some praising Chevy for toughing it out after the talk-show fiasco, although Chevy repeated many times that the film was completed before the talk show began. Some critics called it a "comeback" even though it really wasn't.

Chevy was alternately amused and puzzled by the number of comebacks he had supposedly had during his career, especially since he hadn't gone away and seemed to be making films on a regular basis. After the first *Vacation* film came out, *Fletch*, which came out two years later, was called a "comeback film," and this continued through his 2007 release *Funny Money*, once again dubbed a "comeback film." The term "comeback" was applied later in 2007 to his guest appearances on the television series *Brothers & Sisters*.

Among the factors leading to his return to New York was an incident that brought him to the realization that there was no privacy in his LA life, that Jayni and the children were suffering for it, and that he needed to go back home and figure it all out. He knew that he could easily fly back to Los Angeles for work.

Chevy's only trip to jail took place on January 26, 1995. One evening he drove himself to meet his friend Alan Greisman (producer of both *Fletch* movies) for dinner in Los Angeles. Chevy had two or three drinks and believed himself to be in control. Not normally a drinker of hard liquor, and no expert—"normally I ask for Scotch and bourbon"—Chevy was stopped by one of the LA police officers who sometimes hover around restaurants waiting to catch drivers who have been drinking. Chevy was driving too fast and was over the breathalyzer limit.

"Who wants to be cops? Bullies!" Chevy rails against the establishment. They made him do a whole host of tests that sounded more like a neurologist's exam. "My own doctor couldn't do those things when I asked him," Chevy says. Walk a straight line. That was fine. "Close your eyes and touch your nose, while balancing for ten seconds on one leg and angling your head straight up at the sky! Who can do that?" They were determined to book Chevy, although reassuring him that it would all be kept quiet. He had heard that before.

Reporters who listen all night to the police radio, however, had a field day with the news item, just the kind of announcement they love. Chevy called Jayni at one a.m. and she was asleep. "I've been arrested for drunk driving," Chevy explained.

"Okay, honey," the sleepy voice replied. "I'll see you in the morning."

Chevy was released at five a.m., got in his car, turned on the radio, and it was the first thing on the news.

In a March hearing he pleaded guilty, was placed on probation, fined $966, and ordered to undergo therapy. For the next six months, Chevy had no license and was in "driving therapy, where they show you old movies of how to drive, and films of bad wrecks. I had to attend to get my license back."

He knew now it was time to go back home. While Hollywood had been home to Chevy and his family for eighteen years, Chevy was becoming more and more concerned, not primarily about the direction of his career but about what was happening to his family. He didn't like the lifestyle and the values, and he wanted his girls to be raised in a less superficial, more intellectual atmosphere.

Although Chevy realized it would affect his career and access to Hollywood, he was firm in the decision to move. His family came first. So in 1995 they took the plunge. Chevy sold their California home and the family moved to a spacious home in Bedford Corners, New York, less than an hour's drive from Manhattan. Several years later, they added a Manhattan apartment to their East Coast residences, making it easier for them to socialize and attend events in the city.

The twelve-acre property they now call home is a traditional northeastern country house on a rocky and hilly wooded landscape. There are two grass horse paddocks and a tennis court that "seem to have grown out of the land," according to Jayni. "The feel of the property is earthy and overgrown." There are many types of trees: oak, sugar maple, spruce, cherry, hemlock, and other indigenous trees, plants, and flowers. In keeping with their environmental concerns, they have solar panels on any roof space that gets enough sun. They gathered furniture from their California, East Hampton, and Snowmass houses, and now have only one real home, a difference the family appreciates.

"In my opinion," Natasha, a friend of Jayni's who helped her find the house, says, "it was an incredibly smart decision to move East. They did make a very conscious decision, but it still must be extremely difficult for Chevy at times."

It was quite different living in rural New York than it had been in California. Managing a large property was a learning experience, and the size of the grounds meant that someone had to be in charge. Rocco Fava, who was employed by the previous owners, stayed on to work as caretaker and is still there today. When Rocco heard that Chevy Chase had bought the property, he was a little hesitant. He had heard stories that Chevy was not nice to people, "but I don't know how that could have started." At their first meeting, Rocco was impressed with Chevy's attitude. "Some people really think they own the world, but here's a guy who's known in public. No chip on his shoulder. He's so down-to-earth. When we had our first conversation, I thought, 'This guy is not what I had heard.'"

Now, it's more than just an employer/employee relationship. The two are close friends. "When my father was in the hospital with pneumonia, he came with me. He lit a spark under the medical staff, and he uses his celebrity in a good way—never a bad way. He would do anything for me, as I would for him."

Rocco's responsibilities extend beyond the physical care of the property and its buildings. The property includes the main house, the pool house, and the office/studio complex and guest building, several apartments, a gymnasium, an art studio, and stables. It's a lot to keep in order. He needs to be certain that any temporary workers are respectful and will keep the location of the Chase home confidential. "When they are working for the first time, they don't know it's his house." Not until they've been tested. "I don't want them to seek him out, engage him in conversation. Chevy's a shy person, and he shouldn't be startled," Rocco added.

Lorne Michaels describes Chevy as "a family man, not a careerist." Thinking about Chevy's twenty-year run in Hollywood, he says, "It's a long time to have the same success in Hollywood. There's the question of a 'leading man versus a comedian.' I always felt he was a comedian. But there are periods in which certain types of comedy work, some things you can do and say at thirty that don't work at fifty or sixty. Chevy had been playing fathers for twenty years, so much success for a long period. But he was associated with a period. And the talk show had cost him a year or two. It blurred the image."

Chevy's friend Benno Friedman said, "I know there can be pressures to deliver a story even when there isn't a story to be had. Sometimes you create the story. Some people like to hit people when they are down, enjoying the failures of the one-time mighty. Chevy had a big stumble with the talk show. People are not generous in spirit over something like this. Chevy had a great run for a while. Every actor has made some movies that are not so good, yet they are committed to it based on contractual obligations."

Pamela, Chevy's sister, looks at it realistically. "Chev had a twenty-year run at the top, and very few people have a twenty-year run. As an actor you're going to go through a transition period. Too old to be a leading man and not old enough to be [the adults'] dad yet. That's just the way it is."

Chevy and Jayni's youngest daughter, Emily, was six at the time of the move and recalls it affecting each member of the family differently. Now nineteen, and a graduate of the Lawrenceville School in New Jersey, Emily is clear and outspoken about the pros and cons of the move. "I know it affected Dad's career, put a damper on that. It was a good move for me, and also for Caley [who was ten at the time]. But not so much for Cydney." Cydney was twelve then, and well adjusted in school, with many close friends. "Mom is flexible and can adjust to anything," Emily adds.

Emily was also six when she realized her dad was famous. At first, her response was to use it to gain acceptance. But that phase didn't last long. "I look back and it's shocking," she laughed. "Now it's the opposite," she said. "I don't tell kids about it, but I am very proud of Dad and where I come from, and not annoyed if people want to talk about it."

As with many children of celebrities, her dad's celebrity has been a burden. The start of high school was difficult. When she first got there, "There were assumptions and judgments. Kids shouting in the hall, 'That's her!'

"Even with boys. I would have a crush on a junior or senior boy, who would pay attention, and then I would discover it had something to do with being Chevy's daughter. For the most part, it has settled down. My friends know me as a person."

Caley, now twenty-three, has also thought about how her father's celebrity has affected the family. "I did not tell anybody. Sometimes it's appropriate to share it, but if people don't ask I don't share it. That's something that is almost a rule in my life. I like to figure people out. I've seen kids' reactions when they find out. They can be extremely nice or hate you. It's amazing the things they've said."

Caley has only recently and "accidentally" decided to go into acting, "which I've avoided most of my life." But she discovered that she has acting talent, and is studying at NYU and the Lee Strasberg Institute in New York. "My dad has always been supportive of whatever I've wanted to do, and that's really important."

At first unhappy about the move East, Cydney actually found life in New York much easier. "It's so much more quiet. We can go out and not be hounded. I remember in California going to Disneyland a lot, and crowds asking for autographs." On occasions when Chevy didn't want to sign a lot of autographs, Cydney remembers apologizing for him, feeling sorry for the people who asked, while understanding that he couldn't sign every autograph in a crowd.

The film *Cops and Robbersons*, which came out in 1994, was something of a final straw for Chevy, signaling time for a change. "It was the end of my tenure out there, doing films at a lower price, like four million bucks for *Cops and Robbersons*. Films that were not up to par for me."

He knew the film wasn't a good move, but things were closing in on Chevy, particularly after the failure of the talk show. He was beginning to address his feelings of depression and doubting his reasons for living in California. "What was I thinking? Maybe the money, and I always felt I would have some say in the cutting and the postproduction. *Cops and Robbersons* was targeted to a younger, less thinking audience.

"I was thinking about my children getting older, and their education, their living in this terrible place, the consistency of the weather, everything about meaningless hugs, kisses, and the business. And it was beginning to approach that time when it was gonna matter where they lived.

"*Cops and Robbersons* was another piece of crap that I agreed to do for the money," Chevy says. He was very happy to work with Jack Palance, "a wonderful man, a big hulking man almost my father's age. And taller than I am, and intimidating-looking. There wasn't Tinsel Town remotely around this guy. He lived in Pennsylvania on a farm. He was well read. He was quiet and a sweet guy. He was just terrific." Chevy had long and intriguing discussions with Palance while filming, and felt a true kinship with him.

Palance died in November 2006 at the age of eighty-seven. It was not widely known that he was a professional heavyweight boxer in the late 1930s, early 1940s, fighting under the name of Jack Brazzo. He won his first fifteen fights, then went on to fight in World War II, receiving a purple heart, a good conduct medal, and the World War II Victory Medal. His film career began after the war.

In the film, when police discover that a mob hit man has moved in next door to the Robbersons, they set up a stakeout in the Robbersons' home. Jake Stone (Jack Palance) is assigned to the stakeout. The Robbersons are eager to help but they are driving Jake insane. Norman Robberson becomes an amateur detective, causing a full range of problems for the real detectives. There were difficult stunts in this film, and Chevy did some of them himself. "As much as I could—as long as the Stuntmen's Association wouldn't cry out."

One stunt involved swinging on a rope through a window, but the first attempts banged Chevy's character into the outside wall. It was divided between the stunt man, John Robotham, and Chevy. "The initial swing from the roof was me. They would stop the rope, hold it three feet from the wall, and bang into the wall with me on the rope." With clever cutting, it looked as though Chevy did the complete swing. Part of the scene involved Chevy's character flying through the glass window on the rope. "The shot used was a big splash through the glass, from the interior looking out," Chevy explains.

Critic Leonard Klady shared Chevy's assessment of the film. "There's trouble afoot in Pleasant Valley and the postcard-perfect suburb is about to burst at the seams in *Cops and Robbersons*. However, the mixture of mischief and mayhem served up in the antic affair is never quite in balance. It's a tale long on intriguing ideas and always a millimeter short in its realization."

Jayni and the girls are very protective of Chevy, and they take it hard when the press has been flippant or critical of him. Emily has taken an active role in answering the press when she feels they have been unfair. "If I've seen negative things, I've responded over the Internet, and also responded to positive things said about him. Some dialogues and ongoing correspondence has developed over these issues. It's painful. Some of the stuff is so terrible."

Chevy was at odds with Howard Stern for several years, disagreements that arose over two phone calls to Chevy, the first when he was filming the *Fletch* sequel, *Fletch Lives*, and the second after Chevy was called at home at five-thirty a.m. while still living in LA.

The first call was Stern's attempt to get the "dirt" on Julianne Phillips, one of the leads in the film. Phillips was in the middle of a highly publicized divorce from Bruce Springsteen, and Stern's crudely worded questions to Chevy were offensive to him. "She was a very sweet girl who was going through hell," says Chevy, who cut the live on-air conversation short.

Stern had it in for Chevy. A couple of years later, Chevy's friend Richard Belzer gave Howard Stern Chevy's home number. He called at five-thirty a.m. and in the live broadcast gave Chevy's housekeeper a hard time when she would not put Chevy on the phone. He happened to pick up the phone. Jayni did too. "She tried to protect me, said, 'Leave my husband alone.' She didn't realize we were on live radio. So there we were. I was saying, 'Jayni, hang up the phone.' She was saying, 'Leave my husband alone.'" Stern, doing what he does best, played the tape on air many times, ridiculing Chevy and claiming he was funnier than him.

"Finally it began to affect my family," Chevy said. He took Emily, then eleven years old, to a New York Knicks basketball game. "We went to get popcorn, came back, and our seats were taken. We asked the guys to leave. All of a sudden, when they were two steps up, one of them turned around and loudly said, 'No wonder Howard Stern says you're a prick.' This shocked Emily. She turned white. The guys smelled of beer and I could tell they wanted to engage me in some fashion."

Chevy walked up to them and berated them verbally. "I kept my hands in my pockets. I knew if I touched them I would be sued. Again I was at a disadvantage due to Howard Stern and his fans in that section. That was the wrong place for me, for my daughter. The wrong world, the ugly side of America."

After another incident, Chevy came to the conclusion that he could not take his daughters to games any longer. Chevy, Rocco, and Cydney went once to watch the Yankees play and throughout the game one guy was screaming remarks at Chevy. It was the day comedian and actor Phil Hartman, who was a friend of Chevy's, had been shot by his wife Brynn in a murder-suicide. Chevy was very upset about his death. Rocco said they were "wisecrackers looking to push the wrong button. One guy kept harassing him. Finally he said, 'Does your wife have a gun?' and Chevy stood up and yelled at him. He was very upset, but he showed me a lot. Somebody else might have hit the guy. He held back. Security came and removed the heckler."

Chevy was very upset because the incident affected Cydney profoundly. Chevy contacted a producer on Stern's show explaining what was happening to his family. "Strangely," Chevy noted, "a couple of days later, he said on the air something to the effect that 'Whatever you hear happening between me and Chevy Chase is show business. It doesn't have anything to do with personal life and he should be left alone—you shouldn't be doing that in front of his daughters.' He laid off after that."

Speaking of the problems over Stern, Beverly D'Angelo said, "There is something about Chevy's humor that begs people to take jabs at him. It's that 'Oh, so you think you're so smart? Take this!' kind of attitude, and lesser wits throw lines at him that aren't funny, just hurtful, like fastballs aimed at the head or wide swinging punches way below the belt. As Howard himself only lays claim to being a shock jock, it's generous to say he has even half the comedic talents that Chevy does."

Chevy also had some serious problems when the Friars Club roasted him in 2002. His first roast, in 1990, was more traditional and involved many of his friends and colleagues, people who knew him well. It's generally considered a great honor to have a Friars Roast, and unusual to have two. He was quite happy with the first one.

For the second roast, the funds Chevy received were donated to Jayni's charity. Chevy asked his old friend Paul Shaffer to be the roastmaster and Paul was happy to do it. Although some of Chevy's friends were there to support him, the press later used the event to attack Chevy's career.

This was disturbing to Paul, whose friendship with Chevy had only recently been rekindled after some years apart. Paul feels strongly that the traditional Friars ceremony should not be televised. "In private, people can talk as dirty as they want. 'A' and 'two,' as they used to say on *SNL*. It's theoretically people so close to the honoree that they can say anything about him in jest and it's understood by the honoree as said with love. Put that on television and you lose both 'A' and 'two.' The backlash? Well, Chevy's was the last of the Friars Roasts that was televised. Many didn't want to do it because they didn't want it to be on television. They were legendary—Don Rickles, Milton Berle."

Some of Chevy's old friends and costars refused to participate because Chevy had not had a "hot" movie in a while. So the roast ended up being done by some people who were not close to Chevy, some who didn't even know him personally. "A lot of comics, favorites of Comedy Central, were booked and had no relationship with him," says Paul Shaffer.

"You can't have an elephant in the room and not comment," Paul said. In order to make light of the turn of events, Paul opened with a Tom Leopold musical number entitled "We Couldn't Get Anybody Good." "I did an opening monologue that was appropriately nasty. Chevy had no problem and loved my monologue. We had that kind of relationship."

"It was written completely with affection from us," Tom says, "but the thing just had a bad chemistry to it. The people [who roasted Chevy] didn't know him very well. By that time it was already happening—it just wasn't fun."

One of Paul's comments, said completely in jest, was, "You made us laugh so much. And then inexplicably stopped in about 1978."

Al Franken said, "No one laughed harder than Chevy when the town of Chevy Chase, Maryland, tried to change its name to Not Funny, Maryland."

Others followed suit. Only a few of his real friends were there besides Paul: Beverly D'Angelo, Steve Martin, Laraine Newman, and Richard Belzer. The first time, Paul says, it was more in keeping with how a roast works. The second time around, Beverly points out, the producers gathered together comedians who were less than familiar with Chevy.

"So here is this group of comedians, in some cases who had never even met Chevy. And with all due respect, a lot of unknowns who hadn't done any roasts. Paul had worked with Chevy, opened the show with a great musical number complete with dancing girls and just the right balance between acerbic wit and respect to the man who created an identifiable brand of humor the minute he looked straight into the camera and said, "I'm Chevy Chase and you're not."

"Then came this onslaught of people Chevy had never met, who focused on the drug problems he'd had in the past, and it turned into a kind of insult fest—really weird. It was like the new comedians were trying to top each other in an insult humor contest, and using Chevy, just because he was there. They knew nothing about Chevy's background, his life. They kept doing 'spins' on the same things, even the same movies."

Part of the Friars Club tradition, Beverly points out, is camaraderie, but there was "very little sense of camaraderie that night. I guess Chevy knew who his comrades were that night. The audience was probably full of managers who were watching their fledgling artists try out material on the dais, using Chevy's roast as a place to audition for who knows what. Anyway, that's the feeling I got. True to form, Chevy thanked me profusely afterwards for coming," Beverly added.

"At the end of the roast," Paul said, "there's a traditional moment when the honoree gets up and has a chance to be nasty back to the others. Chevy said, 'Wow, that was tough. I don't even know half of you.' He was so painfully honest."

"Paul was so loyal to me," Chevy said. "Some years earlier, Danny, Paul Newman, Bob De Niro, had been at my 'real' Friars Roast. The second one was an eye-opener to me, a perpetuation of myths. I had never fought against things written about me, just let it go. They prepared their material based on what they had read, with no knowledge of me. The horrifying thing is it wasn't funny. It really hurt, and it's not supposed to do that."

Chevy was wearing sunglasses throughout the roast. "Thank God I was. My eyes were tearing. Thinking they really believe this stuff." At the end of the evening, Paul, Tom, and Lew Soloff went up to visit Chevy in his hotel room. "We talked about it, what had happened." Paul offered to have one of his nastier jokes removed before the televised version, but Chevy refused. "He said, 'Don't take it out. I loved your whole presentation.' It was a touching moment, and he has expressed to me so many times how touched he was that Tom, Lew, and I came up to see him. That has cemented our friendship."

Jayni had been looking at Chevy's career in a realistic way, proud that he had been at the top for so many years, and understanding that it can't be that way forever. "For years, he stayed up at number one when pictures opened. Then it started to falter. When it changed, it didn't matter to me. I was assuming Chevy was the same way, but of course it mattered to him. When things calmed down, he went from 'being there' to 'not being there,' just like that. It was kind of a shock to him. I was buried with kid stuff. He was having a lot of fun with us. But after a while he wondered, what happened to all that? It just went away."

The problem is, she explains, "If you disappear for a while, people decide you are drugged up, because of those issues at one point. They assume you are depressed. It's like they want you to be drugged up like a suicidal drunken idiot. That wasn't at all what was going on," Jayni insists emphatically. "He was being a hands-on dad!"

Some of Chevy's friends have theories about what happened to his career. According to Harold Ramis, "The problem with broad comedy is that even the most talented actors have a limited number of moves. With dramatic actors, like Hoffman and De Niro, after a while I can hear that's the way they said a line in another movie. The public is fickle—it likes novelty for its own sake. I've always known that. Prepared myself to fade from popularity. I think it was maybe that Chevy was a little distanced from what he was doing. He said, 'I can't find stuff to do.'"

Harold advised him to "start from something that's really on your mind, from life experience, and age appropriate to who you are. There was a time when our pose was that we didn't care, nothing was sacred—you might be accused of being grandiose. Consequently, nothing is important. He never made a sincere investment in the real literature of what he was doing."

Chevy had been doing a lot of favors and accepting offers he shouldn't have. "I saw that film he did with Aykroyd, *Nothing But Trouble*," says Carl Reiner. "It's horrible. Once you do one of those it's too late. Never do favors! It's their script, but it's your body. He's a loyal guy, but you lose your identity. Give him that advice!" He sings Chevy's praises as an actor. "He had that ability. You believe him as a lover, a father, and a husband.

"It's all in the material that is offered to you. If agents, managers, aren't getting the best material, and you are having to buoy up bad material, the performance is doomed. His performances remained good—his talent never changes—but if the material is not, the career goes down. And as you get older, you are not as cute as you were. Chevy was Cary Grant handsome. Cary Grant retired at the top of his game."

Reiner most admires Chevy's two films with Goldie—*Foul Play* and *Seems Like Old Times*. He found "diminishing returns" with *Vacation*, *Fletch*, and *Caddyshack*, the first of each being the best. "When you are mining the same kind of material, there's a depreciation that happens naturally," he adds.

Beverly D'Angelo has a different take on Chevy's career, and her own theories about its direction. "Chevy was smarter than everyone around him. He did one year on *Saturday Night Live*—one season only. He became a movie star, instantly acting opposite Goldie Hawn at her peak. His humor was biting and sarcastic and full of put-downs. Little people 'suffered,' secretly envied him his success, thought, 'Why him?' Critics don't think he's so hot, so his box office slips. Just like Captain Hook. When the natives suddenly found out he was a mere mortal they jumped on him. That's my theory. What they didn't realize was that Chevy was an extremely sensitive artist, a true human being, and that he would rather leave Hollywood, raise his kids right, than to put up with that Hollywood kind of crap.

"I don't know exactly how it worked. Maybe his agents were trying to hold him off independent projects that could have taken him down a different road because they would have been less lucrative. Maybe they pushed him into the talk show that got him really beaten up by the critics. You have to understand what kind of priorities Chevy really has. His family has always come first. He would give up anything—his career—anything to be there for his wife and family. It's not a sacrifice. He is the most ethical person I have ever known."

Chevy was concerned about Jayni as well. In California she had created a nonprofit organization called the Center for Environmental Education, and Chevy was involved, both putting money into the organization and helping with fund-raising activities. From her teen years, Jayni has been concerned about the environment and has become more and more active in working to preserve our natural resources for future generations. Jayni's book *Blueprint for a Green School*, published in 1995, is a manual of information for teachers, listing publications and methodology for making schools more environmentally responsible. It was the first full guidebook answering questions about environmental issues on school grounds.

In California, Jayni had an office and a staff, and the most productive years were 1989–95, when the groundwork was laid for her environmental activism. With the move to New York, Jayni thought it would be possible to keep the California office open and establish a New York branch, but the assistant left behind to do the job didn't have Jayni's skills as a motivator. Jayni realized that she would have to transport the Center with her. She decided to dissolve the board and hand over the operations to be hosted at Antioch University, where Cindy Thomashow, then academic director of Environmental Education, was based. Jayni continues to head the Board of Advisors and remains active with the Center. In October of 2007, the affiliation moved to Unity College in Maine, where it continues with Thomashow as director.

Chevy wholeheartedly supports the CEE, although, with the exception of fundraising events, he considers it primarily Jayni's venture. "Our mission is to provide the necessary resources, curriculum, expertise and guidance to cultivate environmental leading in K-12 schools," Jayni stated, adding that the three parts of the mission are providing "resources that enable schools to provide healthier meals, educating for climate change and educating for sustainability."

Chevy and Jayni hold an annual Earth Day auction and have garnered support from a prestigious list of colleagues and friends, who have donated celebrity items and appearances. A golf outing with Chevy and Bill Murray raised $25,000 one year, as did lunch with Chevy and Bill Clinton.

After the talk show, Chevy had reached his limit of being able to tolerate living in the Hollywood community. "I'm an intelligent, articulate guy," Chevy says, "and you can't imagine how stupid the world I inhabited is, how filled with—forgetting their educations—people who fail in the production end, distribution end, big-money end. They are continually recycled. In the twenty-five years I was there, people fired from Warners could be heading up Paramount the next day.

"It's so strange, and getting to know all the people I've known there, every mogul—it's always amazed me how taken they are with themselves, what they do, the money they've made. And how lacking they are in a Renaissance view of the world and politics and what's going on in Africa, Iraq, and Iran, nuclear weapons and delivery systems. They haven't the foggiest idea what's out there.

"It's more important to get to wear that black tie at a function the president is going to attend in Hollywood. It's just unbelievable . . . The really smart guys are few and far between. It's only a few of the really funny comedians, like Steve and Marty, who are . . . well rounded and keep up with what's going on in the world."

20. LONG COMMUTE TO HOLLYWOOD

C hevy was back in New York. Several years later he would tell the press that he had not been working and had taken off eight years to raise his family. Between 1995 and 2007, or between the move to New York and the present day, his films include *Vegas Vacation*, *Snow Day*, *Pete's a Pizza* (voice), *Orange County*, *Dirty Work*, *The Great Goose Caper*, *Bad Meat* (made but never released in theaters), *Our Italian Husband*, *Karate Dog* (voice), *Zoom*, and *Funny Money*.

This wasn't your standard Hollywood retirement, although Chevy was correct in the sense that none of the films reached the standards he had set for himself. Yet *Vegas Vacation* had some degree of popularity and *Snow Day*, made in 2000, continues to bring in large royalty checks, including a recent one for more than a million dollars.

Funny Money was released on January 26, 2007 and Chevy's performance was praised by the critics. *Hollywood Reporter*'s Sheri Linden called the film a "deliriously spirited farce," and Chevy's performance "a perfect fit." *The Los Angeles Times*'s critic Michael Ordoña stated it was "nice to see the comic actor in his element," and the *L.A. Weekly*'s critic Chuck Wilson wrote that Chevy was "terrific ... more relaxed and generous than he's ever been." The film is a farce, in the style of restoration comedy, and was listed among the top ten films of the nearly two hundred shown at the Sarasota Film Festival, where it was wonderfully received by audiences. A review in the *Sarasota Herald* said that "*Funny Money*'s best scenes recall vintage *SNL* and *Monty Python* skits. It is probably the most interesting movie Chase has made in more than a decade. Whereas his past films were aimed at families, this picture is clearly intended for adults."

"I'm thinking of it as a comeback," Chevy says, only half a chuckle over his latest "comeback." "*Funny Money* is based on a play that ran in London. It has great potential." It wasn't an easy film for Chevy to make. "I was shooting six days a week for six weeks and they were fourteen-hour days, and I was in practically every scene. It was a killer. For all the movies I've made, to come out of retirement and to star in this movie—I've never worked that hard. The film is a comedy of errors and a farce. It has the rhythm and pace of a *Noises Off* [the 1982 British farce by Michael Frayn]. This film has the possibility of a *Greek Wedding* or *Sideways* kind of response."

It's an ensemble piece, and Chevy had a blast performing with Penelope Ann Miller, whose praises he sings. "She is an excellent actress, very funny, very talented."

Chevy plays the role of Henry Perkins, who is in the wax fruit business. While on a train, he accidentally trades briefcases with another man, and quickly learns there's $5 million inside. Henry tells his unsuspecting wife Carol (Penelope Ann Miller) of their newfound fortune, but she doesn't handle it as well as he does and is reluctant to leave the country, forever, on a moment's notice. As it is Henry's birthday, they're soon joined by their best friends, a cop on the take, a cop on the hunt, and the dreaded Mr. Big.

Much of the filming was done in Romania (which was supposed to be Hoboken, New Jersey), where it was possible to keep the costs down. Being there and working so hard drew the cast together "in a way that made the marriage and the friendship look very organic and real." But it wasn't the easiest of trips for Chevy. Bucharest is a city with the largest stray dog population in the world. "At night it sounds like coyotes. The dogcatchers can't keep up." Chevy, who is an animal lover and has five dogs of his own, was walking alone one evening, in the dark, and heard a dog barking at him.

There had been some dogs on the set and he had played with them. On this particular occasion, Chevy decided to playfully bark back at the dog. There were also puppies nearby, but Chevy didn't see them. The dog was unimpressed by Chevy's barking and felt threatened, providing Chevy with a painful, deep puncture wound. Of course, not knowing the dog's history, Chevy was advised to get a series of rabies shots. In the end, Chevy was not annoyed with the dog. "I felt bad that the dog was threatened by me. I'm not that kind of guy."

Filming also took place in New York and Costa Rica, and was filled with problems, including fights between the cast and directors. Chevy had issues over the filming, the editing, and flying to Costa Rica to find the film crew had been careless about the equipment needed. It was five hours to fly and another five to drive to the right location, and once there they discovered they had the wrong camera mount.

There have been positive words from fans who have already seen the film.

"What a delight to see Chevy Chase back onscreen again, with a great ensemble of hilarious actors. Director Leslie Greif does an excellent job of keeping the audience in stitches from the opening credits to the final smile."

"We saw this movie as the opening film of the 2006 Sarasota Film Festival, in a theater with 1,700 other people. There is no question that the audience loved it. At times, the laughs were so loud and long that if you weren't paying close attention, you might have missed the next joke."

"If you are looking for good, old-fashioned belly laughs, you won't be disappointed in this film. Kudos to Leslie Greif, Chevy Chase, Penelope Ann Miller, Armand Assante, and Chris McDonald."

At the end of the 1990s Chevy made the final *Vacation* film. No longer linked to *National Lampoon*, the 1997 film *Vegas Vacation* "came out of an agreement avoiding a possible lawsuit," reveals Chevy. He had a Warner Brothers deal to do three films for $23 million. The specifics included approval over scripts.

"Something was shoved in my face by Bob Daley, head of Warners at the time—he and Terry Semel. I didn't want to do it, and it was my right to say no." There should have been plenty of time to select the replacement script for the deal, but Warners decided just to drop it—a potential $6 million loss for Chevy. Somehow *Vegas Vacation*, for $4 million, became the substitute film.

Quite a few years had passed between the first *Vacation* movie and the last of the series, and fans of the series had waited impatiently for the grand finale. The constants in the film were the fine team of Chevy and Beverly and Randy Quaid as Cousin Eddie. Chevy's Clark Griswold receives a bonus for developing a food preservative and the Griswolds head to Las Vegas! While in Las Vegas, the family's adventures seem a tad more realistic than heading for Wally World, exploring Europe, or experiencing Christmas with their relatives.

In Vegas, family bonds are put to the test. Ellen finds herself tempted by Wayne Newton, who attempts to seduce her. Clark manages to lose all the money the Griswolds brought along, plus their savings. Underage Rusty masquerades as a high roller and hits a lucky streak as "Mr. Pappagiorgio," and Audrey teams up with Cousin Eddie's daughter Vickie to dance at nightclubs.

By *Vegas Vacation* the original kids would have been about thirty. "The producers never took the fact of the changing children very seriously, and it became an element in the comedy. It also gave new actors a chance to show off their stuff—that mysterious thing. Does the camera like you?" Chevy asked.

Beverly D'Angelo said, "I always thought the coup de grace for *Vegas Vacation* was to use the real aspects of Vegas. In the others, we created a parallel universe—a Griswoldean universe. But in *Vegas Vacation* we used real people that existed independently of Griswold-ville. To me, it became a different thing, a comedy with the Griswolds in it. Instead of Wally World standing in for Disneyland, we had the real Siegfried and Roy, standing in for the real Siegfried and Roy. So I felt we lost an element of satire, and an element of humor."

There was a lot of gambling during the filming of *Vegas Vacation*. The whole crew gambled, Chevy recalls. They were filming during the summer, and they were all staying at the Mirage. "It was 110 degrees and nobody could face going outside. It was like a furnace with no humidity," Chevy says. During one episode filmed at the Hoover Dam, the temperature rose above 130 degrees. He had to climb up some rocks until the stunt man took over, and he had to wear gloves that looked like real hands because the heat of the rocks would otherwise have been damaging. "Every twenty minutes, the cast was *forced* to drink a bottle of water," remembers Chevy.

When not filming, they all stayed inside the hotel, and spent their leisure hours at the tables. Chevy and Beverly often played blackjack. At the end of one evening, Beverly dropped her last two silver dollars into a slot machine. Chevy dropped a dollar into the same machine and proceeded to win a $1200 jackpot. The machine was clanging, bells ringing, and a crowd began to gather.

"And Beverly started to tell me she should have half. I asked why. She said, 'I primed it. I played it twice. You wouldn't have won if I hadn't primed it.' The two of us ended up going at it like a husband and wife," which, after all the *Vacation* movies, they were. It was a loud, albeit light-hearted, argument, beginning to rise in pitch.

People gathered around, realizing it was Chevy and Beverly—or in the eyes of many, Clark and Ellen Griswold. "We started to laugh, seeing how silly it was—me saying, 'Ellen, it's mine ...' 'No, Clark, it isn't.'" With all the commotion, the crowd thought it was a rehearsal, and nobody interrupted. Chevy remembers eventually splitting the winnings with Beverly.

Though the *Vacation* fans turned out to see the film, the reviews ranged from mediocre to negative. At one point, Chevy considered a sequel taking the Griswold family to Europe again, this time the "Swiss Family Griswold," but he abandoned the idea and the series seems to have run its course.

Once back in New York, Chevy's life was different. He had more time to think about the issues that had troubled him for so many years. He was involved in regular therapy, working hard to deal with the one issue that, no matter how he tried, he couldn't escape—his abusive childhood. He had a therapist he trusted who was helping him to work through all the aspects of it, helping him to understand how his actions and feelings, even in his fifties, stemmed from his childhood. He began to speak openly about it in his weekly sessions, and the pieces of the puzzle began to fall into place.

Chevy was finding his commute from New York to Hollywood tiresome, however, and was more inspired to spend time with his daughters, helping them, talking with them, and doing projects and guest appearances closer to home. There were charitable events and guest lectures; many of them he did without accepting a fee. He would be offered $25,000 but he didn't need the money and believed the colleges or other institutions could use it instead.

With certain charitable events, unlike many stars who demand high fees and expensive travel and accommodations, Chevy often picked up his own expenses if he believed in an organization. For the past seventeen years, he has participated frequently in Chris Evert's annual Pro-Celebrity Tennis Classic in Boca Raton, Florida, playing tennis and attending the gala. Proceeds from the event go to Chris Evert Charities, a fund that supports abused and neglected children and helps to counteract drug abuse.

There were a few more films during that time. In 2000, Chevy was persuaded to play a role in the film *Snow Day*. When an entire town in upstate New York is closed down by an unexpected snowfall, a group of elementary school kids, led by Natalie Brandston, try to make certain that the schools stay closed by stopping a mechanical snowplow driver. A variety of antics result in the youngsters trying to hijack the snowplow. This was not a memorable experience for Chevy, who plays Tom Brandston, a TV meteorologist who is in competition with the town's less-than-honorable rival meteorologist. The movie also features a teen romance.

The *Apollo Movie Guide* reported, "Wacky antics in the snow with Chevy Chase in a snowman costume? Sounds like a movie worth skipping, right? Well, that's why there are movie critics—to tell you that there's nothing overwhelming about *Snow Day*, but it's also a cut above what you might expect. There's a sweet love story, fun kids' antics and some appealing juvenile performances that raise it just a touch above the level of average comedy retread."

The fans, writing on various online sites available for film reviews, seemed to like this film. And still do, as evidenced by the influx of royalties from DVD sales.

One fan wrote: "I hate to see people meticulously pine over the details of this marvelous film as if it were *The Last Temptation of Christ*. It's a simple film with heart and hilarity. This film features some of the funniest children actors I've ever seen. It's painfully corny, yes, but at the same time it makes you laugh out loud and feel the characters. Watch this movie. It's pure hilarity and fun."

In 2002, Tom Leopold drafted Chevy to star in the pilot for a sitcom he was writing called *America's Most Terrible*

Things. The idea was inspired by the 1960s sitcom, *My Three Sons*. In Tom's script, Chevy would play a father to three teenage daughters. "In it, I was a family guy, the host of a show called 'America's Most Terrible Things.'" Although the pilot was produced, Tom says, "the sitcom didn't gel." Chevy says the fact that it didn't get picked up by NBC was "not a reflection on Tom—he was as funny as ever." It was a combination of circumstances, including Chevy wearing a toupee that looked silly. "I didn't like the way I looked, I didn't feel good, and the director stank," Chevy says.

Since 2000, Chevy has struggled with some arthritis and physical problems, including a painful hip that was treated with repeated cortisone shots until they were no longer effective. He was set to play the role of Max Green in a Broadway play called *The Bottom Line*, in which he was to play the head of Good Samaritan Hospital—recruited from a Las Vegas casino. It was an interesting take on the health system. His character was brought in because of the similarities in running a casino and a hospital. "Getting people in and out fast, and based on true hospital stories." A comedy, it looked like a good role for him, but he couldn't get insurance because of his hip problem.

In April 2005, Chevy finally had a hip replacement, which was very successful. The producers of the play had expected him onstage by June, doing eight shows a week, but it would have been impossible. He needed six weeks of recuperation before walking easily with a cane. After three months, he was walking normally and without pain, but it was too late to get the play up and running on time.

Chevy also discovered, after recovering from the hip surgery, that he was without most of the back pain he had suffered for many years.

21. JUST UNDER THE RUG

If Chevy could have blocked out his childhood and erased it from his memory, he would have been well served. But he continued to struggle with the effects of his early abuse and to review his relationships, especially the one he retained with his mother, in the context of his success as an adult. He never spoke openly about his childhood while his mother and stepfather were alive, and he never used it as an excuse for things that went wrong, but he began to realize that his childhood explained a lot about his struggles.

Chevy's mother had followed in her own mother's footsteps, with three important relationships in her life. As Chevy's sister Pamela observes, "In terms of patterns, my grandmother [Cattie] had three relationships—the first with a navy man, the second with a business/professional guy, the third with an artist/painter. My mom had a navy guy, a professional, and a musician. Both women were happier with their third husbands." Chevy, too, was married three times, and his marriage to Jayni has been the only happy one.

Chevy had not spoken to very many people about his childhood, and he had not yet had therapy to address the causes of his underlying depression. He worked hard to maintain the facade of a relationship with his mother, as did his siblings.

Today, Chevy and his brother Ned lead very different lives. "We're not very close. We don't talk often." But they shared the same childhood, and Ned says, "I've always loved Chevy." Pamela worked hard to reestablish her relationship with Chevy as an adult. She moved to Los Angeles, but a short time later Chevy moved back to New York. "We had both come from a family that was and continues to be dysfunctional," Pamela explains. "I made a commitment to pursuing a relationship with Chevy, and it was a rocky road at first. He had just hit big money, and the phase when you don't actually know if people are hanging around because they like you or your money. He was just going through that phase: 'Don't know who's my friend and who isn't.' That made it difficult as well. I was very clear that I wanted a brother—not a movie star, a brother."

They began talking, a lot, about their childhoods, and family, and eventually became much closer. "What was important was creating a relationship with him. It was difficult but we have that today. Our family didn't teach you how to interact.

"One of my favorite stories about Chevy—we were watching a football game at his house. I've done every type of job on film sets. I'm a member of the Directors Guild, and he's a member of the Screen Actors Guild. We were at the house and he had ten, fifteen years in the industry. He asked me, 'What's a best boy?' It's one of those questions. Nobody in the industry doesn't know what a best boy is unless you're an actor. It's the second man on base. No matter how much I know he's smart, sophisticated, etc., he's an actor!"

Pamela's sister Catherine Anne has been down a difficult road for many years, dealing with addiction and having been diagnosed with post-traumatic stress disorder from her upbringing. Being twenty-one years younger than Chevy, she felt he was more like an uncle than a brother to her. "It was difficult for him to see me as an adult with my own contacts. He's a good man, charming and sweet, and an amazing dad. He also has a dark side," she says, and this has affected work situations. "Not knowing how to deal with people and people misunderstanding him. But also gentle, kind, supremely gifted."

Catherine Anne was the only one who physically cared for her parents in their old age. She was with her father when he died and subsequently took care of her mother until the end of her life, dealing with her mother's "dementia, mood swings, and psychotic interludes. I waited for her to calm down. The demons were coming from a sick person," she explains. "I understood my mother was a lost child." Her mother's verbal attacks and statements that she wished Catherine Anne had never been born hurt a lot but were symptoms of her mother's illness, she says.

Their mother had eventually reached a point where she couldn't stand Cederquist's abuse of her any longer. Chevy remembers his mother's theatrics when she heard her husband coming home. "I saw John try to kiss her after work. She had suddenly become ragged, as if working in the kitchen all day. When she heard his footsteps, she would transform into a woman slaving to make dinner. John would grab her from behind, arms on her waist, and kiss her. She would rebuff him."

Pamela adds: "She had an affair, and my father [who had hired detectives to uncover the affair] locked her out of the house. [Chevy was out living on his own by then. Pamela was in her teens.] At the time, John was fifteen years old, and was away at boarding school [the Kent School in Connecticut]. "My parents put me away in a private boarding school in lieu of jail, I guess—in hopes of steering me back to a 'normal' existence. It didn't work."

John received a letter from his father that he destroyed after reading. It began, "Dear Son, I don't know how to tell you this in any proper way, but you must know. As your father, it is my duty to prepare you for what lies ahead. My marriage to your mother is at an end. She has taken up with another man, her piano instructor at Juilliard . . ."

John found the news devastating, and it sent him spiraling into a decline. "I've never understood why that news was, in effect, the last straw. My grades plummeted. I failed second-year Latin and American History (the only courses I've ever failed), and returned to Manhattan in disgrace." John ran away immediately after returning home. The family's East Side townhouse "had become a haunted place, as both parents laid claim to it, and it was thick with tension and animosity. A total nightmare."

Cathalene married Lawrence Widdoes, a composer and faculty member at the Juilliard School, in 1976, and they remained together until her death on January 1, 2005. By all accounts it was a better relationship than her marriage to Cederquist. They had music in common, wrote a number of songs and ballads together, and even wrote an opera, music by Widdoes and libretto by Cathalene.

For a time this new marriage seemed to bring the children back into touch. Cathalene was happier. Widdoes reached out to them. When Pamela graduated from school, "Larry was the only one of my parents who called me to go out for a drink. Neither of my other parents bothered to mark it in any way."

For a while, there was a renewed sense of family; the opera, Pamela said, provided "possibly the only family endeavor—the only time we all pulled together that I know of." The original intention was a concert version performance of the opera, without staging. Widdoes and Cathalene asked Pamela to direct it. "I saw it partially as another thing I could add to my résumé to support my desire to direct, and as a chance to support my mother in her artistic endeavors. I think she was a good artist. It was just that she'd never been a mother, so was no relationship like that on the table.

"I wanted to see them both recognized. I think it ended up being good for everyone. As to putting aside our differences, I don't know that I'd call it that. From my end it was much more the realization that if we were strangers, there was no way I'd be friends with her," Pamela said.

The family project resulted in three staged performances at the Kathryn Bache Miller Theater. Ned and Chevy were the producers, putting in $50,000 to finance the production. Their brother John and sister Catherine Anne were also asked to work on the set. According to Chevy, he put the money in and did see the production, but was not very involved in it. "It was beyond me, not lyrical, not traditional like going to the opera." It didn't appeal to Chevy's musical taste. "It was minimal, strange, dissonant. I assume in some mathematical way, it was lyrical to him [Widdoes]."

A January 15, 1994, review by Bernard Holland in the *New York Times* calls the opera, *How to Make Love*, a "somewhat disorganized, altogether pleasant one-act comic opera," and goes on to call the words and music "a nice fit," praising both the music and the dialogue.

The opera was set in a dress shop and the main character was a frustrated young saleswoman, who brings her sexual fantasies to life through illustrated books outlining sexual techniques. Store mannequins in the opera came to life to dance her daydreams.

In his assessment of the opera, Holland states, "There are no surprises. Evil, despite the odds, is vanquished; poor-but-pure wins the girl."

The opera happened to take place at a time Chevy was "very generous with money to everybody in the family. They looked up to me and my help." After moving back to New York, he said, "I thought I had the strength to get through getting to know my parents again. As soon as it got to the point my name wasn't being mentioned all the time, I saw parts of my family turn. It was ugly. I saw my father a little more of the bully he was. I slowly watched my mother care less and less."

Chevy never cut himself off from his family and made sure his own children had a chance to know their grandparents. The family dynamics were always complicated by money, though, as they had been when Cathalene was married to John Cederquist. She was always "clawing to get money from her mother, who got some from her divorces—some from Miles Browning, and much more from Cornelius. But she never gave Mom enough."

Cathalene did, in fact, leave money to four of her five children. Chevy, who had supported her for the last thirty years of her life, was the one exception. According to Ned, who is executor of his mother's will, she put a note into the will saying, "I have intentionally excluded my beloved Chevy because he has no need of my bounty."

Chevy says, "I never thought of it as weird until my shrink brought it up. That was her final blow."

Since Chevy was supporting her and had enough money, it made sense that he could be excluded. The practical implications and the emotional impact of it all seemed to clash inside Chevy. While Chevy had told his mother she didn't need to leave him money, he nevertheless felt slighted. In reality, it might have been a better option for him to receive his share and then give it away to his siblings, or to charity. Nobody could have predicted that his reaction would, once again, trigger emotions familiar from the abuse in his childhood. Chevy will, in fact, ultimately have an equal share of the possessions that remain in the apartment as a "life estate," for use by Widdoes.

Ned also helped their mother financially by hiring her as his secretary for several years, until she was no longer able to work. Ned says Larry Widdoes wasn't earning a large salary at Juilliard, and her secretarial work kept them going. However, attempting to maintain their beloved West Hurley property was a major burden, with taxes, repairs, and the like. "There were periodic financial crises, and Chevy came to the rescue more than once. Upon her death, he was repaid some of the money spent to retain the property."

The West Hurley property had originally belonged to Cathalene's mother, Cattie. After her marriage to Cornelius ended, Chevy's grandmother married Rudolf Anton Bernatschke, a portrait painter who was only ten years older than Chevy's mother. He is now in his nineties and living in New York City in the family house that will eventually go to the five children, Chevy included. It is a brownstone on East Sixty-second Street and has been declared a New York City landmark.

Upon Cattie's death in 1987, she left the West Hurley property to Rudolf and $300,000 to her daughter. But Cathalene loved the West Hurley estate and traded it with Bernatschke for the $300,000 that she had inherited. It was her intention to use the West Hurley property with her husband and to hold on to it. According to Ned, keeping the place was bleeding his mother and stepfather dry.

Cathalene's will was changed in 2002. Her previous will was signed and executed on August 23, 1976. According to Ned, her previous will would have given the West Hurley (Catskill) property to her two daughters. Her new will had been discussed for several months and was signed on September 9, 2002, witnessed by three hospital employees while she was about to undergo surgery to repair an aortic valve.

According to Ned, his mother understood that she could no longer make use of the property, and that maintaining it was a financial problem for her. According to John, Widdoes ultimately "liquidated the Catskill manor house and its fifty-plus acres of virgin lake and mountain-view land for the bargain-basement price of $750,000 to developers three months before her death, thus stripping my sisters of the beloved property she had [originally] left to them. The new [2002] will also left Widdoes our mother's million-dollar apartment on Central Park West," John said, which in the previous will would have remained in the family. Setting it up as a "life estate" was not recommended by the lawyer handling the will for Widdoes and Cathalene, Ned explained.

When the West Hurley property was finally sold, Widdoes put the money into their joint account, not the original intention. Ned had recommended a separate account for the funds from the sale. But when Cathalene died shortly after, the money from the sale constituted the bulk of her estate.

There were arguments over the money after Cathalene's death. Ned said that he hired a lawyer, as Widdoes attempted to keep more money from the West Hurley sale than the will specified. "Larry had views about Chevy and the Cederquist kids. They had not behaved as he thought they should have. He used it as an attempt to take more than what our mother's will provided for. He thought they didn't deserve it." Eventually, Ned said, a settlement was reached.

Although Widdoes received the Central Park West apartment outright, the possessions and paintings in it will go to all five children after his death. After Chevy was paid back for the taxes and some other expenses on the West Hurley property, the remainder was divided among his four siblings.

And what happened to all the old family money? There's a second "life estate" in the family that will also benefit Cathalene's five children. Cattie had lived in the brownstone on East Sixty-second Street from 1940 until her death in 1987. She stipulated that her husband Rudolf would have use of the property and its contents during his lifetime, and it would go to her only daughter, Cathalene, upon his death, or to Cathalene's five children if she predeceased Rudolf, which was the case. It is a substantial home, worth several million dollars according to current New York prices.

According to John, Cattie "bought a countship" for Bernatschke, a source of amusement for some members of the family. In political records showing the details of financial contributions, Rudolf Bernatschke is listed as a portrait painter and Cathalene Crane Bernatschke is listed as a concert singer. They gave modest contributions to Republican candidates: $500 to Jim Abdnor for the Senate and $500 to Ronald Reagan for president.

"It's very convoluted," Chevy said. "He was an Austrian 'busboy,' as my dad liked to say. He lived off Cattie, and they began to be known as Baron and Mrs. Bernatschke, which made my father laugh." After Chevy's grandmother died, Bernatschke remarried, and there were newspaper clippings referring to "Count and Countess Bernatschke." Even so, Chevy added, "He was patient as a saint, a funny, clever man who was patient with Cattie's erratic behavior and Mom's."

22. TODAY

"Who is Chevy?"

"That's too Oprah a question," quips Chevy's good friend Martin Short.

"Who is Chevy?" says his brother Ned. "Chevy is obviously one of the most successful people of the last fifty years. He rose to the top of an extremely competitive enterprise. I've always loved Chevy. The first thirty years, you could be concerned what was going to happen to him. It's a wonderful thing for all of us that he had the success he's had."

In many ways, though, Chevy is an enigma and people don't always know what to expect. One reporter, shocked to find him so personable and forthcoming in an interview, wrote, "I'd heard rude, so I was surprised when he was charming, and willing to speak at length."

Heidi Schaeffer, Chevy's publicist for twenty-five years, says, "At the core, he's a sweet, gentle man. He's devoted his life to his kids."

Natasha Garland is a close friend of Jayni's and knows the whole Chase family very well, having lived with them, sometimes for months at a time. The two families serve as godparents for each other's children.

"Chevy is a very serious person," Natasha says. "His humor comes from a deep understanding of sadness, difficulty, and the pains of life. He's very sensitive, and he's one of the most generous human beings you will ever meet. You can't imagine the thoughtfulness. Their house is a gathering place—it's an open house to a lot of people. They are family to a lot of us. Chevy has given financially to his friends and family, but also of his time and thoughtfulness."

Chevy has a few close friends, "but I don't have one closest friend," he says. "Friends come and go in my life. The sense of self comes and goes, assurance and self-confidence. I've never held on to any one thing," he adds, "excepting my wife and children."

A small group of his closest friends have remained with him over the years, however. Attorney Bruce Bodner has represented Chevy for more than thirty years. Bodner says, "I adore him. He's a loyal, generous friend. One thing that stands out for me is that he was fabulous when I saw him on the sets. The crew loved him. He was generous, kind, always knew people's first names. One thing with a lot of celebrities, they are shy. In a nonthreatening situation, a wonderful quality of his, he is so charming, polite, and courteous.

"Some of the directors would get rough on the crew. Chevy would, in a very nice way, pull the guy aside and say you shouldn't talk to people that way. People think he's inaccessible or arrogant. His kindness comes out around crews—a lot of stars couldn't care less—these are faceless people. For Chevy, they are never faceless wall dressing, they are always real people. He talks to them, he remembers their names."

As soon as Dan Aykroyd began working with Chevy on *Saturday Night Live*, they became close friends. Aykroyd says, "He was my most ardent confidence builder and promoter. He was always behind me in everything I did. I perceived comic genius. Chevy stands out in the industry— he's a great actor. He has a masterful film career," adding that he has always been impressed "with the versatility of the man!"

According to Paul Shaffer, one of Chevy's close friends and a longtime colleague, "Chevy is a musically oriented guy and a piano player. He's absolutely hilarious. His humor is juvenile and intelligent at the same time. When I first met him I thought he was incredibly talented and good-looking. He was perfectly set up to become a movie star."

But friends always had to know his humor could be tough, biting, warns Paul. "I was the eighties bandleader on the *Letterman* show. Chevy, in an interview, would say, 'Paul was gay, we've always known.' It was just his humor. I'm not gay—another person might have been offended but I understood Chevy's humor. He does cross the line a little bit."

Beverly D'Angelo has maintained a close friendship with him for many years. "Chevy is very loyal, extraordinarily protective of his loved ones. Chevy is a great advice giver [with a] crystal-clear vision."

As an actor, Beverly adds, "Chevy always knew what would work and what wouldn't. He was always right. Whenever someone made him do something he thought was wrong, it wasn't funny, in every one of the four [*Vacation*] films. If I got any laughs 'of my own' it was because Chevy gave me a specific thing to do. No one gives Chevy credit for being an actor. He is. Chevy's brand of humor is one that feeds on someone's insecurities, and the need to laugh at that. Really intellectual and classic. He leads you down a road, and then you do a U-turn." And, she adds, "He tells the best 'Aristocrat' joke, bar none."

Try as I might, though, begging and pleading could not get Chevy to serve up his famous version of the joke, so you won't be reading it here. And none of his friends would agree to tell his version of it, for fear of getting it wrong.

In fact, Chevy had filmed the joke for the 2005 film *The Aristocrats*, in which a hundred well-known comedians each tell their own version of the joke—an hour and a half of obscenity on film. However, Chevy refused to sign the release forms when he realized his daughters might see the film.

"I do tell the best Aristocrat joke, but it requires a certain persona and a cellar filled with men." Telling the idea of the joke was acceptable, but Chevy was only willing to give a clue about its content.

"A guy goes to a producer and says, 'I've got a great act for you, a family act, a stage act. I come out on the stage and jerk off all over the audience.' The joke goes on for five minutes, and you could get a busload of nuns laughing. It's about the oddest, most filthy, abhorrent sexual acts. It's about the rhythm and the over-the-top nature of it, socko puncho, and you can't repeat yourself! I told it to a couple of professors at Bard, over a couple of beers, and they laughed so hard I think it changed my mark in one of the classes."

And what about Chevy on Chevy?

"I'm a normal guy who likes normal things. I don't eat beef—it makes good sense not to. I tend to eat whatever my wife or kids are cooking, invariably vegetarian or fish. I do like to sneak out and get a Sausage McMuffin occasionally," he adds, looking around to make sure no one at home can hear him.

Chevy appreciates French wines, mostly red, his favorites being Haut-Brion and Lynch-Bages. "I used to drink a glass or two every night. My cardiologist told me it was good for me." He doesn't drink hard liquor, although "in the old days I went through a period of vodka to assuage stress and complications. I was never drunk. I didn't like a 'buzz.'"

Chevy shares his wife Jayni's concerns for the environment and supports her charitable efforts. He is sensitive and spiritual but on his own terms. "I hate organized religion," Chevy says. "It's always a question of 'my God's better than your God.' I'm an agnostic. The fact of the matter is the only thing I believe comes out of religion is the golden rule—that is the best ethic. If that ethic were really utilized, we wouldn't have the horrible kinds of things that are going on now . . . In my family, we celebrate Christmas as if Santa came."

Chevy is an animal lover—all sorts, from wild animals to pets, including his five dogs and two parrots. One of them talks and sings and taunts him with an annoying tune when Chevy has been out of town too long. On his property are two Icelandic horses (shorter than Arabian horses) named Tvister and Sverna (or Bob and Candy in the Americanized versions). "I'm not much of a rider. Why would horses want people on their backs, if you really think about it? I'm close to Bob and Candy. I give them bread and they come to me."

In October 2006 Chevy was on the set of *Law & Order* at its Chelsea Piers studio in New York City. He was there for an exciting new development in his career—his first serious dramatic role, a role that was completely the opposite of the way he thinks, feels, and lives his life. The opposite of how he has raised his children, how he and his wife have established standards of tolerance and goodness, kindness and consideration.

Chevy played the role of Mitch Carroll in a dramatic episode based loosely (like many *Law & Order* scripts) on a real case or incident—"ripped from the headlines," as the saying goes. NBC made its obligatory statement that the script was entirely fictional, and that any resemblance to actual people was entirely coincidental. In this case, they stretched coincidence as far as possible. Chevy was playing the role of an anti-Semitic celebrity, a role based on Mel Gibson and his highly publicized DUI (driving under the influence) arrest in July 2006, with the plot carried a few paces past the real-life incident, as a warning about the dangers of prejudice unchecked.

The episode, called "In Vino Veritas" and aired November 3, 2006, was preceded by a lot of attention from the press and followed by a generally positive response to

Chevy's strong and enthusiastic performance. His colleagues and representatives heard that his appearance was under discussion for an Emmy recommendation in the "Guest Actor in a Drama Series" category.

On the set, Chevy looked very serious. He had struggled, not with acting the role but with the idea of playing a character filled with so many prejudices. "In my life, I've never had a prejudiced thought. Here, my character says 'Jew' many times in a derogatory way—something I can't imagine ever doing."

Breaks between the scenes, in rehearsal and on camera, were sprinkled with comic relief, however. Chevy and Sam Waterston, as the very serious *Law & Order* prosecutor, traded fake barbs, joking threats. As soon as the director, Tim Hunter, shouted "Cut," something funny was bound to happen and the cast and crew were ready for it. At the end of one courtroom scene, Chevy jumped out of his seat and shouted at his character's fourteen-year-old son, "You've betrayed me!" The laughter seemed a necessary release.

Back in character, Chevy looked stern—a look not often seen in his screen roles up to that point. He was experiencing a mix of feelings: satisfaction over being able to do so well with a serious role, excitement about being involved as guest star in a major role on a prime-time television program, and sadness over the theme of the episode.

The script of "In Vino Veritas" addressed the murder of Danielle Hertzberg, a Jewish producer of a television show in which Chevy's character had been starring. Shortly after the fictional show's cancellation, the producer is murdered. Mitch is accused of murder, and convicted, although the real murderer is his fourteen-year-old son.

The episode was broadcast during Sweeps Week, when US viewership is measured; it was advertised heavily and gained a great deal of attention. Being his first very serious dramatic role, Chevy did not hesitate to admit that he had sought advice from his two eldest daughters, Cydney and

Caley, both of whom have acted. They gave him tips on getting into the character and loosening up for the role—and crying, as required at one point in the script.

Chevy was not at all concerned that playing a highly visible role as a prejudiced person might typecast him or cause trouble for him. A few days after filming was finished in New York, he and Jayni and their daughter Cydney were scheduled to fly to Florence, Italy, for a few days of vacation before going to London, where Chevy was to participate in a comedy ensemble performance as part of the Secret Policeman's Ball to aid Amnesty International. The show was to be recorded for broadcast on Britain's Channel 4.

The day before the trip, Chevy was disturbed to discover that an online news service had released an article with a headline indicating that Chevy had defended Mel Gibson. Chevy was furious. "The whole point of the *Law & Order* episode was about the dangers of prejudice, about what happens when you teach prejudice to your children. I was upset over Mel's comments, and feel sorry for him that he has a father who believes the Holocaust never took place."

The Internet news piece quoted Chevy as excusing Gibson's prejudiced remarks because he was drunk. It was in reality the scripted remarks made by the lawyer for Chevy's *Law & Order* character, who had attempted to excuse his character's actions. Of course, Chevy had said no such thing.

It took swift action on the part of Chevy's powerful press agent, Allen Eichhorn (at the public relations firm PMK/HBH), to get to the source of the error. Chevy insisted on strong action, believing that if he were viewed as sympathetic to prejudice, it would not only ruin his career but, more important, completely misrepresent the kind of person he had been his entire life.

In less than two hours, the Internet rumor mill had stopped spreading the story, and the source of the article printed the following note:

> *In a story published by* PR-inside.com *on 4 October (06), quotes attributed to actor CHEVY CHASE about MEL GIBSON were actually lines taken from a script spoken by his character and not by Chevy Chase. "These statements were made under the influence of alcohol and sleep medication," are actually quotes from the script from his upcoming episode of LAW & ORDER and Chevy Chase in no way implied he was defending Mel Gibson. We apologize for this error and any inconvenience. Our apologies to Mr. Chase for this mistake.*

With news of this correction, Chevy was greatly relieved and ready to leave for his first trip to Florence. There had been occasions in the past when Chevy felt his words had been twisted by the press. In this instance, responsible action was taken by the news service to correct a damaging and mistaken impression.

The Secret Policeman's Ball in London was a highly publicized appearance for Chevy, as well as an opportunity for him to remind the public of his strong liberal politics. The ball is an infrequent but legendary event first organized by John Cleese in 1979, with "sequels" in 1981, 1987, and 1989. This was Chevy's first appearance there, and he performed in a satirical political sketch in which he played a guard at the Guantánamo prison.

The British press were eager to hear what liberal American Chevy would say to a strongly anti-Bush British public, and Chevy didn't disappoint. In fact, he was called upon to do several dozen interviews during the few days he was in London to rehearse and perform.

"I'm so glad at this time that we can bring attention to the whole concept of torture and the idea of 'my God' being better than 'your God,' the killing of hundreds of thousands of people," he said. "The idea of going into Iraq, going into a sovereign country, the ethics of Bush doing that is outrageous."

Chevy was called upon to do only the one sketch. While the British public and press greeted him eagerly, and many elements of the trip were a success, the Albert Hall performance was a disappointment for him. His sketch was early in the evening, and a technical glitch prevented his part from being televised on the giant screens, which remained dark during his performance. This was a big problem in the cavernous Royal Albert Hall, which seats eight thousand, and people were unaware it was Chevy onstage. Chevy was very amused that as he went offstage, in darkness, the announcer said, "Ladies and gentlemen, the legendary Chevy Chase." Thinking he was about to come onstage, the audience gave a thunderous round of applause. He was assured that this glitch would be remedied for the edited televised version of the evening.

Once back home, Chevy was pleased to see that the news of his dramatic *Law & Order* role had spread like wildfire. His character had helped to propel him back into the public eye once again. He had been eager to play a serious role for some time, and he had the drive and energy in his performance to confirm that such parts would be a good vehicle during a transitional time.

Chevy had been struggling with elements of his career for a number of years but in 2005 things began to look like they were turning around. In 2006, that was confirmed when he accepted the part in *Funny Money*.

A few small though intriguing roles in less successful films had set him apart from his comedic stereotype. In the 2004 film *Ellie Parker*, for example, his small part as the depressed agent of an actress, portrayed by Naomi Watts, showed a more exaggerated sort of personality than he had played in most of his films. He was humorous, but with no hint of physical comedy or slapstick. Also in 2004, Chevy played the unusual role of Paul Parmesan, a sleazy manufacturer/salesman on a home shopping channel in the film *Our Italian Husband*, a character he would never have agreed to play years earlier. Brooke Shields and the Italian actress Maria Grazia Cucinotta played the leading roles in the comedy.

Hair slicked back, pushy, and dishonest, Chevy negotiated the demands of the role with mockery and achieved a fascinating takeoff, again a character humorous through exaggeration, although in this role it was a bizarre sort of exaggeration. It confirmed that he was still a highly imaginative actor even in a less than a leading role.

As he had done throughout the years, Chevy continued to accept roles that he wasn't entirely sure about, and to do favors for friends, sometimes to his detriment. Such was the case with *Zoom*, a 2006 film designed for children and preteens. It was the story of an aging superhero brought back into action to train a band of youngsters to be the new superheroes. Tim Allen and Courteney Cox costarred in this film, and in the end Chevy was not happy with his role. In fact, he felt that many of the funny things he had done during the shoot had "mysteriously been cut out." This was a film he was quite happy to forget.

Despite the fact that the public continued to view him as an American icon, adoring him, watching all his old films, despite the words of friends, family members, colleagues, and professionals in the entertainment industry reminding him that careers are cyclical, that there are lapses and dry periods, Chevy wasn't satisfied. He (and Hollywood circumstances) had taken himself out of the limelight for a while, but things seemed to be turning around.

At the age of sixty-three, he was experiencing some of the same challenges of his early years, but from a different perspective. What direction should he take now? He wasn't likely to repeat such hits as the *National Lampoon's Vacation* series, *Fletch*, or *Caddyshack*. In the year 2006 he was ready for a new phase in his career.

By early 2007, Chevy was being offered more appearances and more scripts to read. It seemed that things were, indeed, starting to turn around. "There has been a huge upsurge in attention to me. What's happening in my life

really is great." Chevy praises his new management team—
Erik Kritzer, his manager, and his agents Ben Press
and Michael McConnell, who took on Chevy's career last
year.

"There's a widely held view that I'm fresh meat and in
good shape, but was forgotten somehow. Now I'm waiting
for the right thing." There was a time when Chevy did not
want to consider doing a sitcom; now he says he would.
"Now I feel the kids are safe, and I'm eager to work. We're
keeping at bay the bad material, and the offers keep coming.
I can't remember in the last ten years a better time than
now," he adds. Chevy has received offers for several films
and sitcoms, and they are being given serious consideration
by his manager and agents. At the time of publication, he
has not yet signed contracts.

Ben Press said that he has been fielding a lot of offers.
Two episodes of the television drama *Brothers & Sisters*
have been filmed. Chevy's character, Stan Harris, is portrayed as the liberal ex-hippie first love of Sally Field's
character, Nora Walker. Nora searches for Stan and they
meet for the first time in forty years. "He loved it. This is a
drama, very touching and with some light moments. A
wonderful cast," says Press.

Chevy speaks very highly of the cast of *Brothers &
Sisters*, particularly working with Sally Field, whom he has
always admired. "Sally raises your game. Shooting an hour
episode takes weeks," Chevy says, adding that he had "a lot
of fun with the cast, and being Sally's old flame.

"This is a wonderful show, and filming is intense—all
day, every day—so it better be damn well creatively worth
it because the waiting alone can be enervating." The process
reminded Chevy of the reasons he had refused to do
sitcoms, but in this case, it seemed worth it to work with a
superior cast in an acclaimed show.

Jayni is pleased with all the new developments in Chevy's
career. She adds, "It's wonderful that Chevy worked with
Sally Field. She is one of the most talented actresses of all

time. Chevy has a lot more in him. He's so much better than he has ever had the opportunity to demonstrate. I know. I see it all the time."

Although Chevy has expanded into dramatic roles, with *Law & Order* and now *Brothers & Sisters*, his manager and agents say that it's not a transition into drama. "He will continue to take on irreverent roles and comedies," Press says. "He's one of the great comic legends of film."

Erik Kritzer says, "When Chevy signed with me, we sat down and made a plan. He had never done a drama. We made it happen with *Law & Order*. We showed the tape to the producers of *Brothers & Sisters*. Wonderful things are happening. His new agents—Michael McConnell and Ben Press—these guys are treating Chevy the way he should be treated." Kritzer, who is forty-one, says he grew up on Chevy's movies. "I'm representing someone I idolized as a young man." He's happy to be working with Chevy in "the second part of his career. It's not about finding a comedy for Chevy, but finding the right one, that we can really be proud of."

During August of 2007, Chevy was invited to host the Newport Jazz Festival for the first time. "I took it pretty seriously," he says. And he unexpectedly had an opportunity to play when Dave Brubeck's entrance was slightly delayed. Chevy chose a Bill Evans tune that is one of his favorites, "Waltz for Debby." He thought of it playing for the sound check. "I couldn't resist—the piano was there, perfectly tuned, and the sidemen were there ready." But he was surprised when he received a huge round of applause. Then a nod from the stage manager, and it was time to introduce Dave Brubeck. "As I was walking off and he was coming out, he stopped me, grabbed my hand. 'I had no idea you could play like that. I've been sending you music over the years thinking—how the hell could he play that? I heard you play just now and that was beautiful. You really are good.' This was so nice. I was blown away," Chevy adds. He continues to attend jazz performances at the Blue Note, Birdland, and other Manhattan locations.

While not a career development, there was one intriguing occurrence that involved Chevy's former feud with 'shock jock' Howard Stern. It was a rather unusual meeting of minds, finally, and great fodder for the gossip columnists, some who stated bluntly that just a few years ago peace in the Middle East would have seemed more likely. For many summers, Chevy and Jayni had been part of the East Hampton social scene. During August of 2007, they joined other celebrity guests at an East Hampton party thrown by Jon Bon Jovi. Jayni, spotting Howard Stern, walked up to him and introduced herself. Stern expressed surprise that Jayni was even speaking to him, after the incident during the 1990s, when their middle-of-the-night phone conversation had been played over and over on his radio show. At the party, Stern had separate conversations with Jayni and Chevy and, it seemed, all differences were resolved.

A few days later, Jayni phoned Stern to ask if he would contribute something to their online auction, and he readily agreed. Stern's donation of a studio visit to his show drew the top bid among auction prizes. During the two-week-long auction, Chevy and Jayni joined Stern on-air on his Sirius satellite radio show to discuss their past disagreement, and to speak about the Green School Auction. The winning bid for the Stern session was, surprisingly, far higher than the next item, lunch with Chevy and Bill Clinton, an item that had taken top prize in the previous auctions.

During that same summer, Chevy felt strongly that he wanted to return to *SNL* in some capacity, and conceived of an election-based segment of Weekend Update in which he would address the most bizarre elements of the political candidates seeking the presidency. He discussed his idea with Lorne Michaels and was subsequently contacted by the producer of the Weekend Update segment. The result was an open-ended appointment as the "Senior Political Correspondent" of Weekend Update. With several film and television projects under discussion, Chevy would have been unable to commit to a regular feature but was invited to do occasional spots, schedule permitting.

The first one took place on October 6, and Chevy was surprised by the strong reaction of the audience, as well as his own emotional response to sitting in the old seat. Chevy opened with a familiar scene, talking on the phone, at first unaware of the audience. This time, however, instead of a mock conversation with a female companion, Chevy began "You're my son; I love you. You're going blind? You are doing it right. I gotta go." He hangs up the phone—"Good evening. I still am, and you're still not," followed by huge laughter.

Chevy was enthusiastic about the idea of doing a spot on *SNL*. But he was unprepared for the emotional reaction that would overtake him in the weeks before his appearance. "I was living in a state of anxiety and had dreams that were typical of a fear of exposure." He related a clashing of forces inside of him—the fear that he would not do a good job, playing against "that other side—don't they know how great I am?" all coming out in his dreams. In one, he was in the writers' room with a group of young people. All were showing tremendous disrespect and calling him names. "There was obviously a lot of anger, bitterness that I don't face consciously in my life, but I do subconsciously.

"Then I got there [in reality] and was given a small nondescript office." Chevy, who prefers not to use a computer, asked for a legal pad, some pencils, all the recent newspapers, and he started writing. "I also realized my head is in a tizzy—this isn't going to be easy because of all the fear. At the same time, I felt very welcomed by the producer of Weekend Update," and the young writers, who gave him a grand welcome. "They were not officious, not contentious; they were just there to help. They gave me their ideas and jokes. My feeling was 'I can do this—I damn well better do this. I'm not gonna go out there and succumb to some kind of stage fright.'" Chevy shared all his fears openly with the writers and producer of the segment. "I have to be honest—I told them it's been thirty years and I'm scared to death. They said—'don't worry, we'll help you.' I got to know ten or eleven of the nicest kids I've ever known there—the cast, all of whom have some great talent."

By the time of the dress rehearsal, Chevy fully expected to need tranquilizers. "But there was such a huge response from the audience at the dress rehearsal," he said, that he began to relax. "My mind was racing—do it right, give it energy, underline every word you think you can make something of. I almost overplayed it. All the applause gave me more time to figure out they were so happy to see me, it wouldn't have mattered if I just spoke German for four minutes and left. They were ready to laugh, and wanted me to feel comfortable. That gave me great confidence. I didn't have to worry too much."

The segment was not advertised, simply treated as a surprise guest spot, although several weeks earlier Chevy had publicly mentioned that a return appearance to *SNL* was under consideration. It was only after the fact that the episode received attention from the press and blogs.

Being in the hot seat—it was in fact the old grey Weekend Update set so familiar to Chevy—he noticed differences. He had to remind himself to keep up the pace. "I'm not as young, not as quick. I was pretty fast at thirty-two, and stayed with the camera."

Between dress and air, Chevy reports, Lorne Michaels still calls the whole cast and top crew into a small office, "He cuts this, cuts that—all that stuff in his head." Chevy admires Lorne's brilliance in pulling together an operation that is much bigger than it was in the 70s. Back then, "it was just the two of us, and I miss that." Lorne makes the cuts and it comes in at exactly an hour and a half. "He clearly does have his hands on. Now, it's two and a half million a show—it was a hundred grand then."

The first gag on the episode, following the mock phone call, was what Chevy termed "a physical gag." As he was preparing his pages, he turned the first one upside down, reading gibberish until he 'realizes' the mistake. "It immediately brought the audience to me." The segment was a combination of Chevy's ideas, the writers' ideas, and small adlibs and alterations that Chevy felt brought the material closer to his own style. His plan was to deal with all the political candidates in swift fashion. Once his page was turned right side up, he began, "In a startling moment during Wednesday's democratic debate, former Senator Mike Gravel's head exploded. Then in a chain reaction spreading from one candidate's lectern to the next, John Edwards' hair parted itself on the opposite side, Barack Obama's ears flapped uncontrollably, Hillary Clinton shot up in the polls, and Dennis Kucinich simply . . . vanished, leaving his little blue suit splayed out over the podium," the final description, according to Chevy, being a visual image intended to create a little scene in the mind of the audience member.

Also in early October of 2007, a high-visibility month for Chevy, he was in LA for the premiere and press event surrounding the short film, *Cutlass*. Chevy plays the owner of a Chevrolet Cutlass in the tale about family relationships and traditions. The whole project originated with *Glamour* magazine's "Reel Moments" competition of stories submitted by the magazine's readers. The contest's goal is to empower women by producing female-friendly short films and providing opportunities for actresses to direct. The 2007 theme was to capture the essence of happiness.

Cutlass was one of three short films produced in this project. The films were subsequently screened October 13 in the hometowns of the *Glamour* readers whose stories were selected.

For the film, Chevy was in the company of friends: Kate Hudson, who directed, and co-stars Kurt Russell, Dakota Fanning, Virginia Madsen, and Kristen Stewart. "It was great fun working briefly with Kurt, and most particularly being directed by Goldie's daughter, whom I had held when she was a baby," Chevy says.

23. TOMORROW

Lately, a lot of people have been telling Chevy what he ought to be doing now. People want to see him in new films, both serious drama and comedy, writing, directing (which he hasn't yet done formally), playing the piano, doing television shows, performing a live show, maybe off-Broadway; the list goes on. The fact is that Chevy has affected a lot of people in a very positive way, and they want to see more of him. He has millions of fans and many friends and supporters in "the business," and he remains very much an American icon.

Chevy's role on *Law & Order* opened some new doors for his career, and following the appearance he had a flurry of new offers. With his daughters now grown, he is moving back into films and music and making more public appearances, but he is determined to pick and choose his projects carefully.

Heidi Schaeffer has had the benefit of working with Chevy over the course of many years. "I'm thinking that right now, he's in a place where he really wants this to happen. He is working with new people, a new manager [Erik Kritzer], who is a good match. He has a new direction right now. There's not a real long list of those guys—Steve Martin, Bill Murray, Dan Aykroyd."

For the past few years, Chevy has stated that he does not want to do a sitcom. He is not an admirer of the type of humor generally found in sitcoms. "I come from a darker side of satire. *Mad* magazine but close to *National Lampoon*, leading to *SNL*.

"Your work is not nine to five on a TV show. It's all over the place, long nights, or just at night. It's a year-after-year endeavor—trying to get picked up for six years so you can get residuals the rest of your life, back-end money. A real tough job." A film, on the other hand, is finished in three months. However, several intriguing sitcom roles were offered to him in 2007, and he now says that he would consider a carefully-chosen and well-matched sitcom role.

Jayni would like to see Chevy writing more. "I think that would fill his soul. Acting is a quick fix, more superficial. There's a lot more that he can do. On-screen, it's a huge loss if people don't get him back in films." She understands people not wanting him to do serious roles, since he has been so typecast in comic roles. "It has been suggested that he go and study at the Royal Shakespearean—and I think he should send a film crew," she adds. Jayni was glad to see Chevy on *SNL*. "Rejoining *SNL*'s Weekend Update team this season may be just what the doctor ordered for both the show and for Chevy," she says. "He has missed the energy and camaraderie of working on the show all these years and everyone knows that loads of *SNL* fans would come back to the show just to see him. It's a win-win and I hope that he doesn't get so busy that he can't fit more shows into his schedule."

Family friend Natasha Garland says, "Cary Grant, but Cary Grant with a Jack Nicholson twist. Chevy has done the family films. I think it's time for him to go back to being a little less safe/correct ... to make the audience squirm while keeping the twinkle in his eye, which is what he did so brilliantly on *Saturday Night Live*. He has the capacity to make us all *think*."

Carl Reiner says: "Chevy should be writing." And only doing good films, maybe serious roles, he adds.

"The industry typecasts people," says Harold Ramis, who thinks Chevy should go for serious roles. "Why not drama? Comedy is hard to write and there are few great scripts. For guys like Chevy, it's a huge weight. Comedy is at the mercy of specific writing, inspiration. Drama is rich, and easier to write well."

Dan Aykroyd wants to see Chevy make more films. His plan is a version of *Spies Like Us* with Chevy and Dan as senior statesmen. "I enjoy his eccentricities, his insecurities. I think we have another one in us." Dan places Chevy along with all the great actors, all the remarkable comedic actors. "Gleason, Candy, Steve Martin, Desi, Lucy—he's in that pantheon. The leading men like Walter Matthau and Jack Lemmon—they go on and work forever. It takes producers and directors with the vision to put him in the right thing. The young producers and directors will hopefully see his value. And as a musician, he should keep cutting tracks." Andy Aaron is involved with underground comedy and has encouraged Chevy to join him. "I took him to see an improv group that included people from *30 Rock* and the executive producer of the *Colbert Report*. They invited Chevy to be in it, in the role of narrator."

Beverly D'Angelo says, "Chevy has a really strong persona. Maybe he needs a Quentin Tarantino to come along! Stranger things have happened. I don't know why they use the term 'comeback.' It's a career. Chevy began as a writer. I'd love to see him write, see what comes of that—a one-man show? A whole new career as a novelist, short stories, film scripts? Remember he rewrote much of *Vacation* and he improvises so brilliantly that the writers will end up going with his dialogue."

Bruce Bodner agrees that Chevy should take on serious roles in the future, but says, "I've always encouraged him to branch out, to direct. Good comedy directors are much more rare than dramatic directors. Chevy is a very smart, astute person. He knows shooting—and production and postproduction—as well as anybody I've seen. When he has taken a large role with an inexperienced director, he has helped to set up and block the scenes, and I've always thought he could do that. And he should do live theater."

Chevy looks at it all philosophically. He has a realistic view of his life, and he understands his priorities. He is proud of his family and thrilled that so many people have been able to, and will continue to, share his satirical view of life. Chevy is gratified that he is an American icon, but he is ready for new challenges.

The concluding words of this biography by rights should go to Chevy:

"For those of you who have been my steadfast fans, I owe you more than can be measured. For those of you who doubt my talents and my will, in the words of Governor Schwarzenegger, 'I'll be back.' I have a wonderful, beautiful wife with whom I've been in love for twenty-seven years and will continue to be forever. I have three of the most beautiful, loving, and talented daughters one could possibly have. 'Any time I cash in now, I win,' in the words of Charles M. Russell.

"I believe in living a life of grace. I believe in honesty. I'm a survivor. We're not all so different—it's just degrees—and in the end one's intentions are what counts."

CHEVY'S DESK III

Chevy had a wonderful time writing phony commercials. Some of the commercials were pretaped; others were done live. The commercial for "Triopenin" was taped using a close-up of Chevy's hands, made up to look old. Because he knew how to use his hands and fingers in flexible, imaginative ways, Chevy's hands had starred in several previous productions, starting with Channel One.

[Open on extreme close-up of hands, black background. A droning stinging note of music is played while the hands run themselves together. The feeling is one of extreme pain.]

Narrator (V/O): Arthritis in the adult is painful, lonely, and sometimes difficult to manage.

[Hands continue rubbing, painfully feeling each joint.]

Arthritis is particularly annoying when coupled with neuralgia and severe muscular tension.

[Lights: flash of lightning.]

[SFX: Thunder.]

Abrupt weather changes can add discomfort, inflame tissues, and cause local swelling, calling for special relief.

[Place bottle in scene. It has obvious safety-feature cap designed to foil children from opening it. Hands anxiously reach for bottle.]

Triopenin, a compound of powerful antiarthritic spansules and antihistamines, speeds soothing relief where needed.

[During V/O hands are painfully trying to open the safety cap with extreme difficulty.]

Triopenin is gentle, non-habit forming, aids in soothing muscles and liberating stiff, painful joints.

[Hands continue trying unsuccessfully to open bottle. The safety feature is too effective. Pain is apparent; frustration mounts. Music becomes happier, bouncier.]

Soon, you're "handling life" again, feeling better and getting a firm grasp on the situation.

[Unable to open bottle, hands give up completely.]

[Product shot: of two bottles of Triopenin, one standing, the other lies beside it, the bottom smashed open, pills littering the area.]

Triopenin gets your hands working again. Now with the new child-proof safety cap.

Any samples of Chevy's writing for *SNL* would be incomplete without the bizarre and hilarious "Jaws" episodes—a *Jaws* spoof taken to its extreme. This episode is "Jaws 2," taken from *SNL* 4, November 8, 1975. Candice Bergen hosted the show. The original manuscript bears the date of November 6 and was typed by Chevy in one of many late-night sessions. There were some changes in the actual broadcast but this is the script as written.

Part of the comedy is inherent in how long the sketches go on. (This one is slightly trimmed.) Chevy was always the voice of the land shark, and he wore the shark head since he also played the part of the shark. He recalls speaking into a small microphone hanging off set just by the door that he would open to grab his victims. The script was hanging on the wall, and Chevy would have to hold open the shark's jaws to read the script. Some of these off stage antics were as funny to the cast as those the audience could actually see.

JAWS II
[Music: from the film *Jaws*.]
[SFX: doorbell, "ding-dong."]
[Gilda moves to chain-locked front door.]
Gilda: Who is it?
Muffled voice [mumbling so that the name isn't clear]:
    Mrs. Ramilarghh?
Gilda [suspicious]: Who is it?
Muffled voice: Plumber.
Gilda [perturbed]: "Plumber"? I didn't ask for a plumber.
    Who *is* it?
[Pause.]
Muffled voice: Telegram.
Gilda: Oh. Telegram. Just a moment.
[She opens the door.]
[The head of the shark appears, grabbing her arm and pulling her into the hallway shrieking, out of our view.]
Gilda: Aarrgh!!
[Dissolve to: Sheriff's office. Danny behind desk, dressed in sheriff's khakis. Michael dressed in jeans, work shirt, sweater; snorkel mask is strapped around forehead. On desk is a three-foot-long metal tub covered with a sheet.]
Michael [looking under sheet at remains; he winces]: Oh,
    my God!
Danny: What was it?
Michael: Land shark. The cleverest species of them all.
[Dissolve to: Apartment, Stage 3.]
[SFX: radio, door knock.]
[Laraine comes to the door.]
Laraine: Yes?
Muffled voice: Mrs. Arlsburgerhh? [Voice trails off.]
Laraine: Who?
Muffled voice: [Pause.] Mrs. Johannesburrrrr? . . .
Laraine: Who *is* it?

Muffled voice: [Pause.] Flowers.

Laraine [suspects]: "Flowers"? From whom?

Muffled voice: [Long pause.] Plumber, ma'am.

Laraine: I don't need a plumber. You're that clever shark, aren't you?

[Pause.]

Muffled voice: Candygram ...

Laraine [convinced she knows]: "Candygram" my foot. Get out of here before I call the proper authorities. You're the shark and you know it.

Muffled voice: I'm only a dolphin ...

Laraine: A dolphin? Well ... Okay. [Unlocks door but leaves the chain on.] Just slip the candy through here.

[The shark attempts to pass the box through the opening width-wise, so that it can't possibly fit.]

Muffled voice: You'll have to open the door a little wider, ma'am.

Laraine: Well ... just a moment.

[She closes the door, unlocks chain, shark pulls her screaming into hallway.]

[Dissolve to: Apartment. Candice Bergen is reading a paper with headline "More Shark Killings" and listening to the radio.]

Don (as radio newsman V/O): ... considered the cleverest of all sharks. Unlike the great white, which tends to inhabit the waters of harbors and recreational beach areas, the land shark may strike at any place any time. It is capable of disguising its voice and generally attacks young single women. Experts at the University of Miami's Oceanographic Institute suggest that the best way to scare off the shark in the event of an attack is to hit or punch the predator in the nose ... Now for the weather ...

[Turns off radio.]

[SFX: doorbell.]

Candice: Who is it?

Muffled voice: Sorry to disturb you, ma'am. I am from

the Jehovah's Witnesses and thought you might be interested in a copy of our journal, *The Watchtower.*
[Throughout this, she has tiptoed to a table near the front door and removed a large wooden mallet from a drawer. Her expression tells us that she knows it is the shark and will surprise him upon opening the door.]
Candice: Why, I'd be very interested.
Muffled voice: Would you mind opening the door, ma'am?
Candice: Certainly. [She unlocks the door, opens it a crack, and reaches out with the mallet, slamming it into the head we don't see.]
[SFX: watermelon being broken with a mallet.]
[To Candice's horror, the door opens and Garrett with a suit on, dropping journals all over the place, reels dizzily into the apartment, hands covering a bloodied face. He mumbles and hits the floor, unconscious.]
Candice [confused expression]: Oh . . . sorry!
[Blackout.]

Chevy was distinguished by receiving two Emmys for his work on *Saturday Night Live* during the 1975–76 season. He was honored for his writing and acting and was presented with the awards during the twenty-eighth annual Emmy Awards.

The May 22, 1976, *SNL* was hosted by Buck Henry, and Gordon Lightfoot was the musical guest. The episode took place just after Chevy had won the Emmys. Chevy wrote the scene to include Laraine Newman, he said, because there weren't enough scenes for the women in the cast. His intention with the sketch was to get Laraine "pissed off enough after what I'd said about women to make me do the fall. The point again, with all these falls, is that the more stuff you have—the crutch, the more of a noise you make, and the more stuff you fall through—the better. Also the easier it is on your body."

[Chevy Chase hobbles onto the stage with a cast on his right leg. A red card table and folding chairs are at the left corner of the stage.]

Chevy: Uh . . . good evening, everybody. I'm afraid I have some disheartening news, for some of you. Unfortunately, I've injured my leg earlier this week, accepting an Emmy Award . . . uh, thank you very much. [Audience chuckles.] And it may be broken, I haven't had it X-rayed yet, but, um . . . Actually, I *have* had it X-rayed, I haven't *seen* the X-rays. Anyway, obviously, I can't do a fall for you, and I wanted to do the opening fall.

However, Laraine Newman—one of the Not Ready for Prime Time Players—has very graciously consented to do the fall instead. She's gonna fall over this table to my right. I say "gracious" because the entire show, the entire staff of the show has been very, really terrific about my winning the Emmy—thank you again. [Audience chuckles.] There has been no enmity, no hostility, no jealousy. They've just been very warm and natural, and congratulated me.

And I must say, even Laraine, who I, at times, thought didn't maybe even like me that much, has actually volunteered and consented to come and do the fall. And I—some kind of pratfall, I don't know what it will be. Of course, it won't be as good as . . . my falls. But that's not her fault. She's not trained at that. She's a mime, I believe. She's a woman. Of course, women are clearly not built that way. They're not built for physical schtick, or physical falling, and that kind of stuff. Physical comedy. So I understand the hissing and all that. It's just a fact, they're just not built. So, as I say, anyway, she probably won't be as good as *me*—the winner. Uh . . . but she's gonna give it her all, I imagine. And, well, why don't you give it a shot, Laraine?

[Laraine Newman struts across the stage, stopping in front of the red card table.]

Chevy: Thank you once again.
Laraine: Thank you for this opportunity, Chevy.
Chevy: Oh, you're welcome.
[Laraine stretches her arm out wide in preparation for her scene, then yanks Chevy's right crutch forward and sends him toppling over the card table, which falls off the stage and sends itself and Chevy and his crutches to the floor.]
Chevy [pushes the broken card table off his body]: LIVE FROM NEW YORK! IT'S SATURDAY NIGHT!

FILMOGRAPHY

1978 *Foul Play*
1980 *Oh Heavenly Dog*
1980 *Caddyshack*
1980 *Seems Like Old Times*
1981 *Under the Rainbow*
1981 *Modern Problems*
1983 *National Lampoon's Vacation*
1983 *Deal of the Century*
1985 *Fletch*
1985 *National Lampoon's European Vacation*
1985 *Sesame Street: Follow That Bird*
1985 *Spies Like Us*
1986 *Three Amigos*
1988 *Funny Farm*
1988 *Caddyshack II*
1989 *Fletch Lives*
1989 *National Lampoon's Christmas Vacation*
1991 *Nothing But Trouble*
1992 *Memoirs of an Invisible Man*
1992 *Hero* (uncredited)
1994 *Cops and Robbersons*
1995 *Man of the House*
1997 *Vegas Vacation*

1998 *Dirty Work*
2000 *Snow Day*
2001 *Pete's a Pizza* (narrator)
2002 *Orange County*
2003 *Bad Meat*
2004 *Our Italian Husband*
2004 *Karate Dog*
2005 *Ellie Parker*
2006 *Doogal* (voice of train)
2006 *Zoom*
2007 *Funny Money*
2007 *Goose on the Loose*
(Note: the three below are films of live shows)
1973 *Lemmings*
1974 *The Groove Tube*
1975 *Saturday Night Live*

FEATURE FILMS

Foul Play (1978)

Goldie Hawn, as librarian Gloria Mundy, finds her peaceful existence shattered when a film cassette is by chance left with her by a dying agent. She unwittingly uncovers a plot to assassinate the pope. Chevy plays the San Francisco detective Tony Carlson. In this wacky and complicated comedy spoof, Chevy and Goldie prevent the dreadful crime from taking place. Dudley Moore plays the role of Stanley Tibbets, a famous opera conductor, and he conducts *The Mikado*, a focal point of the pope's visit to San Francisco. Love blooms between Gloria and Tony. *Written and directed by Colin Higgins. The cast includes Chevy, Goldie Hawn, Dudley Moore, Brian Dennehy, Burgess Meredith, Eugene Roche, and Rachel Roberts.*

Oh Heavenly Dog (1980)

Browning (Chevy) is a private investigator who gets killed while on a job. When he arrives in a government-like halfway station waiting room, he is assigned a trip back to earth to solve his own murder. However, the only available body is a dog (Benji). Working around his limitations as a dog, Browning attempts to solve the case, save the girl, and put the world to rights. *Written by Rod Browning and directed by Joe Camp. The cast includes Chevy, Benji, Jane Seymour, and Omar Sharif.*

Caddyshack (1980)

The setting for this farcical romp through class warfare is the Bushwood Country Club, an exclusive golf club. Between the local wisecracking millionaire (Dangerfield), whose desire it is to turn the country club into a development, and the resistance of the club president (Knight), are a broad variety of bizarre characters, some wealthy and some poor. Many are members of the club and many are employees. They include a caddy who will do anything to raise money to go to college (O'Keefe), a laconic golfer who uses Zen to improve his golf game (Chase), and a psychotic groundskeeper continuously pursuing a gopher (Murray). *Written by Brian Doyle-Murray, Harold Ramis and Douglas Kenney and directed by Harold Ramis. The cast includes Chevy, Rodney Dangerfield, Ted Knight, Michael O'Keefe, Bill Murray, and Cindy Morgan.*

Seems Like Old Times (1980)

The second Chevy Chase/Goldie Hawn movie, following *Foul Play* (1978), was written by Neil Simon in his inimitable romantic comedy style. Reclusive writer Nick Gardenia (Chevy) is taken hostage by two gunmen and forced, at gunpoint, to rob a bank for them. His ex-wife, Glenda Gardenia Parks (Hawn), is now an attorney married to the Los Angeles district attorney, Ira Parks (Grodin), who is under consideration for state attorney general. (Nick's face was the only one picked up by the bank security cameras.) He seeks refuge at the home of his ex, where he finds a collection of bizarre assorted characters, all former clients, whom Glenda has employed around the house, along with dozens of stray dogs that Glenda cannot turn away. The story revolves around Ira's embarrassment at having the public aware that his wife's former husband is wanted for bank robbery, and (typical of a Simon story) his fear that Glenda is still in love with Nick. Hilarious scenes are featured on and under beds, including the film's most unforgettable scene where Nick, replacing the "indisposed" butler, serves dinner at a formal party for the unfortunate governor and his wife. Simon's witty repartee shines through the movie. *Written by Neil Simon and directed by Jay Sandrich. The cast includes Goldie Hawn, Chevy, Charles Grodin, Robert Guillaume, Harold Gould, and George Grizzard.*

Under the Rainbow (1981)

In 1938 Los Angeles the Culver Hotel is left for a weekend under the direction of the owner's nephew, who books a broad variety of characters including Munchkins auditioning for roles in *The Wizard of Oz*, secret agents, Japanese tourists, and European royalty. Annie Clark (Fisher), who is the casting director for *Wizard*, and Bruce Thorpe (Chevy) manage to find romance in this chaos. *Written by Fred Bauer, Pat Bradley, Pat McCormick, Harry Hurwitz, and Martin Smith and directed by Steve Rash. The cast includes Chevy, Carrie Fisher, Eve Arden, Joseph Maher, Robert Donner, Billy Barty, and Mako.*

Modern Problems (1981)

Air traffic controller Max Fielding is having problems with life—his career is in trouble and his girlfriend has dumped him. In a bizarre traffic accident, nuclear waste is dumped all over him and his car, leaving him with a new power of telekinesis, the ability to move objects around using only his mind. He tries to rekindle his relationship with his girlfriend by using his powers to make the lives of any other interested suitors very difficult. His powers get out of control at a beach house he shares with a friend; the result is pandemonium. *Written by Ken Shapiro, Ken Sherohman, and Arhus Sellers and directed by Ken Shapiro. The cast includes Chevy, Patti D'Arbanville, Dabney Coleman, Mary Kay Place, Nell Carter, and Brian Doyle-Murray.*

National Lampoon's Vacation (1983)

Clark Griswold (Chevy) plans to take his family on the trip of his dreams from Chicago to Wally World. As usual the best laid plans . . . Everything on the meticulously planned trip goes wrong—daughter Audrey (Barron) is introduced to pot, son Rusty (Hall) finds porn, Cousin Eddie (Quaid) dumps sharp-tongued Aunt Edna (Coca) on them, they get stuck in a ghetto, Clark drives off the road, their money is stolen, and Clark gets shot. Finally they arrive at Wally World only to find it closed for renovation. Clark, now driven to insanity, refuses to be deterred by this final irritation. *Written by John Hughes and directed by Harold Ramis.The cast includes Chevy, Beverly D'Angelo, Dana Barron, Anthony Michael Hall, Imogene Coca, Randy Quaid, and Eddie Bracken.*

Deal of the Century (1983)

American arms dealer Eddie Muntz (Chevy) is trying to sell a high-tech military vehicle to a South American dictator, General Cordosa (Marquez). To seal the deal he wants his girlfriend, Catherine DeVoto (Weaver), to sleep with the general. Complications arise as Frank Stryker (Edwards) tries to undercut Muntz and when Muntz's partner Ray Kasternak (Hines) has a religious conversion and wants to quit the business. *Written by Robert Garland, Robert Towne, Paul Brickman, and Bernard Edelman and directed by William Friedkin. The cast includes Chevy, Gregory Hines, Sigourney Weaver, William Marquez, Vince Edwards, and Eduardo Ricard.*

Fletch (1985)

Irwin "Fletch" Fletcher (Chevy) is a Los Angeles journalist who gets into his work and delivers news articles that bring about change. Now he is a beach bum researching drug dealing. While on the beach in disguise he is approached by a wealthy man, Alan Stanwyk (Matheson), who asks the bum to shoot him for $50,000, saving him from a painful death from cancer and enabling his wife to collect the insurance money. Fletch returns to his role as an ace reporter and determines that Stanwyk is not dying and has a connection to drug dealing and shady real estate deals. *Written by Gregory McDonald and Andrew Bergman and directed by Michael Ritchie. The cast includes Chevy, Tim Matheson, Joe Don Baker, Dana Wheller-Nicholson, Richard Libertini, and Kareem Abdul-Jabbar.*

National Lampoon's European Vacation (1985)

The Griswald family appears on the game show *Pig in a Poke* and wins a trip to Europe. This middle American family, who seem to have no clue about anything outside of the USA, set off for Britain, France, Germany, and Italy. Long-suffering wife Ellen (D'Angelo) does her best to hold the family together while learning to drive on the left side of the road, running down Stonehenge, visiting the wrong relatives, assisting thieves in a holdup, having erotic pictures of herself on a billboard in Italy, and finally being kidnapped. There's a cameo role by Eric Idle as the "accident prone" bike rider trying to avoid the Griswalds. *Written by John Hughes and Robert Klane and directed by Amy Heckerling. The cast includes Chevy, Beverly D'Angelo, Dana Hill, Jason Lively, and John Astin.*

Sesame Street: Follow That Bird (1985)

A Sesame Street social worker realizes that Big Bird is not living among his own kind—birds. She decides to send him away to live with the dodos, intending for him to be adopted and live in Ocean View, Illinois. Poor Big Bird is unhappy living with this strange family and he runs away. His adventures as he crosses the country and meets with different people make him realize that the only place he is happy is at home—on Sesame Street. *Written by Judy Freudberg and Tony Geiss and directed by Ken Kwapis. The cast includes Chevy as the newscaster, Carroll Spinney, Jim Henson, Frank Oz, Richard Hunt, Paul Bartel, Sandra Bernhard, John Candy, Waylon Jennings, and Dave Thomas.*

Spies Like Us (1985)

Emmett Fitz-Hume (Chevy) and Austin Millbarge (Aykroyd) are selected as espionage agents on the basis of their incompetence in order to draw attention away from the real spies. They end up in Pakistan and Afghanistan where eventually the real spies steal a Soviet missile launcher and launch a missile, all to test a new American laser defense system. Needless to say, the defense system fails and, while the Pentagon decision is to let World War III occur, this pair of "spies" saves the day through their own ineptitude. *Written by Dan Aykroyd, Dave Thomas, Lowell Gins and Babaloo Mandel and directed by John Landis. The cast includes Chevy, Dan Aykroyd, Steve Forrest, Donna Dixon, Bruce Davison, Frank Oz, and Bernie Casey.*

Three Amigos (1986)

Three out-of-work silent movie stars are mistaken for real sharpshooting caballeros by Carmen (Martinez), whose Mexican village, Santa Pico, is being terrorized by the bandit El Guapo (Arau). A letter brings the three to Mexico—Dusty Bottoms (Chevy), Lucky Day (Martin), and Ned Nederlander (Short)—where they mistake El Guapo and his bandits for movie stars. Naturally, the trio saves the day and find romance as well. *Written by Steve Martin, Randy Newman, and Lorne Michaels and directed by John Landis. The cast includes Chevy, Steve Martin, Martin Short, Patrice Martinez, and Alfonso Arau.*

Funny Farm (1988)

Sportswriter Andy Farmer (Chevy) and his wife Elizabeth (Smith) decide that life in the big city is too hectic. They buy a house in Vermont. He quits his job and knows that the peace and quiet of the country will be a perfect place for a writer! The movers get lost trying to find their house, they deal with a maniacal mailman, they find a body buried in the backyard, and the inhabitants of this idyllic country village are far from normal. Andy finds that he can't write the great American novel and also has to deal with the fact that Elizabeth has written a successful children's book. *Written by Jay Conley and Jeffrey Beam and directed by George Roy Hill. The cast includes Chevy, Madolyn Smith, Kevin O'Morrison, Joseph Maher, Jack Gilpin, and Caris Corfman.*

Caddyshack II (1988)

This story of new money facing off against an old-money golf club involves some of the characters from *Caddyshack* but isn't really a sequel. Jack Hartounian (Mason) and his daughter Kate (Lundy) apply for membership at the exclusive golf club. They are turned down and Jack retaliates by buying the club and its rights and turning it into an amusement park. *Written by Brian Doyle-Murray, Harold Ramis, Douglas Kenney, and Peter Torokvei and directed by Allan Arkush. The cast includes Chevy, Jackie Mason, Robert Stack, Dyan Cannon, Dina Merrill, Randy Quaid, Jessica Lundy, Dan Aykroyd, and Jonathan Silberman.*

Fletch Lives (1989)

When reporter Irwin "Fletch" Fletcher (Chevy) inherits Bell Isle, an estate in Louisiana, he quits his job and heads South, intending to live out his life as a wealthy landowner. The estate is not quite what he expected and he finds himself in prison for murder and up against Jimmy Lee Farnsworth (Ermey), a TV evangelist whose local Bibleland wants to buy his land. Fletch the reporter surfaces and he starts digging into what is really behind Bibleland and its shady business. *Written by Leon Capetanos and Gregory McDonald and directed by Michael Ritchie. The cast includes Chevy, Hal Holbrook, Julianne Phillips, and R. Lee Ermey.*

National Lampoon's Christmas Vacation (1989)

Clark Griswold (Chevy) is expecting a big Christmas bonus and believes it will be the biggest Christmas ever. He has ordered a swimming pool and knows that his bonus will cover the cost. He invites the whole family—his parents, Clark (Randolph) and Nora (Ladd), his in-laws, Arthur (Marshall) and Frances Smith (Roberts), and Uncle Lewis and Aunt Bethany. According to tradition, Clark covers the outside of his house with 25,000 Christmas lights, which fail to work. He drives his uptight ultra-modern neighbors crazy, and cousin Eddie and his family arrive uninvited in their ancient RV—their only home. To top it off Clark's bonus has been canceled by his cheap boss this year. Cousin Eddie takes it into his own hands to fix the situation. *Written by John Hughes and directed by Jeremiah Chechik. The cast includes Chevy, Beverly D'Angelo, Juliette Lewis, Johnny Galecki, John Randolph, Diane Ladd, E. G. Marshall, Doris Roberts, and Randy Quaid.*

Nothing But Trouble (1991)

Financier Chris Thorne (Chevy) agrees to take Diane Lightson (Moore) to a business meeting in Atlantic City. On the way, they get lost in the "wilds" of New Jersey and are stopped for speeding. They are hauled into a place called Valkenvania and appear before a maniacal 106-year-old wreck of a judge (Aykroyd). They become prisoners in a crazy world of booby traps and deadly machines, and spend the rest of the movie trying to escape from the maniac and his hallucinogenic family. *Written by Dan Aykroyd and Peter Aykroyd and directed by Dan Aykroyd. The cast includes Chevy, Demi Moore, Dan Aykroyd, and John Candy.*

Memoirs of an Invisible Man (1992)

Chevy appears to have issues with nuclear power. In *Modern Problems* he is attacked by nuclear waste. In this film he plays Nick Halloway, a San Francisco stock analyst who gets caught in a nuclear fusion accident and becomes invisible. An unscrupulous CIA agent, David Jenkins (Neill), sees the opportunity to recruit him into the world of espionage. The conventional Halloway attempts to elude the agent, engage in a challenging romance with lawyer Alice Monroe (Hannah), and find a cure for his invisibility. The film incorporates many effective special effects as a result of Halloway's invisibility. *Written by H. F. Saint, Robert Collector, Dana Olsen, and William Goldman and directed by John Carpenter. The cast includes Chevy, Daryl Hannah, Sam Neill, Michael McKean, Stephen Tobolowsky, and Jim Norton.*

Hero (1992)

This is a reverse Cinderella story. Bernie LaPlante (Hoffman) is divorced, out of work, and a deadbeat dad. He witnesses a plane crash and sees an opportunity to loot the crash site; however, upon entering the plane he becomes involved in saving passengers. One such passenger turns out to be a television reporter Gayle Gayley (Davis). After leaving the crash site and losing a shoe in the mud, Bernie ends up being given a ride by John Bubber (Garcia). He tells Bubber his story and makes it clear that he wants no recognition for his part in the rescues. Meanwhile Gayley offers a million-dollar reward for the person who saved her life. John Bubber collects it. Gayley discovers the true identity of her savior. Chevy plays the director of Channel 4 News, for which Gayley is a reporter. His role is uncredited, by choice. *Written by Laura Ziskin, Alvin Sargent, and David Webb Peoples and directed by Stephen Frears. The cast includes Chevy, Dustin Hoffman, Geena Davis, Andy Garcia, and Joan Cusack.*

Cops and Robbersons (1994)

When a mob hit man (Davi) moves in next door to the Robbersons, the police use the Robbersons' house for a stakeout. Jake Stone (Palance) and his cute young sidekick Tony Moore (Gray) persuade conventional suburbanite Norman Robberson (Chevy) to take over his home. Helen Robberson (Wiest) and the two kids treat the guys like family and drive the hard-nosed Jake Stone crazy. Eventually Norman comes to the rescue of both Jake and his family. *Written by Bernie Somers and directed by Michael Ritchie. The cast includes Chevy, Jack Palance, Dianne Wiest, Robert Davi, David Barry Gray, Jason James Richter, Fay Masterson, and Miko Hughes.*

Man of the House (1995)

Sandy Archer (Fawcett) has met Jack Sturgess (Chevy) but Sandy's young son Ben (Thomas) is determined that this relationship is going nowhere. Jack involves Ben in the Indian Guides and the two somehow manage to bond through the experience. *Written by David Peckinpah, Richard Jeffries, James Orr, and Jim Cruickshank and directed by James Orr. The cast includes Chevy, Farrah Fawcett, Jonathan Taylor Thomas, George Wendt, and Chief Leonard George.*

Vegas Vacation (1997)

Thanks to one of Clark Griswold's (Chevy) inventions, he gets a big bonus and takes the family on a trip to Las Vegas. In Vegas they meet up with Cousin Eddie (Quaid), who now owns land just outside of Vegas on a former H-bomb test site. Another "perfect" vacation turns into a series of disasters involving Wayne Newton, Siegfried and Roy's tigers, a blonde in a red Ferrari, fake IDs allowing Rusty (Embry) to become a high roller, a cage-dancing cousin, and Clark managing to lose the family bank account. *Written by Elisa Bell and Bob Ducsay and directed by Stephen Kessler. The cast includes Chevy, Beverly D'Angelo, Randy Quaid,*

Ethan Embry, Marisol Nichols, Miriam Flyn, Shae D'Lyn, Wayne Newton, Siegfried Fischbacher, Roy Horn, and Sid Caesar.

Dirty Work (1998)

Unemployed Mitch and his buddy Sam start a revenge for hire business in order to raise $50,000 that Sam's father needs to get a heart transplant. Their plan goes awry when they hire hookers to pose as dead bodies during a TV ad. A wealthy developer hires the duo to destroy a building. It's a plot and a movie filled with unexpected difficulties. *Written by Frank Sebastiano, Norm MacDonald, and Fred Wolf and directed by Bob Saget. The cast includes Chevy, Norm MacDonald, Artie Lange, Jack Warden, Taylor Howard, Don Rickles, and Christopher McDonald.*

Snow Day (2000)

A heavy snowfall in an upstate New York town brings out a group of elementary school kids who decide that the only way to keep the schools closed is to stop the snowplow. The plot deals with four separate but intertwined stories, each involving a member of a single family, the Brandstons. First, Natalie (Gray) leads the group of kids in an attempt to prevent the evil-looking and apparently insane snowplow driver from clearing the streets. Her brother, Hal (Webber), uses the day to try to win the affections of the local high school princess who has just broken up with her jock boyfriend. The mother of the family, Laura (Smart), is a high-energy career woman whose business suffers due to the snow. The predictor of the snowstorm is the local TV weatherman, Tom Brandston (Chevy), the father of the family, who spends his day in great frustration as his untalented competitor on another TV channel gets all the credit for his prediction. Roger, the plowman (Elliott), steals the show with his bizarre and comedic snowplow antics. *Written by Will McRobb and Chris Viscardi and directed by Chris Koch. The cast includes Chevy, Chris Elliott, Jean*

Smart, Mark Webber, Zena Gray, Connor Matheus, Damien Young, and John Schneider.

Pete's a Pizza (2001)

A short animated film for children. Chevy narrates the story. *Written by William Steig and directed by Gary Goldberger and Peter Reynolds. Animated by Noah Jones.*

Orange County (2002)

Shaun Brumder (Hanks) has a dream—to go to Stanford University, become a writer, and leave his dysfunctional family behind. He's rejected, however, when his guidance counselor sends in the wrong application. He decides that any lengths are acceptable to get into Stanford; with help from his brother Lance (Black) and his girlfriend Ashley (Fisk) he tries any means to an end. *Written by Mike White and directed by Jake Kasdan. The cast includes Chevy, Colin Hanks, Jack Black, Schyler Fisk, John Lithgow, Lily Tomlin, Kevin Kline, and Ben Stiller.*

Bad Meat (2003)

Butcher's Mill, Illinois, has a meatpacking plant, a junk yard, and Earle (Worley), whose desire in life is to marry Pam (Fosse-Dunne). First, however, he needs to own his own trailer (Pam's requirement of home ownership). His friend Buddy (Berber) hatches a plot to kidnap a corrupt US congressman (Chevy) and hold him for ransom for the down payment on a trailer. Unfortunately the congressman ends up dead and his body chopped up for bologna and sent to market. If Buddy and Earle are going to survive they have to find the "bad meat" and provide a body for the congressman's family to bury. *Written by Scott Dikkers and Michael J. Hirsch and directed by Scott Dikkers. The cast includes Chevy, Billie Worley, Lance Berber, Judah Friedlander, Ellie Weingardt, Becky Boxer, and Melissa Fosse-Dunne.*

Our Italian Husband (2004)

Chevy plays the unusual role of Paul Parmisan, a sleazy manufacturer/salesma n on a home shopping channel. Brooke Shields and the Italian actress Maria Grazia Cucinotta play the leading roles in this comedy. The film opens in Italy where Maria Scocozza is making sandals to support her two children from her marriage to artist Vincenzo Scocozza (Favino), who left for America to make it big in New York. She comes to find her husband and discovers he has married another woman, Charlene (Shields), who is now pregnant. With no place to go, Maria and her two children move in and the two women eventually join to plot against Vincenzo. *Written and directed by Ilaria Borelli. The cast includes Chevy, Maria Grazia Cucinotta, Brooke Shields, and Pierfrancesco Favino.*

Karate Dog (2004)

Cho Cho the dog (Chevy, voice) is not only the eyewitness to his master's murder, he can also speak to humans and is an expert in martial arts. Detective Peter Fowler (Rex) links up with Cho Cho and between them they set off to solve the murder of an old man in Chinatown. The path to uncovering the truth places both of their lives in serious danger. *Written by Steven Paul and Gregory Poppen and directed by Bob Clark. The cast includes Chevy, Jon Voight, Simon Rex, Jaime Pressly, and Nicolette Sheridan.*

Ellie Parker (2005)

Naomi Watts portrays the role of an actress struggling to become a success in Hollywood—endless auditions and financial struggles. Chevy has a small role as the depressed agent of the actress, showing a more exaggerated type of personality than he had played in most of his films. *Written and directed by Scott Coffey. The cast includes Chevy, Naomi Watts, Greg Freitas, Mark Pellegrino, and Gaye Pope.*

Doogal (2006)

Doogal and his friends Dylan, Brian, and Ermintrude set out to save the world from the evil sorcerer Zeebad. To prevent the world from being frozen forever they must find three magic diamonds before Zeebad finds them. Through their dangerous adventures they discover that their friendship is their most powerful weapon, which even Zeebad cannot destroy. *A large team of writers includes Paul Bassett, Martine Danot, Serge Danot, and Todd Edwards; directed by Dave Borthwick, Jean Duval, and Frank Passingham. The cast of voices includes Chevy (as voice of the train), Daniel Tay, Jimmy Fallon, Jon Stewart, Whoopi Goldberg, William H. Macy, Judi Dench, Kylie Minogue, and Ian McKellen.*

Zoom (2006)

Zoom is a film designed for children and preteens. It's the story of an aging superhero brought back into action to train a band of youngsters to be the new superheroes. Tim Allen and Courteney Cox costar. *Written by Adam Rifkin, David Berenbaum, and Jason Lethcoe and directed by Peter Hewitt. The cast includes Chevy, Tim Allen, Courteney Cox, Spencer Breslin, Kevin Zegars, Kate Mara, Michael Cassidy, Ryan Newman, and Rip Torn.*

Funny Money (2007)

Chevy plays the role of Henry Perkins, who is in the wax fruit business. While on a train, he accidentally trades briefcases with another man and quickly learns there's five million dollars inside. Henry tells his unsuspecting wife Carol, played by Penelope Ann Miller, of their newfound fortune but she doesn't handle it as well as he does and is reluctant to leave the country, forever, at a moment's notice. As it is Henry's birthday, they're soon joined by their best friends, a cop on the take, a cop on the hunt, and the dreaded Mr. Big. It's an action-packed farce. *Written by Ray Cooney, Harry Basil, and Leslie Greif and directed by*

Leslie Greif. The cast includes Chevy, Penelope Ann Miller, Armand Assante, Christopher McDonald, Robert Loggia, Guy Torry, Rebecca Wosocky, Kevin Sussman, Alex Maneses, and Marty Belavsky.

Goose on the Loose (2007)

Randall, a talking goose (Foley), is kidnapped by Congreve Maddox (Chevy), the principal of the local elementary school, in order to fatten him up, cook him, and enter him in a contest. Eleven-year-old Will Donnelly (Morrow) becomes his best friend. Will has not spoken since the sudden death of his mother. With the help of Randall and a shared love of rude noises and butterscotch, Randall brings Will back to speaking again. Will, in turn, is determined to prevent Randall's culinary fate. With the help of his sister and classmates Will sets up a kidnapping and a hostage exchange—a true wild goose chase! Aka *Goose! Written by Charles Dennis and directed by Nicholas Kendall. The cast includes Chevy, Dave Foley, Kari Matchett, James Purefoy, Joan Plowright, Max Morrow, Isabella Fink, and Cheyenne Hill.*

ACKNOWLEDGMENTS

M y warmest thanks to Chevy for sharing the story of his life in such an honest and open way, and for giving of his time and energy without restrictions. There cannot be enough words of praise for Jayni Chase, whose tireless assistance, generosity with her time, and trust in me made it possible to complete this biography. Many members of Chevy's family and professional team helped with this book: Chevy's daughters—Cydney, Caley, and Emily—all spoke openly about their relationships with their Dad. Chevy's brother, Ned Chase, and his half-siblings—Pamela, John, and Catherine Anne Cederquist—were enormously helpful in sharing their recollections.

My loving appreciation to my wonderful family for their confidence in me, and their constant support. To my husband Brian Dallow, for endless and unconditional support. To all my children and their spouses, for helping whenever help was needed, and for knowing when it was: Ruth and Stuart Southland; Karen and Kevin Burr; Elise and Vincent Latona, and Joel and Mary Ellen Dallow; and to my sister and brother-in-law, Felice and Jay Platt, and to my sister Dorothea Cahan.

My grateful thanks to a wonderful team of perceptive and demanding readers, including my husband Brian, my sister

Dorothea, my daughters Ruth and Karen, and my friend and attorney Stephen Rodner.

My sincere thanks to my agent Sophie Hicks, at Ed Victor Ltd., for her faith in me, and to Edina Imrik and colleagues at Ed Victor Ltd.; to Claire Kingston, Commissioning Editor at Virgin Books, UK, for her ongoing encouragement; and to a wonderful team including Davina Russell, Editor at Virgin Books, UK, Ken Siman, publisher of Virgin Books, US, and to an expert group of editors including Wendy Hollas in the UK and Marc Haeringer in the US.

Chevy has a devoted team including Allen Eichhorn and Heidi Schaeffer at PMK/HBH, his attorney and friend Bruce Bodner, his manager Erik Kritzer, and his agents Ben Press and Michael McConnell. Thanks to the whole team, and to the Chases' personal assistant Tori West, for all their assistance.

Special thanks to photographer Ron Slenzak, for the cover photo, and to photographer Steve Schapiro, for sharing many film photos taken over several decades.

To those people and organizations who helped to provide rights, permissions, information, and copyright clearances— Florence Phillips and Lorne Michaels at NBC's *Saturday Night Live;* Britta von Schoeler, Jack Anderson, and Maya Handelsman at Broadway Video; NBC; Warner Brothers; Roger Ebert, Paul Newman, and Sylvester Stallone; and Hannah Richert and Jenna Bond-Loudon in the Clinton Foundation Office.

Many of Chevy's friends, colleagues, and associates assisted in a variety of ways. Recognizing that a brief listing barely gives sufficient credit, I thank the following people with an enthusiastic shout of "Bravo!":

Andy Aaron, Peter Aaron, Dan Aykroyd, Bruce Bodner, President Bill Clinton, Beverly D'Angelo, John Clements, Rocco Fava, Benno Friedman, Christopher Guest, Goldie Hawn, Tom Leopold, Lorne Michaels, Bill Murray, Florence Phillips, Harold Ramis, Carl Reiner, Paul Shaffer, Martin Short, and Neil Simon.

INDEX

Author photograph © Arthur Paxton

ABOUT THE AUTHOR

Rena Fruchter is the author of the critically acclaimed *Dudley Moore: An Intimate Portrait*. She is a concert pianist, writer, and educator and for twelve years was a music columnist for the *New York Times*. Rena made her solo debut with the Philadelphia Orchestra at the age of six, and has toured internationally as a pianist. She is a graduate of Brandeis University in Massachusetts and holds graduate degrees from the Royal College of Music in London, England. She is the cofounder and artistic director of Music For All Seasons, an organization that presents musical programs for people confined to all types of institutions. Rena lives in New Jersey with her husband, Brian Dallow, and they are parents of four adult children, including a set of triplets.